Welfare Transformed

Welfare Transformed

Universalizing Family Policies That Work

ROBERT CHERRY

OXFORD
UNIVERSITY PRESS

2007

OXFORD
UNIVERSITY PRESS

Oxford University Press, Inc., publishes works that further
Oxford University's objective of excellence
in research, scholarship, and education.

Oxford   New York
Auckland   Cape Town   Dar es Salaam   Hong Kong   Karachi
Kuala Lumpur   Madrid   Melbourne   Mexico City   Nairobi
New Delhi   Shanghai   Taipei   Toronto

With offices in
Argentina   Austria   Brazil   Chile   Czech Republic   France   Greece
Guatemala   Hungary   Italy   Japan   Poland   Portugal   Singapore
South Korea   Switzerland   Thailand   Turkey   Ukraine   Vietnam

Copyright © 2007 by Oxford University Press, Inc.

Published by Oxford University Press, Inc.
198 Madison Avenue, New York, New York 10016
www.oup.com

Oxford is a registered trademark of Oxford University Press

Library of Congress Cataloging-in-Publication Data
Cherry, Robert D., 1944–
Welfare transformed : universalizing family policies that work / Robert Cherry.
    p. cm.
Includes bibliographical references and index.
ISBN: 978-0-19-518312-2
1. Public welfare—United States—Evaluation.
2. Welfare recipients—Employment—United States—Evaluation.
I. Title.
HV95.C44 2008
362.5'5680973—dc22   2006102753

9 8 7 6 5 4 3 2 1

Printed in the United States of America
on acid-free paper

This book is dedicated to three generations of working women who shaped my life: Jean, Shelley, and Sara.

Preface

This book is a radical departure from most critiques of welfare reform. It acknowledges welfare reform's inadequacies but argues that focusing on those aspects that have been shown to work is the best way to address the flaws that leave some families behind. Welfare-to-work policies have moved millions of mothers into paid work and their families further away from abject poverty. If we are serious about wanting to strengthen our families and communities, we cannot afford to ignore these lessons.

Thirty years ago, I could never envision adopting such a policy perspective. Living in Boston in the 1970s, my wife was employed by Model Cities, a government-funded health clinic in a poor neighborhood. We did some political organizing with clients that involved visiting families in public housing projects. Walking into those projects was depressing. Garbage was strewn through the hallways, broken windows leered at visitors, and it seemed impossible that people lived there. Once inside the apartments, however, we were transformed into another world: clean and orderly. In their oases, these mothers did their best to maintain the dignity that they were not afforded elsewhere.

At the time of these visits, two of the most influential books were William Ryan, *Blaming the Victim* (1972) and Frances Piven and Richard Cloward, *Regulating the Poor: The Functions of Public Welfare* (1971). Ryan's book showed how the "culture-of-poverty" thesis that black poverty was primarily the result of a dysfunctional culture was simply a way to rationalize systemic oppression. Piven and Cloward demonstrated how welfare was a necessary component of a system that was unable to provide full-time, year-round employment for its black workforce. These visits and books reinforced my belief that poverty was a result of a system in which the powerful exploit the powerless.

During the early 1980s, the right-wing apostle Charles Murray focused on shiftless men and the growth of female-headed households. He claimed that only by ending welfare as an entitlement could welfare dependency and dysfunctional behavior be countered. My response was predictable. I condemned the racist stereotypes that Murray and his ilk popularized.[1] When, a few years later, welfare rolls and teenage pregnancy rates increased, I convinced myself that they were rational adaptations to a racist system.

I still reject suggestions that dysfunctional behavior in poor urban black neighborhoods during the 1980s reflected deeply rooted cultural norms. Instead, I have come to believe that there were quite specific—maybe even unique— circumstances that victimized these communities. The great exodus from the South after World War II provided modest upward mobility for most black workers. They moved from being impoverished sharecroppers, domestics, and agricultural workers into unskilled factory employment. These factory jobs began to disappear in the 1970s as manufacturing firms began to move out of central cities. As a result, the postmigration generation—black children born in the late 1960s and early 1970s—grew up in a harsh environment where even unskilled jobs became scarce. This widespread joblessness was only intensified by the deep 1980–1982 recession that caused black unemployment to reach levels not seen nationally since the Great Depression. The problems faced by these young blacks only worsened when the crack cocaine epidemic hit in the mid-1980s.

I also became convinced that welfare was not as helpful a safety net for single mothers and their children as I once thought. New evidence on sexual coercion and domestic violence indicated that welfare had a much more damaging effect on the lives of many mothers than previously thought. The most dramatic evidence was presented by Jody Raphael in her book *Saving Bernice: Battered Women, Welfare, and Poverty* (2000), which documented the experience of a poor African-American teenager. Unlike the culture-of-poverty viewpoint, Bernice was neither shortsighted nor enamored with the fast life. Indeed, it was a desire for a traditional family that trapped her on welfare and in an abusive relationship. Bernice's partner was responsible for her frequent pregnancies and repeatedly sabotaged her efforts to leave welfare. Other research documented how typical Bernice's story was and motivated Raphael to spearhead the aptly titled "Trapped by Poverty, Trapped by Abuse" biennial conferences.

It is this snapshot of black youth coming of age in the 1980s that is most useful for understanding the drive toward reform in the 1990s. Rather than rehash the history of welfare policies since the New Deal, it is more important to focus on the structural factors unique to this era that prompted the New Democrats to take the initiative. The growth of dysfunctional behavior, including a rise in teen pregnancy; increased welfare dependency and the resulting rising government expenditure on safety net programs; and the entrapment of many welfare recipients in abusive relationships go a long way to explain the bipartisan embrace of welfare reform in the 1990s. It was obvious that welfare required an overhaul that would address this constellation of factors that effectively closed off any meaningful economic opportunities for the postmigration generation.

Against this backdrop, there is a distinct story to be told that sharply differs from both conservative and liberal critiques of reform. Whatever the overall evaluation of welfare reform, there were many positive lessons that can be drawn from the policy initiatives that accompanied welfare legislation. High-employment and tax policies, government-funded child care, strong community colleges and vocational programs, and healthy relationships can give more of America's families a chance at economic success. The following pages blend empirical data with interviews with key Clinton-era policy analysts, directors and staff at welfare-to-work programs and community colleges, and—most important—welfare leavers themselves, to craft lessons from the aftermath of welfare reform that can help enhance the lives of a large proportion of working women, most of whom have never been on welfare. By strengthening these women, their families, and, by extension, their communities, welfare can work for all of us.

As should be clear, I owe a debt of gratitude to many people. My ability to interview welfare leavers was the result of contacts made for me by Heidi Hartmann (Oakland), Rick Holt (Milwaukee), Susan Greenbaum (Tampa), and Raphael (Chicago). The directors Anita Rees (LIFETIME), Nydia Hernandez (STRIVE), and Julie Kerksick (New Hope) not only arranged for the interviews but also were generous with their own time.

In Washington, D.C., I was able to speak with analysts at the Institute for Women's Policy Research (Avis Jones-DeWeever), the Center for Law and Social Policy (Vicki Turetsky and Mark Greenberg), the Center on Budget Policy and Priorities (Sharon Parrott), the Economic Policy Institute (Max Sawicky and Jared Bernstein), the Urban Institute (Bob Lerman), and the Center for Economic and Policy Research (Heather Boushey).

I also thank Ron Haskins for his willingness to discuss with me his role while working in Congress on welfare reform both during the Clinton years and then as special aide for President George W. Bush during the first two years of the reauthorization debate. From the Clinton administration, I thank Donna Shalala, David Ellwood, Wendell Primus, and Peter Edelman for their time, which enabled me to gain a richer understanding of the welfare reform process than I would have by just reading accounts.

I thank Roberta Mathews and Linnea Weiland for facilitating my interviews at community colleges. At LaGuardia Community College, Audrey Watson and Sandra Watson were extraordinarily generous with their time and resources, and at Union Community College (N.J.), John Farrell, Paul Jurmo, and Shirley

Hollie-Day provided me with important insights into the development of new programs. In addition, at Brooklyn College, Lillian O'Reilly discussed with me the value of adult education.

I was also lucky to have friends and colleagues who read draft chapters and made important suggestions: Steve Fraser, Myra Kogen, Nicole Trujillo-Pagan, Anita Podrid, Janet Johnson, Alex Vitale, and Deb Shanley.

I was most fortunate to have Maura Roessner as my editor at Oxford University Press. Her extensive, thoughtful comments on chapters as they were drafted not only increased their readability but also allowed me to rectify many inconsistencies and shortcomings that I would not otherwise have attended to. She also chose reviewers that uniformly aided my project.

Finally, I thank my family for creating an environment in which I could work effectively. In addition, my wife, Shelley, and my children, Josh and Sara, provided useful comments on the project, particularly prodding me to be less long-winded and more positive in my presentations. Finally, I should mention my grandson, Jacob, whose cheery disposition invariably buoyed my spirits, particularly when I was having some downbeat moments with this project.

Contents

PART I

Setting the Stage for Reform

1

Moving Families Forward

On July 30, 1996, President Clinton signed into law a comprehensive revision of the federally funded welfare program, fulfilling his 1992 campaign pledge to "change welfare as we know it." The prereform program, Aid to Families with Dependent Children, was a federal entitlement. The majority of indigent mothers with dependent children who applied would receive cash assistance.

The level of cash assistance was determined by each state. In 1996, monthly cash payments averaged $347 nationally, with nine states— all in the South—providing monthly payments below $225 and six states, including New York and California, providing monthly payments of more than $500. Along with these welfare allotments, recipients would automatically be eligible for food stamps, which provided an additional $321 monthly to welfare mothers with two children. As an entitlement, recipients were not required to demonstrate any effort to improve themselves in order to collect their cash payments.

Critics claimed that this system bred welfare dependency, trapping women and their children in a cycle of poverty, abuse, and neglect. By contrast, virtually all liberal advocacy groups recoiled at the prospect that the entitlement would be terminated. They feared that mothers and their children would fall deeper into poverty. Most outspoken was Marian Wright Edelman, chair of the Children's Defense Fund, who wrote,

> Both the Senate and House welfare bills are morally and practically indefensible. . . . They are Trojan horses for massive budget cuts and for

imposing an ideological agenda that says that government assistance for the poor and children should be dismantled and cut while government assistance for wealth individuals and corporations should be maintained, even increased.... The Old Testament prophets and the New Testament Messiah made plain God's mandate to protect the poor and the weak and the young. The Senate and House welfare bills do not meet this test.[1]

Despite this outrage, the proposed legislation passed. Under its new name, Temporary Assistance to Needy Families (TANF), the federally funded program required a certain percentage of recipients to be engaged in work-related activities for at least twenty hours weekly. Each state could, however, determine what constituted a work-related activity. For some states, recipients were required to enter workfare programs where they performed menial tasks, such as sweeping streets, in return for their cash payments, while in other cases, mothers attended college classes to fulfill their work-related requirement.

In addition, the federal government placed lifetime limits on the number of years each mother was guaranteed the ability to collect cash payments. The federal limit was five years, although states could set a lower number of years. At the state's discretion, 20 percent of its recipients could exceed the federal time limit. In Connecticut, it was at the state's discretion whether a recipient could extend enrollment beyond two years. By contrast, California decided that the restrictions covered only mothers, so cash payments continue to all children beyond the federal five-year limit.

The federal legislation also gave states wide discretion on the sanctions that they could place on recipients who did not meet work-related requirements. For example, some states allowed welfare offices to terminate cash payments to the entire family the first time the mother did not meet her work-related requirement. By contrast, other states would cut off mothers but not their children, regardless of the number of times work-related requirements were not met.

Not surprisingly, there were many instances where local administrators could be arbitrary and insensitive to the needs of the families they served. In his 2002 film *Bowling for Columbine*, Michael Moore looked into a case in his hometown of Flint, Michigan, where an eight-year-old boy brought a gun to school and shot a classmate. It turned out that the boy's mother was in a mandatory workfare program. Because of the dearth of employment in Flint, she was required to get on a bus at 7 A.M. to travel 90 minutes each way to a shopping mall where she had custodial responsibilities in a Dick Clark–franchised restaurant. With little supervision, her son developed behavior problems, leading to the gun incident.

Despite my own initial misgivings, I have come to believe that the process President Clinton began effectively altered certain behavioral traits that were impeding the well-being of many poor mothers and their children. Moreover, my assessment of the available evidence has led me to conclude that the legislation not only has shifted three million women off of welfare, most into the paid workforce, but also gave rise to many support services that can serve as a foundation for future policies aimed at strengthening families and communities.

Specifically, the Clinton administration's "Making Work Pay" vision of welfare reform included financial supports and government services so that single mothers could accept even low-wage employment and yet escape official poverty. The financial supports included raising the minimum wage and increasing the earned income tax credit (EITC)—a refundable credit that is available to working families with low incomes. These credits supplement wages earned. With wages of $12,000, in 2005 a mother with two children received $4,400 in credits from the federal government. During the 1990s, more than a dozen states enacted their own EITC programs so that total credits could be as much as $5,700. In addition, there was a substantial increase in the minimum wage enacted just before welfare reform was legislated. Together with food stamps, housing credits, and child care subsidies, working mothers would escape poverty even if they could only sustain employment in low-wage jobs. Unfortunately, many critics ignore these credits, thereby substantially understating the benefits to mothers when they shift from welfare to paid work.[2]

Government services included access to subsidized child care, educational and training programs, child support collection policies to obtain payments from nonresident fathers, and more recently, counseling services to improve relationships between fathers and mothers. These services enabled many welfare leavers to sustain employment, improve earnings, have fathers more financially responsible for their children, and improve the stability of parental relationships.

Most of these financial supports and government services are also valuable to a larger group of working mothers. There are tens of millions of working mothers who have the same needs as welfare leavers: affordable child care facilities in order to maintain their employment, training and educational enhancements in order to raise their wages, and counseling services in order to improve their personal relationships. Learning from policies initiated by welfare reform and applying them more broadly can help millions of working mothers and their families have more successful lives.

THE BACKLASH

Unfortunately, the hostility toward welfare reform, particularly among left academicians, has stifled any positive assessment. One of the most vocal critics of welfare reform has been Barbara Ehrenreich, author of the bestseller *Nickel and Dimed* (2000). The book chronicled her travails as a low-wage worker in three cities during the Clinton-era economic boom. Summarizing the initial 1998 discussion with her editor, Ehrenreich indicated the book's objective: "How in particular we wondered were the roughly four million women about to be booted into the labor market by welfare reform going to make it on $6 or $7 an hour?"[3] She stressed that if she, a healthy, hard-working, educated women, could not survive, it would be impossible for welfare leavers to do so.[4]

While Ehrenreich effectively highlighted important inadequacies in the low-wage labor market, her application of these lessons to welfare reform were problematic. By ignoring the government programs initiated and enhanced to support welfare leavers, she underestimated the gains that could be made even if welfare leavers obtained only "nickel and dime" jobs—jobs that pay modest wages with limited upward mobility. Of course, these are jobs that the vast majority of this book's readership would never consider for themselves or their children, jobs that will never pay enough on their own to provide a middle-class standard of living. As a result, many welfare reform critics recoil from policies that, even if beneficial, doom women to a lifetime of work at subsistence wages. They belittle the modest financial gains made by many welfare leavers because these critics are angered by visions of mothers toiling at jobs that involve abusive conditions. They consider it better to allow them to remain on the dole than to subject these vulnerable women to such degrading work for such little pay.

Some critics point to those welfare leavers left behind, unable to find work and falling deeper into poverty. While evidence indicates that this group was far smaller than critics suggest, I agree that there were far too many welfare mothers who were needlessly victimized by insensitive welfare requirements. Studies have shown that a substantial share of welfare mothers have multiple barriers to work, including health problems, disabled children, transportation nightmares, or child care needs. Often these barriers were severe enough that mothers could not even meet welfare work-related requirements and thus faced sanctions or were harassed sufficiently that they chose to leave welfare without attaining stable employment. More enlightened policies surely could have reduced the share of welfare leavers whose lives were harmed during the Clinton boom.

Virtually all critics emphasize the adverse impact of the 2000–2004 economic slowdown on welfare leavers. Nationally, the official unemployment rate rose from 3.9 percent in summer 2000 to 6.0 percent by spring 2002, peaking at 6.4 percent in the summer of 2003. The unemployment rate of African-Americans was much higher, rising from 7.0 percent in March 2000 to 11.2 percent by December 2002. As jobs became more scarce, many welfare leavers were unable to improve their well-being by shifting to work.

Tamara could be a poster child for these critics. In quest of a better life for her and her child, Tamara left TANF in 2002. Unfortunately, she did so just when the economy went into the tank, so all she could find was sporadic employment. This allowed Tamara to maintain independence despite earnings that were only modestly above the welfare guarantee that she left.

In early 2004, Tamara had to change the child care arrangements for her four-year-old daughter, Shauna. Originally, Shauna had been in a government-funded child care facility that was conveniently located three blocks from their apartment. Unfortunately, the economic downturn created state deficits that caused adjustments to daycare funding. As a result, the only placements available were too far from home and work, forcing Tamara to rely on family and friends, further restricting her employment alternatives.

Reluctantly, Tamara applied for unemployment insurance benefits. The problem is that she lives in Florida, which has one of the most restrictive unemployment policies nationally. Florida eligibility requires minimum earnings that Tamara was unable to meet due to her discontinuous employment record. As a result, Tamara was forced to return to the welfare rolls because, luckily, she still had not reached the five-year lifetime limit.

Despite the limited upward mobility provided, despite its adverse impact on the well-being on some welfare leavers, and despite government indifference to the adverse effects during economic downturns, I believe that Clinton's welfare policies enabled millions of women to lift one leg up—to improve their situation compared to what it would be if they remained on welfare. The persistence of material hardships among near-poor families, however, dampens any rejoicing. We cannot and should not be satisfied with lifting families into the near-poor income range. We must develop additional government policies to help pull the second leg up, enabling welfare leavers to distance themselves and their families from material hardships.

In the past, I fully subscribed to the images Barbara Ehrenreich sketched in *Nickel and Dimed* when she chronicled her experiences in the low-wage labor market. Indeed, the images transport me back to the time. When one of Ehrenreich's Wal-Mart co-workers was unable to purchase a cheap shirt with her employee discount, I thought of coal miners so exploited that they were unable to buy coal to heat their own homes. When supervisors were making sure that Ehrenreich was not shirking her housecleaning activities, I thought of past images of supervisors on roller skates, making sure that telephone operators were not taking unwarranted breaks.

So why do I now believe that low-wage work can improve the lives of welfare mothers? One reason is that I no longer believe low-wage workers generally labor under harsh and oppressive conditions. My current vision does not replace profit-hungry capitalists with benevolent employers, as Charles Dickens transformed Ebenezer Scrooge in *A Christmas Carol*. Instead, bosses increasingly found labor turnover expensive and labor morale important.[5] Turnover raises training costs as seasoned workers were replace by neophytes. Moreover, oppressive conditions reduce morale, making it more likely that the best-performing workers will leave and few remaining workers will embrace the company's goals and interests. Fewer workers also face harsh working conditions because of the shift from a manufacturing to a service economy.

The concern for turnover rates is present even in today's low-wage labor markets. While replacements are generally easy to obtain in this sector, firms still would rather reduce training costs and retain their best workers. Interviewing 300 New York City workers in the early 1990s for her book *No Shame in My Game* (Russell Sage, 1999), Katherine Newman documented how fast-food employers were willing to adjust work schedules to keep their valued workers. Indeed, one of the barriers to employment faced by welfare leavers was employers' beliefs that these women would be unstable employees. Only when studies began to show these concerns were unfounded did this negative stereotype begin to erode.

I certainly do not want to romanticize how changes in labor management have reduced abusive and exploitive relationship. There are still bosses who cherish their ability to be arbitrary and employ heartless supervisors. And there are modern-day sweatshops, most notably in food preparation companies that have reproduced the factory conditions of yesteryear.[6] I now believe, however, that examples of inhumanity and debasement of workers are moving to the periphery of the low-wage sector.

It is still the case, however, that less-educated female workers are underpaid so I agree with Ehrenreich's conclusion that

> the "working poor," as they are approvingly termed, are in fact the major philanthropists of our society. They neglect their own children so that the children of others will be cared for; they live in substandard housing so that other homes will be shiny and perfect; they endure privation so that inflation will be low and stock prices will be high.[7]

As a result, I continue to support unionizing efforts and campaigns to enact living-wage legislation, but I no longer believe that these are the only ways or even the most important ways to increase the incomes of low-wage workers. I now believe that a high-employment economy will induce substantial wage increases for low-wage workers even in the absence of unions or other outside pressures.

Unfortunately, many reform critics believe that the Clinton-era boom did not significantly raise the wages of those who toil at the bottom of the labor market: young workers and single mothers with little education. They claim that even during boom times, there continues to be an abundant supply of low-wage workers available. And as long as this excess persists, wages for these workers stagnate.

SMALL SUCCESS

Economic data paint an entirely different picture. While wage rate increases for longtime employees were moderate, during the economic boom there were significantly larger increases for the lowest paid workers. Very low starting wages were followed by significant increases as workers gained experience and value.

Thus, a high-employment economy can play an important role in improving the economic well-being of the poor.

Unlike conservatives, however, I do not believe that a high-employment economy alone will solve the earnings problems faced by low-wage workers. Despite the rather robust wage increases a high-employment economy would provide, the vast majority of single mothers with little education still are consigned to limited earnings. In 2002, the median earnings of all single mothers with only a high school education equaled $10 per hour, an annual wage of no more than $20,000 if they worked full-time year-round. Of course, half of these single mothers earned less, and these are disproportionately welfare leavers. Many, like Tamara, have been unable to work full-time year-round, and a large proportion will have annual wages in the $12,000 to $15,000 range at least for the first few years after leaving welfare. While the addition of income supports, including the recently legislated federal refundable child credit, raises their incomes to the $20,000 to $25,000 range, these women will continue to suffer some level of material hardships.

I have come to realize, however, that even among welfare leavers who had limited financial gains, many have bettered their lives in other ways by entering the paid workforce. Indeed, I believe one important error made by many reform critics has been their underestimation of the nonfinancial costs of welfare and the nonfinancial benefits from paid employment. Two personal conversations reinforced this new perspective. The first was when I was visiting a friend who was a nursing home administrator. When our conversation turned to welfare, Pam related a recent experience. As part of the welfare-to-work program, her nursing home began a ten-week program that certified nurses' aides. She related to me the joy that many of these women took in the completion of the program. It was clear that these women took pride in their accomplishment that allowed them to move along the road to self-sufficiency and become role models to their children. "They treated it as we treat our children's graduation from college," Pam said. "They would dress up and bring their mothers and children to the graduation, going out to celebrate afterward."

The second conversation was with my son about his trade union organizing experience in Texas. Texas is a "right-to-work" state, so individual workers do not have to pay union dues even at workplaces that have voted for union representation. At Baptist Hospital in Beaumont, Josh's assignment was to raise the share of dues-paying workers. Coming from New York City, he was shocked at the low wage levels. After having worked there for a decade or more, many women were making no more than $1 an hour above minimum wage. What surprised Josh even more, however, was the pride they took in their work. For example, one of the most important grievances that these workers voiced was how the hospital's cost cutting had made it impossible for them to do a quality job. With a reduced staff and less equipment and materials, they could not maintain cleanliness at the levels they desired.

MOVING FAMILIES FORWARD

When I began circulating these ideas, a number of reform critics castigated my efforts. Many dismissed any positive assessments of the welfare-to-work transition given the current political climate. They believed that no matter how well founded, my position on nickel-and-dime jobs would undermine antipoverty struggles. Whatever its weaknesses were, these critics believed that *Nickel and Dimed* resonated with mainstream Americans and could stem attacks on welfare mothers and increase sympathy for unionizing efforts to better the wages and working conditions of less educated workers.

While appreciating these concerns, I have proceeded because I believe that many critics provide the wrong outlook for long-term welfare reform and the needs of less educated workers. Clearly, they were right to condemn many of the mean-spirited proposals made by conservatives during the 2001–2005 TANF reauthorization debates. Welfare must continue to provide a safety net, especially when there is no longer a high-employment economy capable of absorbing large numbers of welfare leavers. Most important, efforts must be made to protect the most vulnerable women—those who are least able to make the transition to work because of a variety of barriers.

While access to welfare must be protected, these critics devalued or dismissed the gains made by welfare leavers, so they ignore the valuable lessons that can provide a foundation for policies to help a broader group of working mothers. Critics of welfare-to-work policies have minimized the positive effects of a strong labor market. Once the official unemployment rate declined below 5 percent in 1997, robust job growth disproportionately benefited those at the bottom of the job ladder, enabling the overwhelming majority of welfare leavers to find employment and experience significant wage increases over their job tenure.

In 2000, I thought it was important to publicize how important tight labor markets had been for welfare leavers and other underemployed groups, particular black men with limited education or criminal records. I published material that documented how low unemployment rates enabled many to gain a foothold in the mainstream economy.[8] Even if these tight labor markets caused a modest increase in the inflation rate, I argued, they should be sustained because of these important social benefits.

What surprised me, however, was the unwillingness of some welfare reform critics to support my efforts. While they desired the maintenance of high-employment policies, while they feared that the Federal Reserve would weaken employment to reduce inflationary pressures, these critics would not be associated with publications that in any way put a positive spin on welfare reform.

Improvement in the minimum wage is crucial to low-wage workers. Indeed, I believe that this legislation should be given priority over unionizing and living-wage efforts. While I have supported efforts to raise wages directly, it is a mistake to focus *primarily* on the market wage received rather than the total incomes obtained. There must be a greater recognition of the role of government supplemental payments, including the EITC, in the lives of low-income families. These supplemental payments are substantial and enable working mothers to escape from stark poverty, especially if the minimum wage is raised.

Even among those who understand the importance of these supplemental programs, there has been a reluctance to support necessary changes. For a few years, together with a colleague at the Economic Policy Institute, I was involved with a tax proposal to correct some of the deficiencies of the current EITC program.[9] While these wage supplements have helped many families escape poverty, it has certain drawbacks that limited further upward mobility. Once annual wages rise above about $15,000, many single mothers begin to lose credits with further wage increases. Further wage increases will also reduce food stamp allotments and increase rents in subsidized housing and parental expenses for children in subsidized child care. As a result, the financial benefits from further wage increases can be quite small until annual wages rise above $25,000.

Our tax proposal was very favorably received by a number of legislators.[10] Unfortunately, it was not as well received by some welfare reform critics., They focused solely on the most vulnerable mothers and their children, those who had been left behind. As a result, they were less willing to give support to tax proposals that would aid primarily lower middle-class families and welfare mothers who had made the successful transition to paid employment.

One of the most important supports provided has been the dramatic expansion of child care for welfare leavers. Between 1997 and 2000, the federal Child Care Development Fund increased child care expenditures from $2.1 billion to $7.4 billion.[11] Rather than highlighting how helpful these funds had been for welfare leavers, some critics decried the loss of the ability of recipients to raise their young children, and others only complained that the child care slots provided were substandard and did not meet the needs of the vast majority of welfare leavers.

While there certainly were some problems with the quality of and access to child care facilities, these critics missed an opportunity to fight to extend these policies to all working women. Fortunately, this opportunity was taken up by a number of Washington policy analysts and child care activists nationally. As a result, one of the main conflicts in the recent TANF reauthorization debate was whether or not subsidized child care should be expanded to all low-income working mothers. Indeed, the expansion of federal funds for child care for mothers making the transition from welfare to work was a catalyst for an expansion of states providing universal prekindergarten for four- and five-year-olds.

In my research, I also found that welfare reform was an important catalyst for changes in program offerings at community colleges. Educational enhancements had to be tailored to a population who had done poorly in school and had family responsibilities. For this group, short-term education that leads to valuable vocational credentials seems to be the most effective path to success. In response, community colleges increased their vocational offerings, reducing their emphasis on academic tracks for students who hope to transfer to four-year colleges. These new programs provided learning tracks that proved to be helpful to a larger group of working men and women.

Instead of praising these programs and supporting their expansion, many reform critics characterized them as dead-end tracking programs because they would provide access only to subprofessional occupations, occupations that often pay no more than $15 per hour. These critics stressed that only four-year college degrees enable single mothers to independently escape material hardships.[12] They ignored, however, the barriers that basic skill deficiencies place in the way of many single mothers, deficiencies that present an insurmountable barrier to academic advancement, as failure rates attested to. I spoke with educators who believe that the most effective educational enhancements for the vast majority of welfare recipients are vocational credentials provided by community colleges, programs that most states currently allow recipients to use to satisfy their work-related requirements and programs that are beneficial to a large group of working families.

Finally, many reform critics reject efforts to increase marriage rates and child support payments, both of which would enable many families to distance themselves from poverty. When the Clinton administration took child support enforcement seriously, critics decried these efforts. They claimed that these efforts at obtaining payments from noncustodial fathers were senseless and mean spirited— senseless because these men had little income and mean spirited because these men were themselves the victims of a system that did not provide stable employment to less educated men. Evidence has proven otherwise, as child support payments have dramatically increased in the last decade, and some of these funds have been used to improve the employment possibilities of absent fathers.

The conservative rhetoric of many of the supporters of President George W. Bush's healthy marriage initiatives are certainly cause for concern. Rather than simply condemning these activities as policies to reestablish traditional patriarchal relations, reform critics should strengthen their positive aspects. Evidence so far indicates that these programs have had positive impacts and even greater potential if shaped to improve relationship skills.

We shouldn't praise nickel-and-dime jobs or trumpet vocational education, but we should see how they can be stepping stones that make sense for many working families. Low-wage employment can better people's lives, especially if government provides the necessary supplements, including income supports, education subsidies and supports for building healthy relationships.

ABOUT THE BOOK AND INTERVIEWS

The story of welfare reform could not be told without hearing from those involved, from senior policy analysts to agency managers to welfare leavers themselves. I learned as much about my own assumptions as I did about how policy plays out in real life from my interviews with 16 welfare leavers in Chicago, Milwaukee, Oakland, and Tampa. These were 90-minute, one-time interviews for which each participant was paid $60. The individuals were selected by directors of welfare support programs. I had asked to interview those who could be considered success stories because, as mentioned above, not only did I feel that they reflect the majority of leavers, but also their stories could give important insights into future policies.

Almost from the first interview, I realized that this activity would yield much more than texture and concreteness for the book I was preparing to write. Together with the interviews of the program directors and staff members at these sites, it provided me with a window into the lives of these women, which were much more complex than I had imagined. I gained important insights that qualitatively affected the structure of the book. For example, I had not anticipated writing a chapter that centered on the role of community colleges. After listening to a number of stories about the way these mothers were victimized by for-profit proprietary institutions when these women sought vocational training and credentials, I changed the book so that this issue could be fully explored. This led to interviews with community college and adult education directors that amplified the stories these mothers told and how programs have evolved for the better since welfare reform.

Most important, these interviews humbled me. I was struck by the time management discipline that many of these leavers forged so that they could be effective mothers and workers. They rose before 6 A.M. so that they could organize themselves before they had to prepare their kids for school and child care, and I was not sure that I would have the strength to do this for a week or two, let alone the years on end that they must. In this context, it seemed not simply foolish but also insensitive, even heartless, to focus on the reasons that they ended up in the situations they were in. As a result, I spent much less time asking them about the (bad) choices that they had made as teenagers and young adults than I had anticipated.

While at times I tried to steel myself in order to maintain a detached "objective" approach, it was impossible not to become emotional and morally outraged at the indignities that these struggling mothers have had to endure. I remain fearful of the way that these very limited personal stories can shape views on welfare reform. I know, however, that these interviews enriched my understanding of the impact of welfare reform on the lives of real people, and I hope they have made this book more truthful than it would have been otherwise.

Interviews with program directors and staff members, some of them former welfare recipients themselves, lend a unique perspective on the story of welfare reform. These women do not romanticize their clients. There were many mothers who could not gain the discipline and circumstances necessary to be as successful as many of the women I interviewed. These directors and staff members, however, did not fault these less successful mothers for a lack of effort or for the bad choices they had made when they were younger. Instead, they uniformly emphasized the difficulties these women faced and the need to find solutions that would move them ahead. These discussions and interviews also made me more attuned to what these mothers and staff workers considered success rather than what might have been my preconceived notions.

This more positive assessment of the impact of welfare reform and the need to adjust rather than replace the 1996 legislation was reinforced by my discussions with Washington policy analysts. Save one important Republican analyst, I spoke exclusively with those who were employed by liberal policy institutes. They all believed that welfare legislation had been much more successful than anticipated during its first five years, thanks to the strong economy that provided the necessary jobs and the tax revenues that enabled states to fund substantial work supports. They were, however, discouraged when I spoke with them because the weakened economy was not providing the necessary jobs and wage increases, and the war and Bush's tax agenda had undermined a fairly broad bipartisan coalition that was prepared to expand further the necessary work and educational supports.

These candid discussions animate the rich empirical data now available more than a decade after welfare legislation. Since neither tells the complete story, this book integrates the two in order to explore how to bring more working families closer to the American dream. Chapter 2 summarizes the legislative dynamics that led to reform legislation. It highlights the make-work-pay philosophy that motivated the Clinton administration and how the rise in social spending on safety net programs provided a fiscal rationale for reform.

Chapters 3 and 4 assess the more ideological reasons that underpinned the broad support for welfare reform. Chapter 3 discusses the widespread public perception that a culture of poverty inhibited the ability of the poor, particularly black men and women, from developing a strong work ethic. Chapter 4 discusses the issues of teenage birth rates and domestic violence within poor communities and their possible link to welfare.

Chapters 5 and 6 look at the impact of the Clinton-era economic boom and the Bush-era economic slowdown on the employment and earnings of welfare leavers. Besides evaluating the impact of the economic boom, chapter 5 indicates why adverse projections at the time of reform proved faulty, and methodological reasons why researchers sometimes obtain conflicting results. Chapter 6 evaluates the impact of economic slowdown and discusses high-employment and tax policies that could better the lives of all working mothers, and why they have not been legislative priorities.

Chapters 7–9 assess the impact of various support programs on the well-being of welfare leavers and how these programs apply to all working mothers. Chapter 7 explores the issue of government-funded child care and its impact on child development and on the provision of universal prekindergarten funding. Chapter 8 assesses educational policies for welfare leavers and their adaptability to all working mothers, emphasizing the critical role of community college vocational programs. Chapter 9 describes the marriage promotion and health relationship initiatives promoted by President Bush and how they can be adjusted to improve father–mother and father–child relationships among the working poor.

Chapter 10 summarizes the 2006 welfare reauthorization legislation. It describes the reason for its four-year delay and potential future changes. This chapter also summarizes the policy proposals that will strengthen families and communities.

2

Changing Welfare as We Know It

Clinton's "Making Work Pay" Philosophy

In any history of the Clinton administration, Donna Shalala figures centrally as the cabinet member directly responsible for developing and implementing welfare policies. Moreover, unlike a number of her senior staff, she did not resign in outrage when President Clinton chose to sign the 1996 welfare bill. Instead, she soldiered on to ensure that its implementation and subsequent adjustments were as helpful as possible to the vulnerable women and children who were affected.

Shalala could be the poster person for a modern-day Horatio Alger story. Born into a working class family, attending a technical high school in a neighborhood where many young men served and died as a result of the Vietnam conflict, Shalala rose to become a member of Bill Clinton's cabinet and president of some of the most prestigious universities in the nation.

Throughout her career, Shalala also practiced what she preached. When she was president at Hunter College during the 1980s, the urban public university had hundreds of female students with young children. Shalala made sure that there was sufficient child care to meet her students' needs. In addition, she assigned the most skilled staff to be available early mornings and late afternoons so that there would be effective counseling available for these young mothers when they dropped off and picked up their children.

Shalala's tenure at Hunter College coincided with the beginnings of the first discussion of a welfare crisis. These claims of a "crisis" were made by conservatives who argued that there was a growing welfare dependency. They suggested that a culture had developed whereby large numbers of families became accustomed to remaining on welfare, generation after generation. These conservatives argued that only by eliminating welfare as an entitlement—by distinguishing between the deserving and undeserving poor—could this cancerous culture be reigned in.

Distinguishing between the deserving and undeserving poor has a long tradition. Indeed, when discussing the needs of the poor, Talmudic rabbis suggested this distinction. On the one hand, they made clear the obligation of society to aid the most unfortunate. They wrote, "One must be careful to give charity promptly, lest the failure to do so result in the shedding of blood for perhaps the poor may die if not given immediately."[1] On the other hand, it was the obligation of the poor to make every effort to provide for themselves: "Skin a carcass in the marketplace and don't rely on charity."[2]

Liberals like Shalala did believe that welfare should be discouraged. Indeed, her convictions were strengthened by the attitude of Hunter students, especially black and Hispanic women who came from poorer neighborhoods. These students believed that many welfare mothers should take more responsibility for their situation and deplored the harmful effects that the presence of large numbers of welfare mothers had on all children in their neighborhoods.

Liberals, however, rejected conservative rhetoric that a welfare crisis existed. They argued that conservatives inflated the number of women who were permanently on welfare and rejected any notion that there was a significant culture that transmitted dependency across generations. Statistics supported these liberal claims. During the 10-year period 1969–1978, one-quarter of all U.S. families obtained some form of welfare. Among these families, almost half obtained payments in no more than two years, while only one-sixth received payments in at least eight years.[3] Moreover, during this time period, despite the economy experiencing its most severe recession since the end of World War II, the welfare population remained virtually constant at 3.8 million families annually. Thus, for most recipients, welfare primarily served as a safety-net program to help pull them through difficult times, and only a small percentage of recipients could be characterized as welfare dependent.

EMERGENCE OF THE MAKE-WORK-PAY STRATEGY

As Shalala headed for her new post as chancellor of the University of Wisconsin, Congress legislated the Family Support Act of 1988. This bill produced an unexpected political consensus. Republicans supported the legislation because it allowed states to require welfare recipients to work. Democrats secured provisions that required states to provide child care, job training, and other benefits for welfare leavers. Congressional debate waned, and it appeared that welfare policies would no longer be a divisive issue. Future events, however, proved that this was just the calm before the storm.

Demographic changes upset the temporary political equilibrium. In 1960, only about one-quarter of all married women with children 6–17 years old worked outside the home. By 1980, this rate reached almost 60 percent, equaling the rate for single mothers. These changes undermined the traditional social norm that women should exit the labor market once their children were born.

Over the next decade, the employment rate for single mothers rose only slightly but for married mothers dramatically, creating a 10-percentage-point gap. The gap continued to grow in the early 1990s, when despite the economic downturn, the percentage of married women with children working outside the home rose while the rate for single mothers fell.[4] This created resentment among married mothers, who became more critical of government financial support for non-working female householders.

Teen pregnancy statistics also began to trouble policy analysts. After decades of continuous decline, the teenage birth rate began to rise. In 1985, the birth rate for black and white women 15–17 years old was 69.3 and 24.4 per 1,000, respectively. By 1989, the rate for both groups had increased by 15–20 percent. Most troubling to some, 95 percent of births to black teenagers were to unwed mothers.[5] Conservatives seized upon these statistics to hammer home their point that welfare provided incentives for dysfunctional behavior.

The political battles became more heated as the welfare population increased. The number of families on welfare had remained fairly constant at about 3.8 million from 1976 through 1988. This all changed, however, with the subsequent economic slowdown. According to Rebecca Blank, "Despite a relatively mild economic slowdown, caseloads rose by 27 percent between 1990 and 1994. This rise was a driving force behind the desire of state governors to implement more radical welfare reform."[6]

Given the continued growth of the employment gap between married mothers and female householders, and the dramatic increases in welfare caseloads, welfare policies move again to the forefront of political discourse. This discourse, however, was not a replay of past politics. Instead, it took a fundamental turn when Clinton, the 1992 Democratic Party presidential nominee, campaigned to "end welfare as we know it." While conservatives dismissed this pronouncement as campaign rhetoric, events proved that it was the starting point for a new "third" way. It also highlighted an emerging difference among liberals.

Clinton's vision rejected conservative views that there is no need for government to financially support women making the transition from welfare to work, and no need to be concerned with their standard of living. It also rejected traditional liberal views that welfare must remain an entitlement available with limited conditions to all single mothers. Under the slogan "Making Work Pay," Clinton's

New Democrats supported a policy that made welfare payment conditional but provided substantial supports for the welfare-to-work transition. Whereas conservatives simply demanded government spending reductions, make-work-pay proponents argued that the reduction in direct welfare payment should be replaced by government financing of child care, job training, and other services to aid welfare leavers. Whereas traditional liberals believed that welfare rolls would decline simply through the voluntary choice of recipients when the labor market offered them sufficient financial incentives, make-work-pay proponents believed that some degree of coercion was necessary to change the choices made by many young women.

As his lead political advisor on domestic policy, President Clinton selected Bruce Reed, characterized by George Stephanopoulos as a "New Democrat of integrity and conviction."[7] For the cabinet position in charge of Health and Human Services (HHS), President Clinton selected Shalala. In a speech at American University some years later, she summarized her support for the make-work-pay strategy:

> I do think any job is better than welfare. But, I don't believe that moving into any job should cause people to live in terrible poverty. I'd rather see government resources supporting working people by providing them with child care and health care, and making sure their income is putting cash in their pockets to raise them above the poverty-line.[8]

The first component of the make-work-pay strategy was to increase substantially the earned income tax credit (EITC). David Ellwood, who was the initial promoter of the make-work-pay perspective, took leadership in devising the necessary legislation that almost doubled the maximum benefits working families could obtain.[9] After passage in early 1993, even if paid only the minimum wage, a single mother working full time year-round would escape official poverty. Elated by this legislative success, Ellwood felt like a kid in a candy store, able to accomplish all the public policies that he could imagine. He was to find that subsequent attempts to change welfare policy would not be nearly as tasty.

These attempts had to wait a full year as Clinton gave priority to his health care agenda. Heath care came first because, unlike welfare, it was an issue that affected the vast majority of families. Clinton felt that voters had given him a mandate to make changes, and it was especially timely, given spiraling health care costs. Moreover, changes in national health care policies would influence how much would be provided to welfare leavers and their children. In addition, the same congressional committees decide upon both health care and welfare proposals, so both Clinton initiatives could not be legislated simultaneously.

Just as important, President Clinton could not move quickly on welfare reform because there was a significant disagreement within his administration over the shape of the proposal. These disagreements were clearly evident when a working committee was set up during the summer of 1993. While there was general agreement on the need to provide work supports, the committee divided over work requirements and the degree to which welfare would be withheld from some applicants. The team at HHS that Shalala directed—Ellwood, Mary Jo Bane, and Wendell Primus—generally favored building on the 1988 bill: limited work requirement and no lifetime limits. By contrast, Clinton's political consultants, especially Reed, favored more stringent work requirements and enactment of lifetime limits. In addition, the two groups differed as to whether welfare should provide additional payments for children born to welfare recipients and if payments should be given to teenage mothers.

THE POLITICAL STRUGGLE OVER WELFARE REFORM

In spring 1994, HHS director Shalala finally released President Clinton's welfare reform bill that had been fashioned by Ellwood and Bane. The proposal accepted some limited employment requirements for younger women (those who were born after 1971). For these women, after two years on welfare, they would be required to take a public-sector or subsidized private-sector job. Some recipients could face sanctions, resulting in termination of welfare for the entire family. States could also refuse to give additional payments to recipients who had additional children. The proposal, however, had no lifetime limits and continued to provide benefits to teenage mothers.

Still smarting from the defeat of his health care initiative, Clinton moved cautiously on welfare reform. There was strong support from some Democratic legislators, including Daniel Moynihan. The bill would have cleared the Appropriations Committee and come up for a vote in fall 1994. The lead Republican staffer in charge of welfare reform legislation was Ron Haskins. He told me, "The majority of Republicans would have supported the bill. There was a crucial group of House Republicans, including Clay Shaw and Nancy Johnson, who always wanted a compromise bill, especially when we were in the minority." However, Clinton was forced to withdraw the legislation as a result of the strenuous opposition from liberal members of the Democratic caucus and advocacy groups. According to Haskins,

> There was no way that Clinton could have passed that bill in 1994—the Democrats would not go along with it. While Democrats always said they were for work requirements, they were not serious because in order to get people to work you had to do something serious to the system. The system coddled people. If you didn't show up for work, they sent you a letter and if you didn't show up again, they just sent you another letter. That's the way the system operated; it just sent checks.

In testimony before the House Ways and Means Subcommittee on Human Resources, many liberals continued to claim that the real problem was lack of decent-paying jobs—jobs that recipients would voluntarily accept if available. As a result, many liberals claimed that all that was needed was "carrots"—better jobs—and continued to reject "sticks": work requirements or time limits. As Mark Greenberg from the Center for Law and Social Policy maintained, "Simply forcing them to leave, or exposing them to the world of work, will not address the underlying problem. Rather, the principal challenge is to help them reach the point where they can support their families."[10]

Deborah Lewis of the American Civil Liberties Union testified against the withholding of additional funds for children born when the mother was already on welfare. She claimed,

> [These policies] violated the right to privacy ... in the same manner that anti-abortion laws and restrictions on birth control violate these rights. ... Just as the government cannot prohibit a woman from practicing birth control or having an abortion, it cannot coerce these practices through the threat of termination of necessary subsistence benefits.[11]

Many liberals were also upset with another set of components of the Clinton welfare bill: child support enforcement and stepped-up paternity establishment. Cynthia Newbille, director of the National Black Women's Health Project, and members of the Congressional Black Caucus cautioned that without a comprehensive job creation strategy, measures such as wage garnishment and the revocation of professional licenses would be largely ineffective within the African-American community.[12]

Shalala aggressively promoted these policies, particularly the withholding of professional licenses. Withholding of licenses and garnishing wages of federal employees would allow HHS to have enforcement initially most heavily on middle-income, professional fathers. Moreover, there was widespread political support for these provisions. Even then Texas Governor George W. Bush advocated withholding hunting licenses from fathers who were in arrears.[13]

Unfortunately, the 1994 elections shifted the control of Congress to Republicans. Flush from victory, House leader Newt Gingrich was intent on implementing his "Contract with America." As a result, a new Republican bill demanded strict lifetime limits with no guarantees of work supports for welfare leavers, and demanded that aid be refused to teenage mothers. Its most controversial recommendation was the reinstitution of orphanages to be available for children of parents who refused to enter the workforce.

The Clinton administration roundly condemned the Republican bill. In a press release, the administration claimed that the bill was "weak on work, tough on kids, and doesn't have all the pieces of child support enforcement that we want it to have and it's simply awful on teenagers." The administration pointed out that the orphanage plan was not only inhumane but also not feasible, given the limited funding provided to states. If fully implemented, the Republican bill would cause 6.9 million people to lose benefits, almost 700,000 of them teenage mothers. The states, however, would be given only $1.1 billion to fund benefits to the children in these families, funding that translated into less than 30,000 spaces in residential care, or 225,000 provisions for foster care.[14]

Hillary Clinton seized upon the orphanage issue. She criticized the Republicans for failing to recognize that "children are best left with their families." Ms. Clinton then went on to write her book *It Takes A Village: And Other Lessons Children Teach Us* (1996) with the central narrative that "it takes a village to raise a child"—government and community must work in partnership with parents.[15]

Not surprisingly, many liberals, such as Marian Wright Edelman, chair of the Children's Defense Fund, spoke out against welfare reform. She claimed, "The Old Testament prophets and the New Testament Messiah made plain God's mandate to protect the poor and the weak and the young. The Senate and House welfare bills do not meet this test."[16]

In order to show his "toughness" on welfare, Clinton chided the Republican bill for having little to say about work requirements. That is, the Republican bill, besides stipulating lifetime limits and reducing funding, left it up to states to determine the responsibilities they had to those on welfare and the responsibilities of welfare recipients. By contrast, Clinton pointed to the work requirements in his bill as evidence that he took more seriously than Republicans the welfare-to-work transition.

At the same time that the Clinton welfare bill was unveiled, HHS greatly expanded waivers to states, allowing them to experiment with new sets of policies. By the summer of 1996, HHS had approved waivers for 43 states.[17] These experiments increased the role that governors played in the congressional welfare debate. As governors claimed success for their pilot projects, the waivers and the social science research that supported their claims helped support Republican proposals.[18] After Clinton vetoed the second Republican bill in January 1996, the National Governors' Association (NGA) unanimously approved bipartisan agreements on welfare and Medicaid reform at their winter meetings. Both House Speaker Gingrich and Senate Majority Leader Bob Dole pledged that Congress would give the governors' policy statements serious consideration.

The bipartisan NGA and congressional support undoubtedly was influenced substantially by budgetary considerations. In particular, the sudden increase in the size of the welfare population in the early 1990s was accompanied by similar increases in other social welfare programs. Between 1990 and 1994, the number of families receiving food stamps increased from 7.9 to 11.1 million. This expansion was also experienced by the Supplemental Security Income (SSI) program, particularly for three categories: noncitizens, children, and individuals suffering from addictions. Projections from the General Accounting Office (table 2.1) suggested that, without reforms, SSI caseloads would continue to grow rapidly in these areas for at least another five years. While we might see these increased caseloads as quite justified, they clearly strengthened support for policies to constrain welfare spending.

Many Democrats were outraged by the damaging effects the NGA bill would have on children. Senator Moynihan claimed that, as a result of lifetime limits, by 2005 five million children would be cut off from assistance and that almost half of these children would be black. He lamented, "To drop 2,414,000 children in our central cities from life support would be the most brutal act of social policy we have known since Reconstruction." Senator Carole Moseley-Braun suggested that the plan might lead to a civil rights suit because it clearly "would have disparate impacts on African-American children."[19]

Shalala distanced herself from this doomsday forecast. She thought that Moynihan and others overstated the dangers because they underestimated the number of welfare leavers who would find employment and the ability of states to exempt one of every five families from the cutoff under the governors' plan. However, Shalala announced that the president could not support the NGA welfare proposal in its current form. It needed to be modified to provide vouchers for children of parents terminated from assistance, to retain the entitlement status of child welfare services and food stamps, and to include fundamental revisions of the immigration section.

Throughout spring 1996, Republicans fine-tuned their proposals. As Haskins related,

> I imagined that Clinton would be in a room with [Robert] Reich and Shalala both trying to convince him not to sign, and I wanted to take away as many of their arguments as possible. Republicans added some additional funding for work supports and child care, separated out Medicaid proposals, and eliminated the Wisconsin waiver that riled many Democrats.

Table 2.1. Supplemental Security Income Caseload (in Thousands)

YEAR	TOTAL	NONCITIZENS	CHILDREN	DRUGS/ALCOHOL
1989	4,700	370	200	16
1995	6,500	785	917	130
2000 (projected)		2,000	1,816	200

Source: Lynn Karoly, Jacob Klerman, and Jeannette Rogowski, "Effects of the 1996 Welfare Reform Changes on the SSI Program" (with comments by Matt Weidinger), in *The New World of Welfare*, ed. Rebecca Blank and Ron Haskins (The Brookings Institution, 2001), 482–499, reprinted with permission.

As the bill reached its final stages, President Clinton called a meeting of his staff to determine his course of action. As Haskins imagined, all of those at HHS urged him to veto the bill, while his political operatives—Dick Morris, Reed, and Rahm Emanuel—thought that it was imperative for him to sign it.

All in the room agreed that the most harmful provisions were with the parts of the bill outside of welfare reform: $54 billion in savings through cutbacks in food stamps and benefits to immigrants. In supporting Clinton's signing the bill, Reed described his position: "A good welfare bill wrapped in a bad budget bill." Shalala was particularly concerned that these cutbacks would adversely affect a million poor children. She strenuously urged Clinton to veto this bill in hopes that Republicans would respond by making improvements as they had in response to previous vetoes.[20]

Emanuel and trade advisor Mickey Cantor rejected the view that Clinton should hope for a better bill. They contended that a veto would cause "more harm by perpetuating a failed system." These advisors also thought that the current bill contained core provisions that were close to Clinton's original proposals and was much better than the ones he had vetoed. Moreover, they feared that a veto would break faith with voters who took Clinton at his word when he promised in 1992 to "end welfare as we know it."

CRITICISMS OF THE WELFARE BILL

When Clinton decided to sign the bill, there were two reactions. Three of the senior staff at HHS—Peter Edelman, Mary Jo Bane, and Wendell Primus—eventually resigned. Clinton's decision was criticized by virtually all liberal advocacy groups. In a Children's Defense Fund press release, Marian Wright Edelman stated,

> This legislation is the biggest betrayal of children and the poor since the Children's Defense Fund began. President Clinton's signature on this pernicious bill makes a mockery of his pledge not to hurt children. . . . This act will leave a moral blot on his presidency and on our nation that will never be forgotten. Today marks a tragic end to our nation's legacy of commitment to our most vulnerable children—this is truly a moment of shame for all Americans.[21]

There was a second group, however, that was willing to support Clinton's decision. Shalala and transportation director Henry Cisneros accepted Clinton at his word, that after reelection he would give priority to eliminating the food stamp and immigrant cutbacks. Stephanopoulos considered it a close call but understood the political reasons that compelled Clinton to sign this bill.

Stephanopoulos (and all those in the cabinet) were well aware that Clinton's decision had little to do with his reelection. Only Morris believed that a veto would cost Clinton a second term. More important was the pressure from congressional Democrats to sign virtually any welfare bill. Many of these Democrats were elected from relatively conservative states or congressional districts allowing them to deviate only so much and a limited number of times from the moderate values of their constituents. They feared losing their upcoming elections if Clinton forced them to support another veto. Thus, the interests of his fellow Democrats, not his own future, played a crucial role in Clinton's political calculations.

The reaction among liberals was predictable. Clinton was pictured as a heartless politician whose sole aim was to regain a more moderate constituency—especially those whose defection proved so costly in 1994. According to Robert Sheer:

> Clinton is buying into the conservative principle that welfare helped to destroy families by offering perverse economic incentives to young women giving birth to babies out of wedlock.... Clinton knows the nuances of the welfare debate as well as anyone and he knows the bill is a disaster in the making. It has nothing to do with serious reform of welfare and everything to do with the random brutal assault on the poor, most of whom are children.[22]

Of course, the Clinton administration trumpeted his signing as a victory. In January 1997, Shalala wrote:

> The belief that dependence must be reduced and dignity increased now transcends party lines. In fact, Mr. Clinton vetoed two welfare bills because they defied this consensus.... In contrast to the two previous bills, the new law does not replace the national guarantee of food stamps and school lunches with block grants to the states. It drops proposed deep cuts in funds for child-abuse prevention, foster care, and adoption assistance, preserving our national commitment to these vital services.... It is tough on parents who don't pay child support. And, to enable parents to go to work, the law adds $3.5 billion for child-care services.[23]

Shalala then made clear how this law fit perfectly into the make-work-pay philosophy:

> The goal of our welfare-reform strategy must always be to make work pay.... We did that by fighting for and enacting budgets that dramatically expanded the earned-income tax credit for 15 million working-poor families and invested in education and training to help people find jobs and keep them. We did it by raising the minimum wage to $5.15 an hour, thereby making it a living wage and giving all full-time minimum wage workers an $1,800 annual raise. And we did it by expanding Head Start and child care and approving several state demonstration projects designed to expand health-care coverage for the working poor.[24]

After the election, Clinton fulfilled his promise to Shalala and Cisneros by successfully reinstituting benefits to legal immigrants and restoring food stamp funding. He also proposed legislation to support the employment of long-term welfare recipients. To encourage private sector jobs, Clinton provided a generous targeted tax credit to employers who hired long-term welfare recipients. He also campaigned for grants to cities to help employers create new opportunities for welfare leavers.

In 1998, Clinton proposed to distribute $1 billion in federal bonuses to states that were the most successful in moving recipients into jobs and keeping them there. In each year, $200 million would be distributed to the 10 states that ranked highest on each of four measures: job entry rates, success in the work force, improvement in entry rates, and improvement in workforce success. Workforce success would be measured by job retention and improvement in earnings for recipients. Through these policy initiatives, Clinton made clear that his focus was on sustained employment, not simply reducing the welfare rolls.[25]

While Peter Edelman resigned soon after Clinton signed the welfare bill, he remained silent during the presidential election campaign. However, three days after Clinton's reelection, Edelman gave a speech in Milwaukee strongly criticizing Clinton's decision. He gave the same speech dozens of times throughout the country over the next six months so that detractors would know that they were not alone in their condemnation of Clinton's decision.

Edelman also mobilized opposition through his writings, in particular, his widely quoted article, "The Worst Thing Bill Clinton Has Done."[26] There he laid out two propositions: Clinton did not have to sign the bill, and the loss of welfare as an entitlement would worsen the lives of millions of children. When I interviewed Edelman in January 2004, he continued to passionately oppose the welfare bill.

Unlike Stephanopoulos, Edelman emphasized the vulnerability of Republican legislators who were under election pressure to show that they had fulfilled something from their "Contract with America." Edelman argued, "House Republicans, especially freshmen, began to worry that they were vulnerable to defeat on the basis that they had accomplished so little of what they had come to Washington to do." As a result, he believed that they were willing to make changes to convince Clinton to sign the welfare bill. Thus, he believed that a third veto would have led to a better welfare bill.

Edelman's criticism went even further. He argued that Clinton had created the problem by his previous actions. First, Edelman claimed that a welfare bill was unnecessary. By 1996, welfare rolls had already declined by more than a million families. Clinton could have declared that these declines reflected the success of his policy of providing waivers to states in which more than three-quarters of all welfare families resided. Clinton also refused to drawn a line in the sand, making clear what he would not accept. For example, Edelman cited Clinton's willingness to attack publicly only the most egregious parts of the first House welfare bill—promotion of orphanages and cutting of school lunch programs—and withheld criticism of its core provision to end entitlements.

Evidence of employment successes did not convince Edelman to change his assessment that the bill caused unnecessary hardship to millions of children. Edelman did not anticipate the extent to which states used their block grant funds to implement work supports. Edelman continued to believe, however, that it was the strong economy and increases in the EITC and minimum wage that were overwhelming responsible for this employment growth, and not the welfare bill. He also cited the success of British welfare policies that rely exclusively on positive economic incentives to work.

Edelman understood that political realities in the United States in 1996 necessitated some set of coercive policies. He cited a number of states that adopted such policies that he could accept. What he could not live with, what he found unconscionable, was Clinton's unwillingness to set federal standards to protect recipients from capricious sanctions and unfair work requirements. He felt that, as a result, a number of states engaged in a "race to the bottom," demonstrating their mean-spiritedness by having the most severe requirements possible to discourage families from remaining on welfare.

Edelman made clear that it was discretionary judgments at the state level that drove the worst policies. For example, federal law required 30 percent of welfare mothers to be in some workfare situation. This provision, however, stipulated that any drop in the welfare rolls could be counted toward the federal workfare requirement. Since every state had a welfare drop of at least 30 percent, they all quickly met their federal requirement without actually having to place any current recipients in workfare programs.

Edelman lamented how the federal government encouraged states to adopt "work first" strategies that were cheap and forced recipients to accept immediate employment rather than invest in training programs that would enhance skills. As a result, he felt that many families sank deeper into poverty when they left welfare but were not able to sustain employment. He complained that state policies worsened the situation of many poor families, needlessly causing some to fall into extreme poverty—families with incomes less than half what was required to escape official poverty.

After working for 15 years on the House Ways and Means Committee, rising to chief economist, Primus joined HHS because of his desire to help shape welfare policies.[27] Unlike Peter Edelman, who returned to a tenured position at Georgetown Law School, Primus had nothing secure to fall back on when he resigned.

Primus's principled stance was applauded by many, including even some, like Arianna Huffington, who favored the welfare bill. In a column written after his resignation, she highlighted how Primus maintained his personal integrity by resigning because "to remain would be to disown all the analysis my office has produced regarding the impact of this bill." She juxtaposed his principled stand to that of other liberals who "didn't give up without a whimper—they gave up with a yawn." Not surprisingly, her harshest criticisms were reserved for President Clinton:

> In his trademark way of holding two diametrically opposed positions at once, Clinton both signed the bill and wrote in his new book that "there are parts of the legislation that are just plain wrong." But once re-elected, he added, he would fix them. So, the president is asking opponents of the bill to re-elect him so he can undo the law that would not be on the books without him—while simultaneously taking credit for a step he called "historic." It is the kind of chutzpah that rivals the young man who, after murdering his parents, asks the court for mercy on the grounds that he is now an orphan.
>
> So here is a tale of two men, Baby Boomer Democrats both: One sailed from Hope to the White House, with no moral compass but with finely tuned instincts about how he can stay there; the other, a man with four children to support, gave up a secure job and a staff of 30 at HHS to stand up for what he believed. . . . I dream of a day when the political battle is between people with distinct visions and strongly held principles, instead of hollow shells tossed about by the political imperatives of the latest polls. Clinton believed that signing the bill was morally the right thing to do by 73 percent to 12 percent. Primus believed that resigning was the right thing to do by the power of one.[28]

Huffington's desire for pure morality to govern political decisions is dead wrong: there is extreme danger if we had a government run by moral crusaders, and indeed, over the last few years she has railed against the moral crusaders in the George W. Bush administration. Moreover, part of the problem of welfare reform was the zealotry of these who perceived themselves as protectors of the poor. If they had embraced his original bill and use of state waivers, Clinton might have been able moved on welfare reform before the 1994 elections and been more willing to hold the line when facing opposition from Republicans. As a result, these defenders of the poor marginalized themselves and had little influence over the shape of welfare legislation. Only at the last moment, thanks to Senator Paul Wellstone, were they able to inject into the bill a domestic violence option and have some influence on the work supports provided.

Indeed, the uncompromising stance of many liberals may have created some of the problems Clinton faced. Whereas many liberals were willing to accept some work and time limit requirements post-1996, they and their advocacy groups adamantly opposed these provisions of Clinton's original bill. While in 1996 many counseled Clinton to claim victory by citing the success of state waivers, in 1994 they criticized these waivers as an abandonment of federal regulation.

After a year at temporary positions, Primus joined a liberal economic policy group, the Center on Budget and Policy Priorities, and in 2003 returned to government service as Minority Staff Director at the congressional Joint Economic

Committee. It was clear from my discussions that Primus was no political zealot. His years of government service conditioned him to understand the necessities of political compromise, so he did not have ill will toward Clinton. Unlike Peter Edelman, Primus's resignation was based solely on the immigrant and food stamp portions of the bill. For him, it was insufficient that Clinton would make reversing these provisions a priority in his next administration.

As to the welfare provisions, Primus agreed with Edelman that it had caused extreme poverty to grow. Indeed, when we spoke he had just finished making a presentation of new data that quantified his assertions that more than a million female-headed households lost income as a result of welfare reform. More than Edelman, however, Primus believed that there were important positive achievements. Indeed, he has documented the substantial decline in the share of children living in lone-mother households, one of the key goals of the welfare reform bill.

What troubled Primus was the growing insensitivity of welfare providers. In a moral society, welfare professionals would be advocates for the poor, trying to make sure that they could obtain all the government supports and payments that they were legally entitled to. Since welfare reform, welfare professionals have instead been encouraged to see themselves as protecting the taxpayers who are funding welfare. As a result, their objective is to save as much money as possible even if it means knowingly withholding information that could aid welfare clients.

As evidence, Primus cited state agencies that made little effort to smooth the welfare-to-work transition. They provided little support to ensure that clients would continue to receive food stamps when they left the welfare rolls. Agencies discouraged welfare leavers from applying immediately for child care slots, requiring them to first seek alternatives. For Primus, this change in values and objectives was more damaging in the long run than the particular provisions of the legislation.

Just as Primus and Edelman, the passing of time had not changed Shalala's assessment of welfare reform when I interviewed her in 2004. While she believed that, in hindsight, a case could be made that welfare reform should have come early in Clinton's first term when, with a Democratic majority and a reasonable consensus, he could have had his original bill adopted. There was evidence, however, that the public was much more attuned to the lack of health coverage that affected working people. Moreover, Shalala believed that the waiver legislation that was effectively coordinated by Bane provided a necessary working model for reform.

Shalala stressed that, after passage of the welfare reform bill, her office was able to make sure that its worst aspects did not materialize. She believes that the waiver period was crucial in developing constructive administrative relationships. As a result, HHS was able to work successfully with many state policy makers to assure that as much money as possible went into child care and other support services. To facilitate implementation, Shalala hired nationally more than 700 individuals, a significant number of whom were former recipients.

Shalala emphasized her role in development of policies to combat domestic violence, citing her 1993 efforts with Janet Reno. While not denying that many welfare mothers are victimized, Shalala was struck by how many immigrants were in domestic violence shelters. She even noted how her efforts were instrumental in convincing Israel to set up domestic violence shelters and found that there immigrant women were also predominant.

When asked about the decline in food stamp coverage, Shalala pointed out that it was primarily due to bureaucratic problems, reflecting inexperience among welfare office staff. She rejected claims that the insensitivity of some states fell along political lines. She cited a number of states with Republican governors—Wisconsin, South Carolina, and Georgia—that had exemplary responses to guarantee that food stamp coverage did not end with the transition from welfare to work. In general, she felt that in the vast majority of states, there was not an attempt to throw off of welfare those women who had the most barriers and that the discretionary judgments of caseworkers were much more humane than official policies.

Shalala discounted any emphasis on the growth of extreme poverty due to the ending of welfare. She pointed out that the data cannot determine whether these individuals were living alone or in extended families and thus thought that the numbers of truly destitute individuals were much lower than the numbers projected by welfare reform detractors.

Shalala suggested that part of the problem was the large number of less educated immigrants who overwhelm the health and school systems and depress wages at the lower rungs of the job ladder.[29] It is not that Shalala is anti-immigrant. Indeed, since becoming president at University of Miami in 2001, Shalala has worked to improve the situation of the recent immigrants that the university hires in custodial positions. She instituted a university policy to provide them with weekly free English-language classes during their working hours. While this creates more labor turnover, Shalala believes strongly that it is a small price to pay for the resulting upward mobility of hard-working Latino and Haitian immigrants.

Shalala thought that the largest corporations played a very positive roll in welfare reform. They were willing to hire welfare leavers because of the good public relations they received as well as gaining access to Clinton, and also because they needed workers as the job market tightened. Importantly, the Clinton administration funded job services for these workers that reduced their risk of failure, and allowed corporations to be more confident in the welfare leavers they hired.

Shalala felt that traditional welfare rights advocates have little understanding of what working people desire in a job. Unlike middle-class professionals, they do not see their lives revolving around jobs and careers. Welfare leavers desire a job that supports their families, so the notion of a "dead end" job is not a meaningful concept to them. It is the role of government not to focus on the "quality" of the jobs but to make sure full-time year-round employment enables these women to better their lives financially and to better support their families.

CONCLUDING REMARKS

The history just presented differs from accounts presented by welfare reform critics. They emphasize President Clinton's errors in judgment and philosophy while minimizing their own miscalculations more than I have.[30] Some of these critics focused exclusively on the link between writings of conservative Charles Murray and the 1996 welfare reform legislation. In 1984, Murray published *Losing Ground: American Social Policy, 1950–1980*, in which he argued that welfare funding was responsible for the growth in poverty rates the nation was experiencing. As a result of generous cash payments, he claimed, "pride in independence was compromised, and with it a certain degree of pressure on the younger generation to make good on the family tradition." Thus, unwed motherhood became the norm and welfare dependency resulted. Many critics contend that Murray's views provided the intellectual rationale that underpinned attacks on welfare that led to the 1996 reforms. By contrast, Peter Edelman contends that Clinton's own initiatives, not his need to respond to conservative ideologues, were responsible for the 1996 legislation. Specifically, Edelman wrote that when he joined the Clinton team in 1992,

> I thought the welfare war was over with the bipartisan passage of the Family Support Act of 1988.... The Republicans gained recognition for compulsory work and the Democrats gained agreement that money would be appropriated for child care, job training, and other supports. I was somewhat concerned that Clinton had brought the welfare issue up again in his campaign . . . but I didn't think it would result in any serious damage.[31]

For Edelman, it was the make-work-pay philosophy, not Murray's vision, that was responsible for the 1996 legislation.

I also find fault with the thesis that welfare reform was dictated by the needs of low-wage employers.[32] If this thesis were valid, we would have seen support for restricting welfare begin during a period of high employment when wages were rising. By contrast, the move toward reform began in 1993 when unemployment was still widespread and firms had little concern about rising wages. Moreover, when state initiatives began forcing recipients into the labor market, reluctance to hire welfare leavers was widespread. And to the extent that employers have been seeking cheap labor, immigrants would seem to be a more likely source. Indeed, the respected academician and trade union advocate Vernon Briggs contends that there was a fundamental link between the ending of Jim Crow and the reopening of immigration in 1965.[33] He reasoned that if black workers were no longer going to provide as much cheap labor as before, a new supply of immigrant labor would be required to depress wages.

Most important, many critics believe that the fundamental problem with welfare reform was the abandonment of welfare as an entitlement, replaced by an emphasis on personal responsibility. This view is forcefully presented by Sharon Hays, who argued:

> The inadequacies of welfare reform ... follow from a serious problem in the cultural logic of personal responsibility itself. ... It is an image of unfettered individualism—of every man, woman, and child as an island unto themselves. This logic most obviously neglects the "dependency" of children and the fact that no parent is "unfettered." ... It makes invisible, in other words, our interdependence.
>
> It is this failure to take account of the full measure of our interdependence that allows for the construction of "us-versus-them" scenarios that not only demonize welfare recipients but also call into question the values and behaviors of all of us who find ourselves unable to mimic the mythological model of perfected self-reliance: seamlessly juggling our multiple commitments without ever needing to depend on our friends, our families, our neighbors, or the nation to support us.
>
> All of this explains why, in the long run, the Personal Responsibility Act will not be a law we can proudly hail as a national "success." Women, children, nonwhites, and the poor will be hardest hit. But the consequences of reform will leave nearly all of us losers, in economic, political, and moral terms.[34]

During the public discourse surrounding welfare reform, there was a substantial amount of demonizing of recipients, sometimes relying upon unfounded racial stereotypes.[35] I believe, however, that Hays overemphasizes conservative views that there is no need for *any* government support while virtually ignoring the make-work-pay approach that commits the government to substantial supports but does require *some* personal responsibility and initiative.[36]

Left academic critics multiplied Hays's errors by demonizing welfare reform and totally ignoring the make-work-pay philosophy. This is most apparent in the 14 papers presented in *Lost Ground: Welfare Reform, Poverty, and Beyond*, edited by Randy Albelda and Ann Withorn (2002). In its preface, Barbara Ehrenreich stated, "It is hard to miss the racism and misogyny that helped motivate welfare reform." Albelda claimed, "As currently implemented, the welfare to work solution is a match made in hell." Gwendolyn Mink believed that welfare's "foremost objective is to restore the patriarchal family" and "exploits women of color to suffocate single mothers' independence." Indeed, Albelda and Mink wonder if one of the objectives of the 1996 welfare reform was to rob poor mothers of their children.[37]

I forcefully reject attempts to demonize all those who have a positive assessment of welfare reform. The interviews I conducted reinforced my view that the difference between those like Shalala (and myself) who believe that the Clinton efforts provided an effective foundation for improving the lives of vulnerable women and their children, and those like Peter Edelman (and Primus) who believe that it was fundamentally harmful, is not individual morality. Shalala and many defenders of the Clinton reform are every bit as concerned with the well-being of vulnerable women and their children as are its detractors. Both groups hope that enforcement would be as compassionate as possible and do not trivialize the unfortunate families who fall through the cracks and sink deeper into poverty and personal despair. As a result, I hope that you keep in mind that reasonable people can disagree.

This chapter has pointed to budgetary concerns that generated legislative support for welfare reform. Clearly there were other factors, as well. Probably most important was a growing perception that a "welfare culture" had developed, increasing the willingness of a significant share of women from poor communities to choose welfare rather than the world of work. This perceived lack of an appropriate work ethic provided a groundswell of support among the general public that promoted coercive components of welfare legislation. In addition, there was a growing perception that welfare was linked to a growth in teenage pregnancies and family disorganization. Chapters 3 and 4 explore these perceptions and their relationship to welfare reform.

3

Work Effort among the Poor

The belief that there are intergenerational communal norms, causing the poor to have dysfunctional behavioral traits, has been characterized as the "culture-of-poverty" thesis. In the United States, a repository of these negative stereotypes has been the black community, which has been perceived to lack a strong work ethic and other proper behavioral traits. Courtland Milloy lamented:

> Not a whole heck of a lot has changed since that 1991 General Social Survey by the National Opinion Research Center, which found that most whites think blacks are lazy, violence-prone, less intelligent and less patriotic. Even sadder, nearly 30 percent of black people felt the same way about themselves.[1]

This culture-of-poverty concept is important because it gave a particular tone and vigor to the critique of welfare. Starting at least in the 1970s, the vision of welfare in the public's mind was an inner-city black woman who did not work but persisted in having children she could not support. Many observers argue that the broad acceptance of this black image was a critical reason why the American public so overwhelmingly supported welfare reform proposals. Martin Gilens found that the U.S. public, as a result of biased and sensationalistic media coverage, associated welfare with undeserving blacks who would rather take handouts than strive to better themselves. Gilens is compelling in his presentation of how these falsehoods mobilized racial prejudice without seeming to be racist.[2]

In their bestselling books, *New York Times* reporters David Shipler and Jason DeParle have highlighted cultural explanations for the causes and consequences of poverty within the black community, which underpin their belief that certain aspects of welfare reform were effective. In particular, this perspective infers that welfare reform can play a transformative role in the lives of welfare recipients by enabling them to overcome their behavioral problems, including poor work habits. Thus, even if there is only a modest improvement in material well-being, welfare reform could be judged successful because of its positive behavioral effects.

In this chapter I present a brief history of the origins of the culture-of-poverty thesis, its application to the black community, and its impact on welfare reform. Most important, this chapter explains why I believe that special structural factors experienced by black communities during the 1980s—not intergenerational cultural norms—explain the dysfunctional behavior that was present in a particular postmigration cohort: black men and women born in the late 1960s and early 1970s.

THE EMERGENCE OF THE CULTURE OF POVERTY THESIS

At the beginning of the twentieth century, industrialization brought millions of immigrants to the United States. The American eugenics movement feared that genetically inferior immigrants from eastern and southern Europe would undermine American values. During his 1903 commencement address at Wellesley College, President Theodore Roosevelt urged the graduates to have many children to stem the tide of "race suicide," which he associated with the high birth rates of these inferior immigrants.[3] Eugenics publications provided a forum for Margaret Sanger to publicize her proposals to reduce immigrant birth rates, including contraception.

While the eugenics movement held out little hope for the uplifting of inferior immigrants, Progressives stressed that immigrants could overcome their inferior cultures by becoming Americanized through compulsory education, settlement houses, and trade unions. Of interest, Progressives considered eastern European Jewish immigrants culturally inferior since they had all of the social disorganization found in other immigrant groups. Jewish criminal activity was widespread and resulted in public outcries. The desertion of families became such a large problem that the *Jewish Daily Forward* routinely ran a "Gallery of Missing Husbands" to assist women in locating their errant husbands.[4] Indeed, Louis Wirth formalized the culture-of-poverty thesis to explain this dysfunctional behavior. Wirth contrasted these newer Jewish immigrants with earlier German Jewish immigrants:

While the Jews of the east lived in large part in rural communities, in a village world, those of the west were predominantly a city people in touch with the centers of trade and . . . with the pulsating intellectual life of the world. While the Jews of the Rhine cities were associating with men of thought and of affairs, their brethren in Russia were dealing with peasants and an uncultured, decadent nobility. While the Jewries of the west were already seething with modernistic religious, political, and social movements, those of the east were still steeped in mysticism and medieval ritual. While the western Jews were moving along with the tide of progress, those of the east were still sharing the backwardness and isolation of the gentile world of villages and peasants.[5]

According to Wirth, the transition to city life was particularly difficult for these eastern European Jewish immigrants. He believed that the urban mode of life was associated with "the weakening of bonds of kinship, the declining significance of the family, the disappearance of the neighborhood, and the undermining of the traditional basis of social solidarity." Wirth considered urban life so difficult that "personal disorganization, mental breakdown, suicide, delinquency, crime, corruption, and disorder might be expected under these circumstances to be more prevalent in the urban than in the rural communities." This would be the case for groups such as eastern European Jews, who, he claimed, "were still clinging to the old bonds that exclusion and oppression had fashioned."[6]

APPLICATION TO BLACK LIFE

In 1925, almost 90 percent of African-Americans still resided in the South, employed primarily in agricultural and service occupations. At the time, there was a broad consensus that their inferior status was a result of character traits. Typical were the views of John R. Commons, one of the most influential Progressives of the early twentieth century. Commons claimed that African-Americans were "indolent and fickle" and that "some form of compulsion" was necessary if they were to adopt the industrious life.[7] In contrast, he believed that immigrants would fiercely compete among themselves for scarce jobs, forcing wage rates below acceptable levels. Thus, unions were necessary to protect immigrants from engaging in this destructive competition, but since African-American workers did not possess these traits, they did not require unions.

When the 1924 national immigration bill effectively eliminated further eastern and southern European immigration, African-Americans were expected to become the new source of industrial labor. This transformation would more fully integrate them into economic life, and their migration north would eliminate any notion that the "negro question" was of only regional concern. To provide an understanding of the difficulties this transformation would create, the Carnegie

Foundation hired the Swedish economist Gunnar Myrdal to coordinate the efforts of a research team. Not surprisingly, the culture-of-poverty thesis developed by Wirth became an important explanation for these difficulties.

Myrdal noted "the low standards of efficiency, reliability, ambition, and morals actually displayed by the average Negro." He attributed African-American laziness to the paternalistic attitude of upper-class white employers, which tended "to diminish the Negroes' formal responsibilities." Moreover, as a result of the lower expectations, Myrdal claimed that the Negro youth "is not expected to make good in the same way as white youth. And if he is not extraordinary, he will not expect it himself and will not really put his shoulder to the wheel." In general, Myrdal argued that these social pathologies could be rectified through education, which would "diffuse middle class norms to the uneducated and crude Southern 'folk Negroes,' emerging out of the backwardness of slavery."[8]

On Negro criminality, Myrdal suggested that racism induces African-Americans to have less respect for laws: "Life becomes cheap and crime not so reprehensible." According to Myrdal, this hostility to whites promoted the "shielding of Negro criminals and suspects." Like Wirth, Myrdal pointed to the social disorganization caused by the urbanization process:

> [D]isorganization only reaches its extreme when Negroes migrate to cities and to the North. The controls of the rural community are removed; and the ignorant Negro does not know how to adjust to a radically new type of life. Like the European immigrant, he comes to the slums of the Northern cities and learns the criminal ways already widely practiced in such areas.... With uncertain sex mores and a great deal of family disorganization, Negroes are more likely to act with motives of sexual jealousy. The over-crowdedness of the home and the lack of recreational facilities augment the effect of all these disorganizing and crime-breeding influences.[9]

The inclusion of so much material on the dysfunctional character of black culture is not surprising since Wirth was deeply involved with Myrdal's efforts. Though Wirth rejected an offer to be deputy research director, he corresponded frequently with Myrdal and was chosen to critique the entire manuscript.[10]

Despite the acceptance of these racial stereotypes, few social scientists associate Myrdal's analysis with culture-of-poverty explanations that were popularized after World War II. Unlike later proponents, Myrdal rejected policies that focused directly on these perceived dysfunctional traits. For Myrdal, reversing white racism would moderate the societal pressures that caused black maladjustment. The differences between Myrdal's thesis and later explanations were summed up by Rebecca Blank in her contemporary discussion of antipoverty policies:

> There is a large gulf between those who see dysfunctional behavior as predominantly the result of flawed personal characteristics and those who see it as a result of

limited external opportunities. For the former, individually focused policies are the appropriate response; for the later, the preferred policy response is to create economic opportunity for historically excluded groups.[11]

The increased emphasis on directly combating dysfunctional traits was most apparent in the 1965 Moynihan Report. Patrick Moynihan was then President Lyndon Johnson's special assistant on urban affairs and provided this report as a background paper for the "war on poverty" policies. Moynihan focused exclusively on the dysfunctional black family life, emphasizing the destructive role of unwed motherhood.

Three years later, after a series of black riots/rebellions in major northern cities, the Kerner Commission Report offered a somewhat different explanation for persistent black poverty. Instead of focusing on family disorganization directly, it emphasized the educational deficiencies of the newly urbanized black population:

> Since World War II, especially, America's urban-industrial society has matured; unskilled labor is far less essential than before, and blue-collar jobs of all kinds are decreasing.... The Negro migrant, unlike the [earlier] immigrant, found little opportunity in the city; he had arrived too late, and the unskilled labor he had to offer was no longer needed.[12]

For culture-of-poverty theorists, the source of educational deficiencies was not primarily racist school practices, such as placing black students in low-end academic tracks or underfunded schools. Instead, low educational attainment was linked to family disorganization and cultural norms. The most recent application of this culture-of-poverty viewpoint is the widely held notion that few black students excel because, according to their cultural norm, those who pursue academic achievement are "acting white."[13]

In addition, culture-of-poverty theorists contend that dysfunctional family life, including sexual abuse, resulted in teenage mothers whose low educational attainment consigned them to a life of poverty. Most relevant to the discussion in this chapter, culture-of-poverty theorists claimed that welfare coddled individuals, enabling them to live a life focused on immediate gratification— drugs and the "street life"—and devoid of the discipline of *steady* work.

In the 1980s, this neo-Malthusian view was most associated with Charles Murray, who linked generous welfare benefits to growing welfare dependency.[14] The liberal sociologist William Julius Wilson also presented the negative images of life in poor black communities. In contrast to Murray, Wilson claimed that external factors, including past racism and industrial adjustments, were most responsible for the destructive features of ghetto life. However, Wilson criticized those who blinded themselves to the massive internal inadequacies present within African-American communities. He identified culture-of-poverty theorists

Kenneth Clark, Moynihan, and Lee Rainwater as visionaries who correctly perceived that "self-perpetuating pathologies" were becoming rampant within poor African-American communities.[15] Not surprisingly, culture-of-poverty theorist Lawrence Mead wrote, "Wilson describes bluntly how crime and illegitimacy have escalated in the inner city. He calls liberals squeamish for refusing to admit such problems."[16]

THE CULTURE OF POVERTY AND WELFARE REFORM

More recently, David Shipler emphasized "culture-of-poverty" explanations when assessing the impact of welfare reform on poor *black* women. At the same time that Barbara Ehrenreich parachuted into the world of low-wage workers, Shipler dropped in to chronicle their lives. Ehrenreich toiled only with white workers, none of whom either had been on welfare or had any deficient work habits. This enabled her to focus in her book *Nickel and Dimed* (2000) on the exploitive nature of the jobs provided by heartless bosses. By contrast, Shipler allows us to look at the experiences of black women, almost all of whom belonged to the postmigration generation. He chose black women who had been long-term welfare recipients and were involved with drugs and the street life, neither planning for their personal advancement nor exhibiting a strong work ethic.[17]

Shipler described the life experience of Debra Hall. Upon giving birth to her daughter at 18 years of age, Debra entered the welfare system. Debra remained on welfare for 21 years, subsisting on cash payments, an occasional "off-the-books" job, and the Supplemental Security Income (SSI) payments she received for one of her children. Debra judged herself lazy because throughout her years of collecting welfare, she never learned a trade. Then, when she was 39 years old, welfare reform demanded that Debra enter training programs. Not surprisingly, Debra had a trying time adjusting to the world of work. With little work experience and few work-related skills, Debra's finances were only marginally improved. Shipler laments: "Her major gain was emotional—she felt better about herself—and so, on balance, she was tentatively glad to be working."[18]

If welfare reform had happened years earlier, Debra might not have developed the weak work habits and attitudes that limited her employment. Indeed, Shipler spends a whole chapter describing the difficulty that many black women have had adjusting to work after living without paid employment:

> They enter [the labor market] burdened by their personal histories of repeated failure: failure to finish school, failure to resist drugs, failure to maintain loving relationships, failure to hold jobs. . . . They admitted gently that they were afraid of making the phone call, of getting no reply, of filling out the application, of going to the interview.[19]

To illustrate how difficult it can be to move poor women into the world of work, Shipler discussed Camellia Woodruff. She had dropped out of high school, started getting into the "street life," became involved in an abusive relationship, and watched her mother die of a drug overdose. Camellia had worked sporadically because "getting up for work everyday seems hard." When a caring caseworker used personal contacts to obtain a job selling jewelry at the local Macy's, Camellia failed to show up for her orientation because "she could not find her way through the tangled anxieties and excuses."[20]

Shipler also reported the evaluation made by a Sprint supervisor in Kansas City:

> She saw two pervasive problems among the mothers coming from welfare. One was an absence of any belief in others, a profound distrust. The second was a conviction that backing down meant weakness. Those two disabilities stole from her employees the ability to manage their anger and to form collegial connections in the workplace.[21]

Washington, D.C. welfare recipient Peaches was also the victim of consistent abuse by men. Echoing the thoughts of the Sprint supervisor, Peaches had trouble in the workplace. Peaches recalled, "I really don't work that well with people, and that held me back." When she lost her job, Peaches used drugs and "partied from Sunday to Saturday, ain't leaving much room in between."

Shipler found that for *black* women like Peaches, even low-wage labor can make people successful when support programs help them develop the self-confidence and work ethic they need for stable employment. Shipler quotes approvingly Options for People director Richard Blackmon when he tries to convince people to take a minimum wage trainee position: "The minimum wage has power. It is a starting point, $5.15 an hour, forty hours a week, four weeks a month, $824. How many of you get $824 a month in public aid?" Like the STRIVE program in Chicago, these support programs transformed the attitudes of Peaches and two other D.C. women who had been battered for decades by abusive men, the drug culture, and an inability to hold stable employment.[22]

Unlike Shipler, Ehrenreich, or me, Jason DeParle writes about welfare from the perspective of having reported on poverty for nearly two decades for the *New York Times*. DeParle tells the story of welfare reform through the lives of three related Milwaukee women: Angie, Opal, and Jewell. Opal and Jewell had the same great-grandfather, Pie Eddie Caples, and Angie's three children were fathered by Jewell's brother, Greg. All had been involved with drugs and worked only occasionally to supplement their welfare checks.

Before detailing how their lives were affected by welfare reform, DeParle quotes approvingly a problematic report written on black life in the South during the 1930s. He states, "Most [black] sharecroppers lived in unsteady common-law arrangements, 'easily entered and easily dissolved.' Nonmarital births prevailed. . . . Domestic violence was epidemic . . . and so were other forms of black-on-black violence."[23]

Leaving no doubt that this described the Caples clan, DeParle reported that the majority of Pie Eddie's children were involved in violent black-on-black encounters that either took someone's life or landed them in jail. Nor is the epidemic of domestic violence absent. Jewell's grandmother, Mama Hattie, recalled being sexually molested by her grandmother's boyfriend at the age of seven. "Men back then didn't allow girls to have much of a childhood," she said. Mama Hattie then recounted how she became pregnant at 12 years of age when her aunt Vidalia's boyfriend raped her. When she married at 15, it was to an abusive man who fathered her next three children. She left him after "years of explosive violence."[24]

Describing Mama Hattie's arrival in Chicago, DeParle echoed Wirth's theory of how urban life intensifies dysfunctional behavior: "There had always been chaos in black southern life. But the stabilizing forces of the rural world—church, schools, communal networks—carried less weight in an anonymous city, where someone looking to live the wild life could do it on a grander scale."[25]

DeParle does mention briefly that the loss of employment opportunities was partially responsible for the intensification of dysfunctional behavior among blacks in Chicago. The lack of employment opportunities, however, never plays a role in his narrative, especially since the women whose lives he chronicled were able to escape the black inner city and grew up in a lower middle-class neighborhood.

While DeParle praised the work ethics of the Caples clan that migrated to Chicago, their children—the postmigration generation—lacked a strong work ethic. DeParle noted, "It took Jewell two and half years in Milwaukee just to apply for a job."[26] When Angie is employed for 18 months, "since no one else [of the three other women and two men] in the compound had a regular job, child care was not a problem."[27] However, as long as Angie was able to receive a welfare check, she was unwilling to be a steady worker. Overall, Angie was employed about half the time during this period, taking breaks when she received her tax refund or when the job was no longer to her liking. As for Opal, work was something to avoid, and her efforts were even more sporadic than Jewell's. And while these women continued to collect welfare, they partied all night long.

DeParle suggests that the reason why so many women left welfare was the undermining of the notion that welfare was an entitlement. When Angie was reapplying for welfare in 1998, the Wisconsin Works (W-2) welfare program required her to take a community service job in order to collect her welfare check. Immediately upon hearing this, she went back to work at the nursing home where she had previously been employed. Jewell made clear that she believed welfare payments were an entitlement. She refused a similar W-2 requirement, claiming that "ain't no way I would wanna be working for free."[28]

DeParle does fault the W-2 program for not doing enough for Opal but admits that "for a surprising number of people, like Angie and Jewell, a small push or pull was all it took."[29] While he thought that some of the work activities required were silly, DeParle concluded,

> But among the early lessons was that even silliness worked: requiring people to do *anything* was usually better than leaving them to do nothing. For Acerbic Angie and Jazzy Jewell, the hassle was a goad to make better plans. For some others, any activity offered a respite from lives stunted by terrible isolation.[30]

I, too, found among those I interviewed that just a little bit of aid went a long way. While welfare-to-work advocates often stressed a need to transform the recipient, for many it was just a little prod, a little support, and a little help in finding the right direction in which to move. I did find, however, that there were women who clearly were helped in much more profound ways. Just as Shipler documented, for these women, welfare-to-work programs had transformational effects.

Cutina exemplified how the development of more realistic goals can be extremely beneficial. She had been on welfare fairly continuously when time limits forced her to enter the STRIVE program in Chicago. She learned from STRIVE's slogan: "Your first job is not your dream job." Cutina said,

> When I came to this program I had expectations of a lot of money and would work for only certain companies. They helped me see that it's okay to have high expectations but there is nothing wrong with starting at the bottom. One instructor gave me faith and hope. . . . I now go out and do the best I can be and it's working out; just the other day they asked me if I wanted to be a supervisor.

For Belinda, an intermittent worker at bars and fast food restaurants, it took a 12-week secretarial training program. This stimulated her to seek a college education for the first time "because I had begun to see what it's like to be a worker in a better environment."

THE POSTMIGRATION GENERATION

Shipler, DeParle, and other culture-of-poverty theorists all make some reference to the employment difficulties faced by the postmigration generation. These writers tend to focus, however, on a set of intergenerational cultural norms that made poor black communities particularly vulnerable to dysfunctional behavior. As a result, they suggest that even modest changes in economic conditions had devastating effects on behavior, undermining fragile work ethics and drawing more and more into the "street life."

Michael Piore offered another explanation for the perceived weak work efforts exhibited by poor blacks in the 1980s compared to those of their parents. He argued that black southern migrants to urban areas willingly accepted the lowest-rung jobs because these jobs still represented upward mobility. Their children, however, perceived these jobs as continued oppression and refused to take them.[31] Christopher Jencks characterized this as rising expectations: blacks thought that once employment discrimination became illegal, they would obtain better jobs, so they were unwilling to take lower paying ones.[32] Elijah Anderson suggested that black youths, having developed a new consciousness and set of expectations as a result of the civil rights movement, now shunned low-status jobs that were once associated with racial degradation.[33] Though their rationales differed, these observers agreed that the postmigration generation lacked a strong work ethic.

These observers suggest that changes in black attitudes toward work explain the joblessness of the postmigration generation. What they ignore or downplay, however, is the most distinguishing feature of the 20-year period beginning in the mid-1970s. The lack of available jobs, not personal choices, explains the massive black joblessness that the postmigration generation experienced.

Though relegated to low-wage blue-collar and agricultural occupations in the Jim Crow South, black men were generally able to maintain paid employment. The great migration north that began in the 1950s when cotton production was fully mechanized did not change this situation. Black men were still excluded from the better paying craft occupations. Economic growth and low national unemployment rates, however, allowed substantial mobility into white-collar positions for white workers, freeing up positions in manufacturing for black workers. By 1975, the share of young black men employed in manufacturing in midwestern cities reached 40 percent.

While this migrating generation was generally able to secure stable employment, the subsequent generation was less fortunate. The economy began to fizzle in the mid-1970s, just when the ending of the Vietnam War brought many young men back into the labor force. At the same time, manufacturing firms began closing their northern and midwestern urban factories, moving from central city to suburban sites and from the older industrial areas to the South.

Beginning in the 1950s, manufacturing firms began focusing on southern production as a way of avoiding unions. Between 1955 and 1967, manufacturing employment in the South expanded dramatically while it stagnated in the Midwest. For example, employment in durable goods industries increased by 74 percent in the South but by less than 5 percent in the Midwest.[34] Part of this strategy was to limit investment in their older urban plants, so by the mid-1970s, many of these facilities were obsolete and economically no longer viable production sites.

Employment prospects for young black men living in central cities were further weakened by the shift of manufacturing to suburban industrial parks. The newly built interstate highway system enabled trucking to replace railroads. In order to avoid traffic congestion, many manufacturing firms relocated to suburban sites adjacent to a highway. And new assembly-line techniques required sprawling suburban factories rather than multifloor central-city locations.

Young black men living in central cities found it increasingly difficult to follow the manufacturing jobs to the suburbs. By 1989, the share of young midwestern black men employed in manufacturing fell to 12 percent. This was the backdrop against which the postmigration generation struggled to find gainful employment.[35]

When the economy suffered a severe recession during the early 1980s, official unemployment rates rose to more than 20 percent for black men and more than 40 percent for black teenagers. Even these soaring figures understated employment difficulties. During the 1980–1982 recession, 21 percent of all black men 20–24 years old who were out of school had *no* work experience in the previous year. This rate was triple the white rate (7.2 percent) and almost double what the black rate had been a decade earlier (12.8 percent).[36] However, this joblessness did not show up in official unemployment statistics. Most of these young men did not meet the government criterion for job search, so they were not considered part of the active labor force.

By the mid-1980s, crack cocaine became a further plague on black communities. Congress and state legislatures dramatically increased the penalties for crack cocaine possession, more than doubling the prison population. Nearly 90 percent of those sentenced to prison for its use and distribution were black. As a result, interaction with the criminal justice system became a common occurrence in poor black communities. For example, in Baltimore, at any point in time during the early 1990s, the majority of black men 18–30 years old were in prison, were on probation, or had a hearing pending within the criminal justice system. Black men born in the late 1960s had a 20.5 percent probability of being in prison by 30–34 years of age; if they were high school dropouts, the probability rose to 58.3 percent.[37]

In his aptly titled book *When Work Disappears*, Wilson surveyed businesses in the early 1990s. He found that employers readily admitted that they selectively advertised job openings to avoid having to deal with inner-city black applicants. These employers embraced the notion that black youths tend to have more dysfunctional behavior than white youths.[38] These employers preferred Latino workers even though they tended to have less schooling and weaker language skills compared with black applicants. Other studies found that the source of this preference was the belief that blacks were more troublesome and less compliant than Latino workers.[39]

Most striking was the broad *black* acceptance of these stereotypes. In Chicago, black as well as white employers used racial profiling to exclude young black men living in public housing projects. Even many black workers embraced negative black stereotypes. As one black resident told Wilson,

> I say about 65 percent of black males, I say, don't wanna work, and when I say don't wanna work, I say don't wanna work hard—they want a real easy job, making big bucks—see? And when you start talking about hard labor and earning your money with sweat or just once in a while you gotta put out a little bit—you know, that extra effort, I don't, I don't think the guys really wanna do that.[40]

Summing up his study, Wilson observed: "The disappearance of work and its consequences for both social and cultural life are the central problems in the inner-city ghetto."[41] Wilson was not surprised that ambitious programs like Head Start generally had no lasting impact. He pointed to the inadequate public schools that poor inner-city black children must attend. However, it was the joblessness that was most decisive. When a majority of adults in many inner-city neighborhoods are jobless, social engineering is doomed.

The crack cocaine upsurge in the 1980s and the resulting increased incarceration rates made it even more difficult for black men from poor neighborhoods to find employment. Devah Pager conducted an audit study in Milwaukee to determine the impact of incarceration on employment. Male applicants were matched by employment history and educational background, differing only in that one had been incarcerated for a nonviolent crime for 18 months while the other had never been incarcerated. She found that applicants with a prison record were less than half as likely to be called back for a second interview as their matched counterparts. And her study was done in 2001, when Milwaukee's unemployment rate was still relatively low, forcing employers to be more flexible in their hiring practices than they would have been if applicants had been more plentiful.[42]

Finally, crack cocaine increased the violence black youth encountered. In New York City, the number of homicides increased by more than 50 percent between 1984 and 1990, and in 1989, 77 percent of those arrested there tested positive for cocaine.[43] In east Baltimore, where the poorest black neighborhoods were located, 5 percent of young people were killed annually.[44] As a result, for a typical young person living in this neighborhood, the probability of being killed at sometime during a 10-year period was 40 percent.

RATIONALITY OR DYSFUNCTIONALITY?

There is no question that, absent paid employment options, it *could* be rational to go on cash assistance, especially if you are allowed to further your education. Indeed, this is just what I found for at least some women in California's Low-

Income Families' Empowerment through Education (LIFETIME), a grass-roots organization that supports welfare recipients attempting to earn a four-year college degree. In Oakland, I interviewed Wendy. She had attended Howard University, but at the end of her freshman year she became pregnant and dropped out. Moving to California, she opened a daycare facility in order to combine raising her child with economic independence. When her child reached school age, Wendy realized that to move ahead she would need to get an education degree so she shut down her facility, went on welfare, and thanks to the support services offered by LIFETIME, completed her degree. In 2004, Wendy was earning $53,000 as a public school psychologist.

In addition, there is always a large number of women for whom welfare is a safety net that enables them to navigate troubled times. These women have a relatively short stay on welfare before getting back into the world of work. The problem, however, is that within poor communities during the 1980s and early 1990s, the sense of hopelessness led many women to use welfare neither to enhance their educational skills nor to regroup before moving forward. Instead, this hopelessness, together with a growing drug culture, caused them to disregard the long-term adverse consequences to themselves and their children of the dysfunctional lifestyle they adopted.

This was certainly the outcome for a number of the black women Shipler interviewed as well as one of the three women DeParle followed. Invariably, these women neglected their children to the point that they had to be raised by family members. This was the childhood experience of one of the women, Sheila, whom I interviewed in Florida.

Sheila was the fifth of 12 children her mother had with seven different partners. By the time Sheila was 11 years old, she had responsibility for the younger siblings while her mother partied virtually all the time. Now in her late 30s, Sheila still voiced bitterness as she spoke about her mother. Recounting the rape and molestation experienced by her siblings at the hands of her mother's various boyfriends, Sheila lamented, "Each one of us has a lot of hurt." Few of her siblings have had steady employment, and a number have persistent drug problems. Indeed, one sister's drug habit and general lifestyle made her so irresponsible that Sheila had to raise her daughter just as DeParle's Angie had to raise Opal's children.

Sheila is, however, one of welfare's success stories. After freeing herself of a problematic relationship, she was able to settle into subsidized housing with her two sons and is working full time. For the first time, she is looking forward to the future, studying to pass the test for a truck driver's license. She has also begun a handicraft business, selling her creations at flee markets. Sheila told me,

> I wanna do something for myself. Spent so much time with my son who had cancer, I spent so much time with my husband trying to make the marriage work, and I now

am trying to find where Sheila needs to be and have a life for myself and finish something in my life that I want to do.

THE PSYCHOLOGICAL REWARDS FROM WORK

There is another fallacy in the argument that welfare was simply a rational choice given the employment difficulties the postmigration generation faced. This approach presumes that work has no intrinsic value, that it is simply one way of obtaining income. Indeed, welfare reform critics such as Ehrenreich often contend that welfare leavers end up in dead-end, meaningless jobs where workers are mercilessly exploited. When she encountered Wal-Mart workers who liked their job, Ehrenreich suggested that they had been brainwashed during their initial orientation sessions. By contrast, in her excellent book on Wal-Mart, Liza Featherstone found that many female workers welcomed the opportunity to get out of the house after years of housewifery. And many of them liked dealing with the public—even workers who did not like working for Wal-Mart nonetheless liked helping customers.[45] Featherstone told me, "That's one of the attractions of retail, despite the low pay."

And these Wal-Mart workers are not alone. Labor researchers have found that low-wage workers in the health-care industry often find their work rewarding.[46] Recall my son's experience while organizing at Baptist Hospital (chapter 1): the workers were upset because, as a result of cutbacks, they had neither the staff nor the equipment to do a satisfactory job cleaning the floors and rooms. DeParle points out that Angie's perseverance as a nurse's aid reflected the intrinsic value she gained from her efforts: her job "tapped a vein of energy and imagination dormant in other parts of her life. She certainly had more patience for her patients than she did for her kids."[47]

I, too, found this with women I interviewed. MiShonda completed the STRIVE program in Chicago and was hired by Avon to package their products. She felt good about her ability to raise her wages from $7 to $11 per hour and two small financial awards she received for her efforts. Her face brightened when discussing the pleasure her job brought her:

> Okay, while I am only working at Avon, I am making products people like to use. I'm helping them be beautiful, feel comfortable, and making them smell good. And I've done it. Gives you something to look forward to. You're doing your part to make someone else happy.

The pride these women felt is not an isolated phenomenon. Many women realize that, through stable paid employment, they become a positive role model to their children. Cutina said,

All of my children think more of me, no longer see me lying around. Can tell them all you want but they go by what they see you're doing for yourself. They respect me more because I respect myself more. I'm way better than I was before. Just can't see myself going back.

The world of work also provides a better set of social contacts. Shipler noted, "Contact with new, more successful people has been a boon of going to work, say many who have moved off welfare and out of the stifling circle of indigence. Encounters with achieving colleagues can revive, broaden, and educate."[48] For Shipler's Peaches, work provided a healthy social environment where "I can enjoy myself and be a real person and have something to talk about besides who screwed who, who shot who, so and so's dead."[49] For another welfare leaver I interviewed, Wanda, it provided "unexpected advice on child rearing from her boss." Heeding this advice, Wanda "stopped hitting them and started doing some of the things that [her boss] suggested, and it worked."

In Chicago, I interviewed Laura. Both her parents had been factory workers, so this was the only world of work she knew. When, through personal contacts developed at her first job, she was able to move into a white-collar position, she recalled, "This new job was different. I had an office, desk, phone, computer, and no one was standing over me. Most important, I got paid for my thinking. It was an introduction into my advancement and career."

MiShonda came from the same environment as DeParle's women: drugs, criminal activity, and a father of her first child who is still in prison. When asked about the neighborhood men she knew, MiShonda answered, "All the men are either locked up, on drugs, or dead. . . . [The neighborhood] black men I knew always believed things were against them rather than seeing things to overcome. They wanted things fast and easy, to get real quick money." For MiShonda, work got her away from this social environment and provided a new partner that she met at Avon.

While important for many low-income workers, finding intrinsic value in work will not be enough. When these women confront barriers, such as domestic, transportation, or child care difficulties, the challenge is how they handle them without losing their jobs. DeParle believes that "new workers ultimately succeed by acquiring . . . a strong 'work identity.' Seasoned workers, when faced with personal turmoil see the job as a pillar to cling to, rather than the thing to let go."[50] After interviewing 300 minimum-wage workers in Harlem, Katherine Newman noted, "These are not people whose values need reengineering. They work hard at the jobs they have because they believe in the dignity of work."[51] Newman cited Kyesha to exemplify this point:

On the way to her Burger Barn job, Kyesha stumbles over drug addicts. She sees young men lingering together on the corner, cell phones in hand, waiting for instructions from the more powerful dealers who control the trade. Many are acquaintances of her older brother, a well-heeled dealer who has moved up in the interstate drug trade.

For Kyesha, these chance meetings are filled with lessons. They are daily reminders of the ease with which she could have found herself on the other side of the counter.... The difference between Kyesha and her less successful friends can be credited to Burger Barn, citadel of the low-paid hamburger flipper, and the salvation for a poor girl from Harlem's housing projects.... It has become the center of her social universe, the place she spends nearly all of her time, the source of all of her closest friends and romantic attachments.[52]

One of the women I interviewed in Florida showed me how work provides meaning and stability in troubled lives. Sally left an abusive relationship and, with her daughter, was forced to move in with her father after being homeless for a time. The situation remained chaotic because of the antagonism between Sally and her father's new wife. At the time, Sally was employed at a center for emotionally disturbed children. When she told me how she liked caring for these children, I asked Sally, "Isn't it sometimes upsetting taking care of these children?" Sally smiled and answered, "I liked being at work to get away from the problems at home."

CONCLUDING REMARKS

This chapter highlights a number of important distinctions. Do we judge the behavior of poor women during the 1980s and early 1990s as simply a rational adaptation to unfortunate circumstances, or do we judge them to be dysfunctional? Welfare was a rational choice for some women that allowed them to further develop skills. It also provided a temporary safety net for others facing a personal setback. For a very large proportion of women, however, welfare trapped them in social environments that only worsened their long-term outcomes and damaged their children's futures.

If we judge their behavior to be dysfunctional, do we believe that it reflects primarily intergenerational cultural norms or a reaction to special circumstances? Returning to Blank's distinction between dysfunctional behavior induced by structural impediments (Myrdal) and that which is primarily the result of internal inadequacies (Moynihan), both Shipler and DeParle virtually ignore the collapse of employment opportunities and the emergence of crack cocaine that victimized the postmigration generation. By ignoring these structural factors, both *New York Times* reporters have more in common with Moynihan than with Myrdal.

Interestingly, both reporters recoil from accepting the seriousness of welfare dependency and were unwilling to support welfare reform. Indeed, DeParle was among the most outspoken critics of Clinton's proposed welfare reform legislation. Centrist Democratic policy analyst Mickey Kaus stated, "He opposed the

1996 reform and did his best, while on the *New York Times* welfare beat, to stop it."[53] Both Kaus and Ron Haskins—the Republican legislative aide most responsible for formulating the welfare bill—expected the worst when DeParle was writing his book: "Having talked with him on many occasions over the years, especially during the great welfare debate of 1995–96, and having read many of the stories he filed with the *New York Times* and other outlets, I expected a diatribe about the evils of welfare reform...."[54] Both Kaus and Haskins, however, hail DeParle's book because it essentially endorses their views that welfare reform was necessary and was successful.

By emphasizing that there were special circumstances that afflicted the postmigration generation, I am more willing and straightforward in accepting the realities of the destructive lifestyles that devastated poor urban black communities during the 1980s and early 1990s. I do not believe, however, that these internal problems were deeply embedded through intergenerational cultural norms.

The cohort born around 1980 did not suffer the same drug problems as those born in the 1960s and early 1970s. By the mid-1990s, far fewer central-city young black men were being victimized by crack cocaine. Whereas 25 percent of D.C. juveniles arrested in the late 1980s tested positive for cocaine, the rate fell to just greater than 5 percent by the mid-1990s, and the test rate among all adult arrestees nationally fell by about one-third between 1989 and 2000. Also, the transition for young adults from marijuana to cocaine (or heroin) declined from 39 to 24 percent.[55]

As a result, I was not surprised by the number of welfare leavers who found and sustained permanent employment during the economic boom. I was not surprised that, for the majority of recipients, only a modest amount of positive support or modest amount of hassle would be enough to transform them into steady workers. I am also hopeful that the next generation of children who will be born to poor working mothers will be better off. Moreover, once past this victimized postmigration generation, the coercive portions of the 1996 welfare reform legislation may no longer be necessary. As a result, positive incentives should play an increasingly prominent role in convincing the poor to choose work instead of welfare. Most important, I remain confident that welfare reform will have long-term positive effects as long as the economy produces enough jobs and government provides the necessary work supports.

4

Domestic Violence, Teen Childbearing, and Race

In 1985, the birth rate for black women 15–17 years of age was 69.2 (per 1,000), almost triple the rate for comparably aged white women. After having continuously declined for more than 20 years, the rate increased over the next five years by almost 20 percent to 82.3, and the rate for black women 18–19 years of age increased by 15 percent to 152.9. Most troubling to some, 95 percent of these black births were to unwed mothers.[1]

In his influential book *Losing Ground*, Charles Murray claimed that welfare generosity was responsible for the growth in nonmarital births as a share of total births.[2] Almost immediately, liberals criticized the linking of welfare cash payments with childbearing decisions. They highlighted statistical studies that found little correlation between a state's welfare benefits and its birth rates to unwed mothers: states with the most generous cash payments did not have the highest birth rates, and some states with the highest birth rates had very low cash payments.[3]

These studies enabled many liberals to separate policies to reduce teen births from the attack on welfare policies. In particular, liberals rejected the notion that young women were calculating when considering childbearing and suggested that they often ignored the long-term adverse consequences of unwed motherhood. For example, psychologists Ellen Freeman and Karl Rickels concluded:

> Like many teenagers, they did not get around to obtaining contraception, and they believed that pregnancy, because it had not yet happened,

would not occur to them. More important, many of these disadvantaged teenagers did not believe that consequences of pregnancy would negatively affect their lives. Although they did not "want" pregnancy, they had no strong motivation to avoid it, because they had no understanding that their lives would be any different.[4]

Conservatives were not troubled by these studies. They believed that by the mid-1980s, welfare was generous enough in most states to be a sufficient inducement to teen childbearing. Indeed, they claimed that welfare and family planning policies created an enabling culture. As one observer stated,

> By the early 1990s, the nation had entered a period of public policy and reproductive behavior that clinical psychologists might label as codependency. Men could father children with little legal or moral obligation to support them; women could bear children with few social or economic sanctions.[5]

A decade later, some economists claimed that these earlier statistical studies were flawed because they did not take into account important state-specific influences. Suppose that some states have cultural norms and other unmeasured factors that encourage teen births. As a result, independent of welfare payments, these states would have birth rates substantially above the national average. Hoping to counter these tendencies, suppose further that when these states lowered welfare payments, birth rates fell. In this case, though a reduction in welfare payments reduced birth rates, these states would still have relatively *high* birth rates despite relatively *low* welfare payments.[6]

When these potential state effects were eliminated, economists found a systematic positive relationship between *changes* in welfare payments and *changes* in birth rates. In general, states that reduced their welfare payments had reductions in teen births, while states that increased welfare payments experienced teen birth increases. One study estimated that, for the typical state, a 25 percent increase in welfare benefits would cause the proportion of young women with a nonmarital birth to rise by 18 percent.[7]

Jason DeParle rejected any direct linkage between welfare payments and the decision to have a child. He believes, however, that teen motherhood reflects conscious decisions: they got "pregnant on purpose, thinking a child would bring ... something to love." In her influential book *Dubious Conceptions*, Kristin Luker contended that "having a baby is a lottery ticket for many teenagers: it brings with it at least the dream of something better, and if the dream fails, not much is lost." Luker concluded, "The high rate of early childbearing is a measure of how bleak life is for young people who are living in poor communities and who have no obvious areas of success."[8]

These more recent studies certainly reinforced conservative efforts to withhold additional welfare payments to mothers who had additional children while on welfare. And these conservatives could certainly find testimony to support their position. Indeed, one of the women I interviewed believed that the behavior of many women in her circle of friends supported this conservative thesis. When I asked a former welfare recipient, Angie, to evaluate the 1996 reform, she stated:

> Before Clinton's law, women were out to have all the babies they could so that their check would increase and increase.... So many babies were born in the early nineties because a lot of my friends were having kids back to back to back because the checks would increase.

When I pressed Angie, however, these generalizations were based on only one or two of her friends. Overall, my interviews were most consistent with Luker's observations. Virtually all of the welfare leavers I interviewed took it for granted that when they had a child, they would simply go on welfare. Typical was Cynthia. When I asked her why she went on welfare, Cynthia just shrugged her shoulders and said, "I didn't think much about it; all my friends went on welfare after giving birth."

While there is clearly at least a kernel of truth in both the conservative and liberal perspectives, they both understate three important considerations. Births to teen mothers may reflect (1) coercion rather than choice, (2) rational behavior independent of welfare considerations, and (3) structural factors that victimized poor communities rather than intergenerational cultural norms.

COERCION, NOT CHOICE

In the 1990s, studies began to document the high level of sexual coercion all young women were experiencing. In a 1995 nationwide study, 23 percent of young women who became sexually active before they were 14 years old characterized their first intercourse as involuntary, and another 14 percent indicated that, while voluntary, they really didn't want it.[9] Among those who became sexually active as 15- and 16-year-olds, these rates, though somewhat lower, were still appallingly high.[10] This contrasted with an earlier survey that found much lower rates of involuntary intercourse among women younger than 16 years.[11] The 1995 survey found that the share of involuntary sexual encounters increased as the age difference between the sexual partners increased. Among girls 15–17 years old, 17 percent reported an involuntary first encounter when their partner was the same age. By contrast, when their partner was at least seven years older, that rate increased to 44 percent.

Unintended pregnancies and sexual coercion have been linked in a number of ways. First, after adjusting for age, the use of contraception was about 10 percentage points lower among young women who felt coerced compared to those who did not. Second, young girls who had an involuntary first sexual encounter tended to have significantly lower levels of protected sex in subsequent encounters.[12] A 1992 Washington State study found that young women who experienced sexual abuse at some point in their lives were twice as likely to have not used contraception during their last intercourse as those who had not. Almost one-half of those young women who became pregnant suffered sexual abuse compared to only 21 percent of those who were never pregnant.[13]

Third, use of contraception was particularly low when the male partner was substantially older. Although men six or more years older than their partners comprised only 6.7 percent of all partners of 15- to 17-year-olds, they comprised 19.7 percent of the partners of those who became pregnant.[14] Finally, coercion influenced the decision of pregnant women to abort or deliver. Among 15- to 17-year-olds, 49.6 percent chose to abort if the age difference of the partners was less than three years, 34.3 percent if the age difference was between three and five years, and 20.9 percent if it was at least six years. As a result, men who were at least six years older than their partner comprised 24 percent of all fathers.[15]

Young black women were particularly at risk for unwanted pregnancies. Studies consistently found that black women become sexually active at a much younger age than do white women. Charles Barone and his associates estimated that 65 percent of black but only 11 percent of white female eighth graders were sexually active. These numbers may reflect a greater degree of coercion experienced by young black women.[16] Another study found that 30 percent of young white women characterized their first sexual experience as either involuntary or not really wanted, whereas the share was 46 percent among young black women.[17]

The image of predatory young black men was presented most vividly in Bill Moyer's 1986 CBS television special "The Vanishing Family: Crisis in Black America." In that documentary, young black men were presented as indifferent to the numerous children they fathered outside of marriage. Indeed, these young men bragged about the number of their children that they felt no responsibility for. One prominently featured young man who had fathered six children by four different women justified his failure to support them by saying, "The majority of the mothers are on welfare. And welfare gives them the stipend for the month. So what I'm not doing, the government does."[18]

More recently, the association of sexual violence with poor black communities is presented in the 2001 hit song by the group City High, "What Would You Do?" (What Would You Do? Interscope, 2001). The song tells the story of Lanie, a young black woman performing as a stripper. Confronted by a former high school friend who urges her to give up her immoral life, Lanie explains that she has a baby and the only way to feed him is to "sleep with a man for a little bit of money [cause] his daddy's gone." When her friend claims that having a child is "no excuse to be livin' all crazy," Lanie laments that she is always in pain from the time "me and my sister ran away so my daddy couldn't rape us."

There are many theories why young African-American women appear to experience more sexual coercion and abuse than do young white women. On the basis of a five-year study he conducted in Philadelphia during the 1980s, conservative sociologist Elijah Anderson claimed that a subculture had developed in which young black males attempt to have "casual sex with as many women as possible, impregnating one or more, and getting them to 'have their baby' brings a boy the ultimate in esteem from his peers and makes him a man."[19] William Marsiglio found that after controlling for some socioeconomic differences, there was a much larger core of black than white young men who were positively affected by their partners' pregnancy.[20] Frank Furstenberg and his associates feared that young black women were at risk for unwanted pregnancies because of their inability to "exercise contraceptive vigilance," whether or not the coercion they experienced met the definition of rape. They concluded that subculture norms put enormous peer pressure on very young black men to be sexually active and that this "has implications for females who are exposed in their early teens to sexually experienced and some have argued, sexually demanding partners."[21]

While coercive situations caused an increase in unintended pregnancies, some liberals emphasize that motherhood enabled many of these girls to leave an abusive family life. At the Crittenton Center for young women in Los Angeles, Almonica recounted how she saw her mother set on fire and murdered by her stepfather during a drunken fight. At age 16, she got pregnant by a 21-year-old man. "It was the only way out," she said. The center's director, Yale Gancherov, stated, "The parents of these young women were violent, were drug abusers, and were sexually abusive. While privileged people can see a detriment in a teenager becoming a mother, these girls see it as a realistic improvement in their lives."[22]

Though teenage motherhood may allow some women to escape abusive families, it often leads to another abusive relationship. From a wide variety of mid-1990s studies, Jody Raphael and Richard Tolman found that 15–20 percent of women on welfare were physically abused during the most recent 12 months, and about 60 percent at some time in their past. Current abuse was about 20 percent higher among recipients who were involved in a relationship with a man.[23] The Center for Impact Research found that among teenage black mothers who were on welfare, 55 percent had experienced some form of domestic violence from their partner in the past year: 23 percent experienced severe physical aggression, 18 percent moderate physical abuse, and 14 percent experienced only verbal aggression.[24]

Many observers project an image of never-married young women living alone surviving on a network of female relationships—sisters, mothers, and friends. The term "lone mothers" minimizes involvement single mothers have with male partners. This vision suggests that welfare is a safe harbor for victims of abuse, while its repeal "threatens to chain abused women and children to their abusers."[25] Indeed, when Wisconsin legislated a "bridefare" program that gave financial incentives to welfare recipients who married, one of the strongest advocates for poor women, State Representative Gwendolyn Jones, made a similar claim:

> The Bridefare program...may place battered women in more danger.... Aid to Families with Dependent Children (AFDC) has traditionally been one way that women could escape from abusive situations that were dangerous for them or their children. Let us not begin telling battered women that if they do not marry, they and their children will be thrust deeper into poverty.[26]

The reality is much more complicated. The vast majority of teen mothers in the Impact study maintained a stable relationship with their abuser. More than four-fifths of teen mothers had boyfriends, and the average duration of the relationships was 2.74 years. These young women often stayed in abusive relationships because their boyfriends provided some financial support or presented a threat to their safety if the relationship was terminated.[27] The financial support was, however, quite meager since half of these men were high school dropouts, only 15 percent had at least some college or trade school education, and only 48 percent were currently employed.

Given the limited financial benefits provided, many of these young men consciously sabotaged efforts of these teen mothers to gain independence, such as attempting to father more children to further limit the teen mothers' independence. Among young women, 31 percent of those who did not experience domestic violence, but 74 percent of those who did, claimed that their partners sabotaged birth control efforts. More than 70 percent of abused black women reported that their partner did not use condoms versus 43 percent of nonabused black women.[28]

Evidence from the U.S. Department of Justice also seems to indicate dramatically higher rates of domestic violence within the black community. Specifically, the justice department calculates an intimate violence rate—the rate of violence women experience at the hands of individuals that they know: husbands, boyfriends, and other friends. During the early 1990s, the intimate violence rate was 43 percent higher for black than for white women.[29]

These black–white differences are not, however, evidence of racial differences. The U.S. Department of Justice found that intimate violence rates vary inversely with the income of the household in which women live—the higher the income, the lower the rate.[30] Since black women on average live in poorer households than do white women, at least a portion of the racial difference could be explained by these household income differences.

Using national intimate violence data, I estimate that more than two-thirds of the black–white difference would be eliminated if black families had the same incomes as white families. As a result, the black–white gap would drop to 13 percent if black and white women had the same family income. Thus, we must be careful not to attribute black–white differences to dysfunctional cultural norms since class differences are much more important, and these class differences are likely to reflect the special economic circumstances faced by the postmigration generation.

Violent partners also sought to limit the ability of teen mothers to gain additional education or outside employment. Among the teen mothers who were currently experiencing a severe level of domestic violence, 57 percent reported some form of sabotage of their employment and school efforts. In contrast, only 17 and 7 percent of those who experienced low levels of domestic violence or no violence, respectively, reported employment or educational sabotage. In a New Jersey study, Raphael and Tolman found that "three times as many abused women as nonabused women (39.7 percent compared with 12.9 percent) reported that their intimate partner actively prevents their participation in education and training."[31] Even if partners did not overtly sabotage their efforts, more abused recipients than nonabused recipients had symptoms of depression, which itself creates a barrier to sustaining employment or educational efforts.[32]

In her book *Saving Bernice*, Raphael concluded that women on welfare are "not abandoned by men but increasingly have difficulty getting rid of them."[33] Raphael's book focuses on the struggles of one former welfare recipient to better her life. Raphael is not a journalist who drops down into the lives of her subjects— she is a former director of welfare-to-work programs where she met Bernice Hampton. Raphael chronicled the poor choices Bernice made in her youth as direct results of an abusive past and welfare-induced isolation. Raphael noted,

> Domestic violence works to constrain the choices and coerce the actions of low-income women. When the issue of domestic violence is squarely faced, we no longer can view many women on welfare as lazy or helpless, but instead see young women like Bernice Hampton struggling to use birth control and trying to sustain employment in the teeth of their partners' violent opposition.[34]

Fleeing a dysfunctional family, Bernice met Billy when she was 14 years old and began living with him a year later. She rationalized his violence and extreme possessiveness, hoping that a stable family life would emerge from the chaos. Billy did not allow her to use birth control, and she had three miscarriages before having a child. She could only leave their apartment to go to the welfare office and Billy enticed her to use drugs to get through the isolation. When Bernice attempted to enter job training programs, Billy sabotaged her efforts for fear of losing her. According to Raphael, Bernice was "not only trapped by her desire for a nuclear family but also by her welfare receipt."[35] Eventually, with the help of social agencies, Bernice freed herself, and over the next few years she and her two children came closer to a hopeful ending to their saga.

In Chicago, caseworker Mimi told me that she believed domestic violence was widespread: "Almost every women coming into the [STRIVE] program seems to have had this problem. . . . These are the stories that I take home with me, especially when the abuse affects the children." David Shipler, too, noted that in

Chicago's Imperial Court, "Domestic violence ran rampant, and of the 1,452 residents only 54 were employed full-time and 12 part-time—and this was in the booming years of a prosperous economy, just before the recession began in 2001."[36]

For Melinda, the domestic abuse she found when taking the case histories of Goodwill clients in Milwaukee reflected their lack of self-esteem. She said,

> Women on welfare already don't have much self esteem. They don't understand how to move forward. They see some money and will accept whatever the man issues out because the money is more than they have been seeing when just receiving the welfare check. And he's seeing she'll let him do whatever he wants; she ain't worth nothing.

A Chicago former recipient, Laura, believes that even when men are not abusing women, they stifle advancement. Reflecting on her own 16-year experience, Laura recounted, "I stayed with him because I thought it was best for the kids. I realized that I was trying to relive my childhood. I wasn't moving ahead because he was very needy. I was focused on being a caretaker for him so that he in return would be a provider."

Leslie, too, found that for her clients "men are a big part of the problem." Leslie recalled that sometimes she had a client who "had a mark that she didn't want to discuss because she was so wrapped up in his life that she couldn't manage hers."

This link between welfare and domestic violence has been rejected by many antipoverty advocates. As Joan Meier noted,

> Emphasis on the values and attitudes which lead to abuse and the need for moral education of perpetrators . . . is anathema to anti-poverty activists who preach the structural and socioeconomic causes of the ills of the poor and see any talk of moral or dysfunctional behavior of the poor as a form of blaming the victim. . . . Such "poverty progressives" are fueled by their belief that both the causes and cures for poverty are social, economic, and political, but not behavioral.[37]

There is no question that generalizations concerning the relationship of domestic violence and welfare are not helpful. There are clearly cases where welfare offers an alternative for battered women. However, by highlighting alternative instances where welfare traps abused women in poverty, Raphael threatens the core beliefs of many advocates for the poor. When forced to acknowledge the existence of domestic violence, many of these advocates, according to Meier, "frame battering in poor communities as another product of poverty; a tragic expression of poor, often African-American men's rage and frustration at racism and their own oppression by white, dominant society."[38]

For a long time, both conservative and liberal policy makers ignored this growing evidence of high levels of sexual abuse and domestic violence within poor black communities. For example, while DeParle is quite graphic in his description of sexual abuse and domestic violence in the premigration generation, his narrative was silent on these matters in the postmigration generation. None of the three black women he followed experienced these problems. When DeParle discussed contemporary sexual abuse, the examples cited were poor white women rather than the experiences of young black women in urban centers. In explaining the unwillingness to discuss abuse, journalist Joe Klein claimed:

> Conservatives are uncomfortable because it posits another victim class: girls who become pregnant aren't just amoral, premature tarts—they are prey. Who could support cutting off these children's benefits, as some Republicans have proposed? But liberals are also uncomfortable because the data are further proof that an intense social pathology—a culture of poverty—has overwhelmed the slums.[39]

Luker devoted a scant two paragraphs on coercive relationships and concluded, "Sexual activity is coerced...for a small but important subset of American teens."[40] She then immediately shifts to alternative explanations for why young women have unprotected sex. This enabled her to remain focused on the broader systemic forces that constrain poor women:

> The increase in the number of teenage and unwed mothers is an indirect measure of the toll that a bifurcating economy is taking on Americans, especially women of poor and minority backgrounds. It would be better to see early childbearing as a symptom, like infant mortality—not a cause but a marker of events, an indicator of the extent to which many young people have been excluded from the American dream.[41]

The 1996 welfare reform legislation brought to the forefront issues of sexual abuse and domestic violence. One important component of that legislation was the Family Violence Option that encouraged states to take into account domestic violence when formulating programs to aid welfare recipients. This option requires each welfare recipient to be screened confidentially in order to (1) identify victims of domestic violence, (2) provide referrals to services for victims, and (3) grant waivers from time limits. The Family Violence Option has been adopted by more than 30 states, increasing the ability of vulnerable women to end abusive relationships.

Some states, most prominently Minnesota, have been effective at reducing domestic violence. Ruth Brandwein and Diana Filiano found, however, that the Family Violence Option had not been fully effective because assessments have sometimes been used to judge the truthfulness of the women's claims and because recipients fear that disclosing abuse risks losing their children if the home is deemed unfit.[42] Raphael and Sheila Haennicke, therefore, recommended that all questions should be linked to potential sabotage and danger around education, training, work, and child support enforcement.[43]

HARMFUL EFFECTS EXAGGERATED

Hostility to teenage motherhood was based in large part on *initial* assessments of long-term studies. In 1972, Furstenberg interviewed women who had become teen mothers six years earlier. He found that half had not completed high school, 70 percent had been on welfare, and many had a second child, increasing the likelihood that they would become welfare dependent. While two-thirds had married their child's father, only a small percentage remained married five years later.[44]

Researchers also believed that serious adverse health consequences were associated with teenage childbearing. In 1960, among black women, the infant mortality rate of children born to mothers 15–19 years old was 5 percent, but only 3.8 percent for those born to mothers 25–30 years old.[45] This bleak assessment of the consequences of teen childbearing was widely accepted and provided the backdrop for an influential National Research Council report.[46]

When Furstenberg and his associates did follow-up interviews of the teen mothers in 1984, however, some of the adverse social consequences had disappeared. The share of teen mothers with less than a high school degree declined from 49.2 percent in 1972 to 32.6 percent. They also found that welfare dependency was not as widespread as in 1972. In 1984, two-thirds of teen mothers had not been on welfare in any of the previous five years because most teen mothers had entered the workforce. The percentage employed increased from 45 percent in 1972—when their children were young—to 72 percent in 1983. These findings indicated that the adverse consequences for teen mothers (from the migrating generation) were not as large as they had thought in 1972.[47]

There is also evidence that the relatively low educational attainment of teen mothers may result from factors other than their childbearing decision. Luker noted that for many young poor women, doing poorly in school *preceded* pregnancy: "As many as one-fourth to one-third of teenage mothers drop out before they get pregnant" and many others "may already be drifting away from school long before pregnancy gives them an official excuse to do so."[48] This is consistent with other research that found lower education attainment was associated with women who have displayed "lower academic ability and had lower educational goals than did their peers who had no children."[49] Thus, the lower educational attainment of teen mothers may reflect their lack of aptitude and motivation rather than the adverse consequences of not delaying childbearing.

School policies can play an enormous role in navigating the consequences facing teen mothers. Until fairly recently, high schools were reluctant to provide support services to pregnant students and teen mothers. Indeed, until the 1970s, it was accepted practice to require pregnant teenagers to leave their regular school once they began to "show." Schools, especially those in poor neighborhoods, reasoned that students would interpret support services as a signal that it was okay to be a teen mother. Today, most urban schools are much more accommodating to the needs of pregnant students, and hence, these students are much more likely to graduate than in the past. Thus, older studies are likely to have overstated the educational disadvantage caused by teen childbearing.

Some more recent studies also indicate that teen childbearing might only have a limited effect on lifetime earnings. To isolate the effect of teen childbearing, Arline Geronimus and Sanders Korenman compared outcomes of sisters, one who became a teen mother and one who did not. Using three different data sets, at age 30, teen mothers lived in households with annual family incomes about one-quarter less than their siblings who did not become teen mothers.[50]

By the early 1990s, there no longer was a consensus that teen childbearing was detrimental to infant survival in poor black communities. Given the devastating effects of joblessness, poverty, and the growing drug epidemic, delaying childbearing to their mid-20s put poor black women at increased risk that they would enter pregnancies with adverse health conditions, such as hypertension and high blood lead levels. Delaying pregnancy increased the risk that these women would smoke or drink during pregnancy and decreased the likelihood that they would breast-feed their infants. As a result, delaying childbearing increased the risk of preterm birth, low birth weight, and neonatal deaths.[51]

Taken together, evidence indicated that during the 1980s the adverse economic and health consequences of teen childbearing were not as severe or as pervasive as suggested by earlier assessments. As a result, for some teenagers, childbearing may not have been as irrational as it seemed, so counseling of young pregnant women should not automatically assume that motherhood is such a harmful choice. Indeed, it was just this type of counseling that caused many in the black community to become hostile to Planned Parenthood efforts during the 1980s.[52]

I think that the criticisms of Planned Parenthood's efforts were overly harsh. The limited economic costs of teen motherhood reflected the special circumstances of the 1980s and early 1990s and still did not take into account the noneconomic costs documented in this chapter. Most important, as a result of improved benefits from employment and the ending of the crack cocaine epidemic (and resulting crime), young women in poor black neighborhoods, at the time of welfare reform, no longer had the same hopelessness and dire futures.

Not surprisingly, black teen birth rates fell substantially during the 1990s. Most dramatically, the birth rate for black women 15–17 years old was almost halved from 84.9 in 1990 to 44.9 by 2001 (table 4.1). Rates fell most noticeably after 1995, suggesting that welfare reform might have accelerated the decline that was occurring. This explanation seems most plausible for white teenagers. Whereas their rates held steady through 1995, they fell substantially thereafter.[53]

Table 4.1. Teenage Birth Rates (per 1,000) by Race, 1990–2001

	BIRTH RATE		
RACE/AGE	1990	1995	2001
Black			
15- to 17-year-olds	84.9	70.4	44.9
18- to 19-year-olds	157.5	139.2	116.7
White			
15- to 17-year-olds	23.2	22.0	14.0
18- to 19-year-olds	66.6	66.2	54.8

Source: Joyce A. Martin et al., "Births: Final Data for 2004," *National Vital Statistics Report* 55 (September 29, 2006): table 8, http://www.cdc.gov/nchs/data/nvsr/nvsr55/nvsr55_01.pdf.

STRUCTURAL EXPLANATIONS REVISITED

Many advocates for the poor, such as Luker, minimize the extent of coercive and violent behavior among the poor and the downside of teen childbearing, especially for black women. The choice, however, is not to rationalize away this behavior or to accept cultural explanations for it. Chapter 3 documented how the loss of employment opportunities and the crack cocaine epidemic created an environment in which dysfunctional behavior flourished among the postmigration generation. This behavior weakened their attachment to the paid labor market and encouraged a fatalism that perceived welfare an inevitable long-term outcome. When black men of the postmigration generation reached their teen years, depression levels of unemployment only made them feel more powerless and, together with the growing prevalence of crack cocaine, translated into their coercive and violent behavior toward women.

The prevalence of drugs also directly affected many women who were on welfare. One study found that in the early 1990s, 27 percent of welfare recipients had used an illegal drug or engaged in binge drinking at least twice during the previous year. This was triple the rate for comparable women who were not on welfare. For 18- to 24-year-old welfare recipients, the rate was 37 percent. When studies looked specifically at cocaine use, the rates for welfare recipients were about twice that of comparable women who were not on welfare.[54]

Finally, drug use among poor women had some harmful effects on children. A study of births in New York City reported that the proportion of birth certificates indicating maternal illicit substance abuse tripled between 1981 and 1987.[55] Both Shipler's and DeParle's narratives verify that drug use not only endangered the health of some children but also adversely affected child-rearing practices. In both books, poor black women lost custody of their children because of persistent drug use.

The poor parenting he observed had a profound effect on DeParle's assessment of welfare reform. In summing up the Caples' family history (described in chapter 3), DeParle concluded,

> *Children who grow up in a household with only one biological parent are worse off on average than children who grow up in a household with both of their biological parents, regardless of the parents' race or educational background....* [They] are twice as likely to drop out of high school, twice as likely to have a child before age twenty, and one and a half times as likely to be "idle"—out of school and out of work—in their late teens and early twenties.[56]

At the end of his book *American Dream*, DeParle returned to this theme. The Manpower Demonstration Research Corporation evaluated the effects of welfare-to-work programs in six states on the well-being of children 3–12 years old. In those families in which work led to an increase in income, "the children actually did better in school than youngsters in similar poor families that simply received cash assistance under the old welfare rules."[57]

DeParle discounted this study and gave his own perspective: "To the extent the programs helped, they appeared to do so not by turning mothers into role models but by getting more kids into formal day care. Reforming welfare, that is, didn't reform the house; it got the kids out."[58]

In a sense, DeParle's evaluation comes very close to the one given by conservatives: substituting work for welfare alone does not help children. Only by increasing marriage and reducing unwed motherhood can the family provide a healthy environment. Thus, it is not surprising that his book is praised by those like Ron Haskins, who developed and supported the 1996 welfare reform bill.

While marriage has the potential to improve the well-being of children, DeParle's sweeping generalizations concerning the weak parenting skills of poor black single mothers are unfounded. In my interviews I, too, found parenting problems. In Milwaukee, I interviewed Belinda. Two minutes into the interview, I realized that she had not been affected by the 1996 reform legislation. Her only child was born in 1980, so Belinda would have been off of welfare by the time the reform was implemented. Going through the motions, I continued the interview and asked, "When did you leave welfare?" Belinda answered, "In 1992 when child services took James away because of my neglect. I was hooked on drugs and not a very good mother to him. I didn't pay much attention then," she recalled, "but looking back now, they were really trying to help me."

James began living with his father but was a troubled kid. Sent to a juvenile home, he assaulted a staff worker and was sent to prison. James was then in and out of prison for various assaults until he was killed in a street altercation in 2003. We had to suspend the interview for a few minutes as Belinda relived her son's death.

Left at this point, her story might be considered an example of the downside of the drug problems that afflicted poor black communities. This narrative, however, does not support the thesis that intergenerational cultural norms put black women at particular risk, nor does it support DeParle's claims that poor single (black) mothers after welfare reform lacked appropriate parenting skills. Rather, it il-lustrated the difficulties faced by women of the postmigration generation when trying to raise their children in an environment where joblessness, violence, and drug use were widespread.

Indeed, Belinda began pulling her life together in the 1990s, gaining stable employment through a secretarial training program and a stable set of social relationships through her church activities. Beginning in 1997, Belinda enrolled at a private four-year college. Working two low-wage jobs over the next six years, she obtained a bachelor's degree in human resource management. There is no doubt in my mind that if Belinda had become a mother in the late 1990s, she would have been much more responsible than she was a decade earlier.

What most dissuaded me from embracing DeParle's pessimist view were the parenting efforts that I consistently found among the successful mothers I in-terviewed. I asked each of the mothers about their time management since leaving welfare. Invariably, they detailed a level of discipline that was truly inspiring. Melinda told me,

> I get up first in the morning. I've learned that I have to get myself ready before the kids get up because once they're up its "Mommy, mommy I need this, I need that, or didn't do that. . . ." I drop the kids off and only then do I turn the radio on and that's my time.

In the summertime, Melinda keeps her kids in child care until 6 P.M. even though she gets off work at 4:30 P.M. "It gives me an hour to pick up something I put on layaway, gives me time to visit my 90-year-old father, or little things like window shopping," she said. "But during the school year, I pick them up right after I finish work so that they can go to the library and other activities."

While Melinda was able to balance work and her children, remaining in school was problematic. She recounted that when her children were young,

> I was enrolled in a two-year business management program. My sister was avail-able on Wednesdays but study group on Saturday was a problem since I had no reliable babysitting. Was getting good grades, but when Friday came around I would be nervous about how I was going to manage the study group the next day.

It was so trying that Melinda was forced to temporarily suspend her educational pursuits. But she was not discouraged. "I enrolled my son in a babysitting cer-tificate program at Blue Cross Blue Shield. Once he turns 12 in two months, I can then go back to school."

Julia has four children, including a son with significant health problems. When this child was four years old, she went back to work. Relating her daily routine, Julia said,

Parenting is more than a full-time job. I was often in a zombie mode because at that time I was a single parent, doing all on my own and not just a mother that had one child but had three other children. . . . My oldest daughter was in kindergarten and I had her at the bus stop by 6:30 every morning, which meant I had to get myself up by 5 A.M., sometimes by 4:30, just to have time for myself. Then I'd get her up and prepare her, then prepare breakfast for all the kids. When I walked her three blocks to the bus stop, it meant my oldest son remained at home with the two younger kids. Being a teenager, he wasn't a happy camper about it but "who cares" was my position. Coming back from the bus stop, I finished getting the smaller ones dressed. At that time my [younger] son was off his monitor and the morning routine depended upon whether I was taking him to the doctor or sending my daughter to daycare. I had to be at work at 8:30 A.M. with a 20 minute drive.

Just as with Melinda, the balancing of work and parenting responsibilities made it impossible to sustain educational pursuits. "When I was still with the father of my two youngest children, he agreed to take care of the children one night during the week and every other Sunday when I went to school," she said. "When we split up, however, the burden fell on my oldest son, and that wasn't fair, so I put off school."

MiShonda's day also begins before sunrise. Her son gets up a 5:15 A.M. After waking her 12-year-old daughter, MiShonda leaves with her son at 5:45 A.M. so that she can be at work at 7 A.M. When she returns home at 4:30 P.M., time is spent on homework and dinner. Then the kids have one hour for TV before baths and bedtime at 8:30 P.M.

After MiShonda described her life, I commented, "Seems like your whole life is dealing with getting to work, getting enough overtime to meet your bills, and taking care of kids. Doesn't that get to be a bit of a drag?" "It tends to be very tiring and sometimes I'm asleep before they are, but it makes me motivated to get my degree," she responded.

CONCLUDING REMARKS

This chapter documents the social downside of the 1980s and early 1990s for poor black women. Victimized by abusive men and facing bleak futures, many of these women succumbed to a present-oriented lifestyle that was harmful to themselves and their children. Many times efforts to escape this situation were stifled by male partners who sabotaged training or paid employment. An outgrowth of this hopelessness was an upsurge in teenage birth rates. By 1990, more than 8 percent of black women 15–17 years old gave birth, and the rate was more than 15 percent for 18- and 19-year-old black women.

Since the early 1990s, however, there has been a remarkable reversal of these trends. Teen birth rates have declined as poor women have become more hopeful and as welfare rules have changed. In addition, there has been a dramatic reduction in intimate violence rates. The rate per 1,000 women fell from 9.8 in 1993 to 7.8 in 1996 to 4.7 in 2000. The number of women killed by intimate partners declined from 1,581 in 1993 to 1,247 by 2000.[59]

There is no denying the *potential* positive effects of marriage, and this certainly has been an important component of conservative policy recommendations. In particular, the George W. Bush administration has made marriage initiatives a central component of its antipoverty proposals and recommendations for reauthorization of the Temporary Assistance for Needy Families program. Thus, the impact of welfare reform on marriage rates, and the Bush marriage initiative proposals are prominently discussed in chapter 9, which looks more closely at legislative proposals. Marriage, however, often has not been a viable option for poor black women, given the behavior and circumstances of their potential partners.

This chapter provides further evidence that the problems poor women faced were not a result of intergenerational cultural norms but instead the special circumstances created by the lack of employment opportunity and the crack cocaine epidemic. When these circumstances ended in the 1990s, together with welfare reform, behavior changed: teenage birth rates plummeted, and employment rates soared. With marriage for many still not a viable option, these women soldiered on, often displaying remarkable perseverance. They rise early in the morning in order to prepare themselves and steal a moment of calm before starting their choirs. This is especially true for those women who, either because they lack a car or had more than one preschooler to prepare, have to rise before 6 A.M. every weekday morning. Then after a full days' paid work, they retrace their steps to pick up children, do shopping, come home to prepare dinner, and then make sure that homework was done before preparing for the next day.

Efforts to escape poverty are also impeded by the skill enhancement programs poor women enter. Many of the women I interviewed gained worthless credentials only to be burdened with the repayment of student loans. MiShonda's experience was one of the worst examples. She had been enrolled in a computer program at a private school that closed its doors before she had even completed the program. MiShonda had no degree but was still responsible for the student loans taken out while in school. Still angered by the experience, she complained, "It took me six years to pay off the loans I took out for this worthless program."

In chapter 8, I discuss how community colleges can play a more prominent role in the skill development of less-educated men and women. Before I evaluate the support services provided and offering recommendations for improvements, the following two chapters will describe the income effects of the 1996 welfare legislation during the economic boom and subsequent economic downturn.

PART II

Measured Successes

5

Welfare Reform during the Economic Boom

Many of the initial objections to welfare reform were legitimate. For many, reform certainly appeared to be an unnecessary overhaul that would only cause more hardships for vulnerable families. Not mentioned in the public debates, however, was that critics based their assessment on a combination of short-term projections and long-term implications. In the short run, many critics forecasted that the labor market would be unable to absorb the volume of women leaving welfare, especially a large number of black women whose barriers to employment seemed insurmountable. Even if employment problems could be minimized during boom periods, critics feared what would happen during periods of high unemployment that would necessarily occur over time.

I return to these long-term concerns when looking at the most recent years in chapter 6. This chapter documents why the dire *short-term* forecasts proved wrong and why some of these critics came to consider welfare reform a qualified success during the Clinton-era economic boom years. It is crucial to understand this distinction because many critics continue to reject the view that welfare reform was effective even during an economic boom. If welfare reform cannot be effective even in the most favorable economic climate in the last 50 years, it is hard to justify my claim that it can provide a foundation for future welfare policies.

FAULTY ASSUMPTIONS

In 1996, many policy analysts believed that welfare served primarily as a safety net for short-term users. They tried to explain why conservative claims that the majority of *current* welfare recipients were long-term dependent was true but misleading. Specifically, table 5.1 illustrates how it is possible over a *10-year period* for the vast majority of welfare recipients to be short-term users while the majority of those *currently* on welfare are long-term users.

Table 5.1 assumes that there are two groups of welfare recipients. One group consists of short-term users who, for simplicity, are assumed to use welfare in only one year during the decade. A second group consists of long-term users who, for simplicity, are assumed to use welfare in every year during the decade. In each year, there are 80 short-term users. Since these are different people in each of the 10 years, over the decade there are 800 short-term users. In addition, there are 100 long-term users who are the *same* individuals in each of the 10 years. Since over the decade 800 of the 900 individuals receiving welfare are short-term users, welfare should correctly be perceived as serving as a safety net, aiding primarily individuals who are having short-term difficulties. If we look at each year separately, however, a majority—100 of the 180 welfare recipients—are long-term users.

The real data are a bit more complicated. Between those short-term and long-term users is a group of "cyclers": women not continuously on welfare but cycling in for a number of short spells. As a result, we might ask, for any woman beginning her first spell, how much time will she spend on welfare during her lifetime? Mary Jo Bane and David Ellwood estimated that, over the 21-year period from 1968 through 1989, 46.5 percent of all welfare users were on welfare for three years or less during their lifetime, while only 22.1 percent were on welfare for 10 years or more.[1] Thus, for *that* time period, even taking into account cycling, it appeared that welfare dependency was a problem for only a modest share of total recipients. For this reason, many policy analysts believed that coercive measures, including workfare and time limits, were unnecessary.

Table 5.1. Hypothetical Distribution of Long- and Short-Term Welfare Recipients

WELFARE USERS	YEAR										TOTAL
	1	2	3	4	5	6	7	8	9	10	
Short term	80	80	80	80	80	80	80	80	80	80	800
(10 years of welfare use)											(89%)
Long term	100	100	100	100	100	100	100	100	100	100	100
(one year of welfare use)											(11%)

In addition, just as welfare reform was being legislated, Katherine Edin and Laura Lein published research results that seemed to indicate that forcing women off welfare would not improve their economic well-being. Edin and Lein interviewed a large group of recipients who left welfare between 1988 and 1992 and found that their wage gains did not compensate fully for the decline in welfare cash payments and food stamp benefits. As a result, welfare leavers had more reported earnings but also more material hardships: missing meals, loss of utilities, and homelessness.[2] When discussing the possible impact of the 1996 welfare legislation in a foreword to their study, Christopher Jencks noted, "No one knows for sure how single mothers will fare, but the evidence assembled in *Making Ends Meet* is probably our best current available guide to the economic impact of this change. Edin and Lein's data bear both on what is likely to happen and how we will interpret these changes."[3]

These two studies illustrate one of the inherent difficulties with social science research. Both Bane and Ellwood and Edin and Lein collected evidence at one point in time that many welfare analysts used to project policy effects on a future point in time. But the changing nature of the welfare rolls made such extrapolations faulty. Between the 1980s and the 1990s, the share of short-term welfare users declined while the share of long-term users rose. For example, Robert Moffitt and David Stevens analyzed welfare use among young women in Baltimore. For the five-year period of 1986–1991, they estimated that 64 percent were short-term users and another 3 percent were cyclers, so only 33 percent could be characterized as long-term users. For the next five-year period, however, Moffitt and Stevens found a noticeable change: only 44 percent were short-term users, while 46 percent were long-term users. More generally, they reported "a marked increase in welfare dependency from 31 percent to a high of 51 percent for the 1991–1996 cohort."[4] Researchers found similar results for Milwaukee.[5] Thus, it appears that welfare dependency had become more prominent than in the earlier time period that Bane and Ellwood analyzed.

Similarly, Jencks underestimated differences between the experience of welfare leavers Edin and Lein studied and what could be anticipated on the eve of the 1996 welfare reform. In the earlier period, if the typical welfare leaver obtained a full-time year-round job at minimum wage, including food stamps and the earned income tax credit (EITC), Ellwood estimated that she could expect to increase her annual net income by $2,005. In 1997, the minimum wage increased from $4.25 to $5.15 per hour while the EITC increased from a maximum of $950 in 1990 to $3,620 by 1997. Thanks to these changes, Ellwood estimated that leavers could expect to receive $7,119 more when taking a minimum wage job after the 1996 legislation.[6] In addition, changes in Medicaid and the passage of the state Child Health Insurance Program made it much more likely that medical coverage would continue for welfare leavers than in the earlier period.

POTENTIAL FINANCIAL BENEFITS

Table 5.2 illustrates the substantial *potential* monthly income increase from a shift to work for welfare leavers in 1997 in 12 representative states. In every one of these states, the family's total monthly income would increase by at least $500 if the household head moved from welfare with no earnings to working 35 hours weekly at the minimum wage.[7] The increases were particularly large in southern states, where welfare cash benefits are quite low.

Of course, table 5.2 assumes that welfare leavers would be able to sustain full-year employment. When Jencks was commenting, however, there was no reason to be optimistic that employment prospects for welfare leavers would be especially robust. Even after five years of economic expansion, the 1996 labor market was still weak. Of particular concern, the employment growth for black workers was not as strong as in previous economic recoveries. Though their official rate had fallen, Jencks pointed out that black unemployment rates still remained at double-digit levels, and hidden unemployment made the employment situation much worse than the official measure.[8]

Even more troubling, outside of the South, there was a core of black women who were distant from employment, neither working nor actively engaged in job

Table 5.2. Monthly Income from Welfare versus Work, 1998

STATE	WELFARE WITH NO PAID EMPLOYMENT	FULL TIME AT MINIMUM WAGE	INCOME INCREASE FROM PAID EMPLOYMENT
Alabama	$479	$1,198	$719
California	825	1,449	624
Colorado	674	1,243	569
Florida	618	1,275	657
Massachusetts	825	1,448	623
Michigan	743	1,257	514
Minnesota	763	1,409	646
Mississippi	435	1,215	780
New Jersey	726	1,300	574
New York	833	1,447	614
Texas	503	1,233	730
Washington	812	1,344	532
Median	**734**	**1,287**	**553**

Total income consists of TANF benefit, cash value of food stamp allotment, earnings, federal EITC, and state earned income and other tax credits, less the employee's share of payroll taxes and federal and state income tax liabilities. Program rules are based on the Urban Institute's summary of state TANF plans, legislation, and regulations as of October 1997.
Source: G. Acs, N. Coe, K. Watson, and R. Lerman, "Does Work Pay?" (Urban Institute, July 1998).

search. This was especially true in the Midwest, where manufacturing employment had declined precipitously. In 1992, 55 percent of black and white women
in the South Atlantic states were employed. By contrast, in the midwestern states,
56 percent of white but only 46 percent of black women were employed.[9] These
figures further suggested to welfare critics that the employment situation for
black women leaving welfare would be particularly grim.

At the time of welfare reform, the national unemployment rate was just below
5.5 percent, the exact point in the previous expansion when Federal Reserve chair
Alan Greenspan had slowed down economic growth for fear of inflationary
pressures. As a result, there was every reason to believe that the already weak
employment prospects that black (and other less-skilled) workers faced would
worsen. Jencks reasoned:

> Since the national unemployment rate seldom falls below 5 percent, we have to as-
> sume that "post-TANF" welfare mothers will be unemployed at least 10 percent of
> the time when the economy is doing well and even more during recessions. In poor
> inner-city neighborhoods and depressed rural areas, the rate is likely to be even
> higher. The least skilled and least reliable mothers will often have trouble finding
> any kind of work. For all these reasons, it seems unlikely that welfare mothers who
> hit their TANF time limit will earn as much (at least in real terms) as the mothers
> whom Edin and Lein interviewed.[10]

Just as Jencks and others predicted, employment difficulties arose in areas where
the economic boom was weakest. For example, black women in New York City
saw their unemployment rate increase from 8.6 to 15.2 percent between 1994 and
1997.

Fortunately, events conspired to create a much more favorable employment
environment over the next four years. As Greenspan was poised to begin slowing
down the economy after the 1996 election, an Asian economic crisis forced a
reappraisal. Rising unemployment and a slowdown in wage growth would have
caused U.S. households to reduce their purchases of goods and services. Since a
significant portion of purchases would have been on goods that were directly or
indirectly produced in these Asian countries, Federal Reserve anti-inflationary
policies would have further weakened economies already devastated by banking and currency problems. As a result, Greenspan decided to allow the U.S.
expansion to strengthen, allowing national unemployment rates to fall below
5 percent.

Greenspan's instincts to pull the trigger and clamp down on the economy may
also have been tempered by an understanding that welfare reform had begun to
thrust hundreds of thousands of new workers into the labor market, and without robust growth, they would likely have difficulty finding permanent employment. He surely understood that welfare recipients suffered from a stigma that
made most employers unwilling to hire them as long as alternative workers were

available. Surveys consistently found that employers believed mothers, especially black single mothers, were employment risks because they would have to take time off to care for their children. Indeed, one employer surveyed lamented that because of federal laws he no longer could ask applicants if their children became sick, "Do you have someone who can take care of them?"[11]

When firms began hiring, it appeared that these stereotypes played out on the job. A Michigan research team reported that many recipients lost their jobs because "they failed to understand the importance of punctuality, the seriousness of absenteeism, and resented or misunderstood the lines of authority and responsibility in the workplace."[12] Other studies from the early and mid-1990s consistently found "that a significant fraction of welfare recipients leave work within three to six months, and most do so within less than one year."[13]

RISING RETENTION RATES

Once more, extrapolating from earlier studies proved faulty. The Michigan research team found that retention rates increased substantially over the next three years, such that by 1999, a variety of studies found employment durations of roughly 16 months on average.[14] As welfare leavers became more consistent members of the workforce, they began to dismantle these stereotypes. One large employment survey found that while black women were disproportionately single heads of households, they had a lower rate of absenteeism or lateness due to concerns about child care than did white mothers.[15] Another national survey found that employers rated the welfare leavers they employed quite highly. These firms judged 35 percent of welfare leavers to be above average, while only 16 percent were judged below average. This study also found that welfare leavers had lower rates of job turnover than the general rates for less skilled workers.[16]

To their surprise, major corporations found that former welfare recipients stayed on the job longer than did other employees. Borg-Warner, Giant Food, Marriott International, Salomon Smith Barney, Sprint, United Airlines, United Parcel Service, and Xerox found that they retained a larger proportion of former recipients than other entry-level employees. United Airlines, for example, had retained 70 percent of the 760 recipients hired one year earlier; the retention rate for others hired at similar jobs was only 40 percent. At Giant Foods, 100 welfare recipients had been hired as cashiers, clerks, and assistants. The retention rate after 90 days was 79 percent, whereas it was only 50 percent for other employees in similar jobs.[17]

The strong economy absorbed a large share of single mothers. Between 1995–1996 and 1998–1999, the employment rate of single mothers 20–45 years of age living in 20 of the largest urban areas increased from 59 percent to 73 percent.[18] The employment rate of black midwestern women increased from 46 percent in

1992 to 59 percent in 2000, completely eliminating the 10-percentage-point racial employment gap mentioned above.[19] Focusing on never-married women—the population most affected by welfare reform—the employment gains were even more striking. The employment rate for black never-married women rose from 47 percent in 1995 to 66 percent by 2000, while the rate for Hispanic never-married women rose from 38 to 57 percent.[20]

One important reason for these rising employment rates was the decision to fund nonprofit companies to improve the work readiness of welfare recipients and supplement the activities of welfare offices. I interviewed welfare leavers at two of the more effective nonprofit agencies that aided the welfare-to-work efforts: STRIVE Incorporated and New Hope. Many of those I interviewed had harsh assessments of the welfare offices and were thankful for the support they received at the nonprofits. Julia noted that at New Hope, the staff would make all the referrals:

> Maybe it would take maybe 15–20 minutes out of a day to make three or four calls, but for a person who needs to focus on her job, it was a relief, instead of missing some days from work. After you miss so many days, they don't care if you are a good worker on the job, or a good person. We need you here and that's understood; those are the rules and what you have to do.

Personal touches made all the difference in these women's lives. "Two caseworkers out of 8–10 actually exhibited the type of attitude that made me confident that they wanted to help," Julia recalled. "Caseworkers can be either encouragers or deterrents. When I had a deterrent, I did everything that I could not to see that caseworker."

In Chicago, I met Mimi, a former welfare recipient who has been working for 10 years at STRIVE, rising from receptionist to evaluating clients. With a salary of $28,000 annually, she felt her life is "10 times better than it ever has been." However, Mimi still had bitter memories of her treatment at welfare offices. She still remembers one caseworker. "It was as if the money was coming out of her pocket. When this caseworker called me a 'doofus' for forgetting something she had told me to do, I blew up and was sanctioned."

New Hope program administrator Julie Kerksick explained that to a large degree, this insensitivity reflected the rocky transition of welfare offices into job placement centers:

> In the new worked-based system of support, caseworkers have to learn to be employment coaches. Helping the TANF participant go to work means starting with an understanding of what she has to offer, and then understanding how to help put support systems in place to do that. It's pretty different from traditional social service approaches, which seem to focus on a professional telling the client what is wrong with her—and how to fix it.

FOOD STAMP POLICIES

A second problematic assumption reflected in the data in table 5.2 was that welfare leavers would continue to receive food stamps as long as their income was low enough to qualify. In reality, many single mothers did not apply for food stamps after leaving welfare because they did not realize and sometimes were not told that they remained eligible.

A particularly egregious example of poor transitioning policies occurred in New York. In April 1998, New York City began implementing a two-day application process where caseworkers urged the poor to rely on relatives, food pantries, and jobs rather than public assistance, delaying application for food stamps to a later second visit. Indeed, at some point, women could not apply for cash payments until they completed a mandatory four-week job search program, and if they missed even one class they "could be forced to start the program all over again."[21]

After a lawsuit, city officials acknowledged that some caseworkers "sent the hungry to food pantries rather than screening them for emergency assistance. Other caseworkers refused to consider food assistance for immigrants or women who showed up without their husbands. Some simply rejected anyone who arrived after 11 A.M." Despite legal actions, nearly 10 months later the city indicated that "workers improperly denied emergency food assistance were 51 percent of those who needed it."[22]

Mayor Rudolf Guiliani defended these policies of diverting the poor because he felt that immediately providing necessary services would send the wrong message: "Offering easy access to applications or encouraging people to apply for food stamps or Medicaid will hinder their efforts to destroy the culture of poverty in poor neighborhoods."[23] A *New York Times* article explained the inherent tension in the new federal policies, reporting that

> The situation in New York highlights the conundrum confronted by welfare officials across the country. They find themselves struggling to juggle two very different Federal mandates. On the one hand, the Federal welfare law allows states and municipalities to discourage people from applying for cash benefits, and offers financial incentives for those with declines in their caseloads. On the other, the law requires states to encourage the needy to apply for food stamps and Medicaid, two benefits described as critical by Federal officials hoping to keep the working poor off welfare and the newly employed from returning.[24]

Kerksick experienced a similar situation at New Hope in Wisconsin, where staff were responding to explicit policy directives from top officials to deter as many potential recipients as possible. Not until April 1999, after public pressure from the courts and the federal food stamp administration, did the Guiliani administration reverse its policy and agree to allow the poor to apply for food stamps and Medicaid on their first visit to the city's welfare offices.[25]

One method of quantifying these food stamp changes is to track changes in the accessibility ratio: the ratio of food stamp recipients to the number of individuals living in poverty. Figure 5.1 indicates that between 1990 and 1995, the accessibility ratio increased substantially as a result of effective outreach and increased awareness among potential recipients. As eligible families left welfare, however, the accessibility ratio plummeted.[26]

Robert Greenstein and Jocelyn Guyer cite the increased burden on working families for this declining participation rate.[27] In response to federal pressure to lower error rates, "a dozen states increased by 50 percentage points or more the proportion of working households with children assigned food stamp certification periods of three months or less."[28] They contend that these changes explain why in these states working families receiving food stamps fell by 29 percent between 1994 and 1999. Greenstein and Guyer do point out, however, that beginning in mid-1999, federal policy makers have begun to "establish procedures to make food stamps more accessible to working families."[29] In response, the food stamp

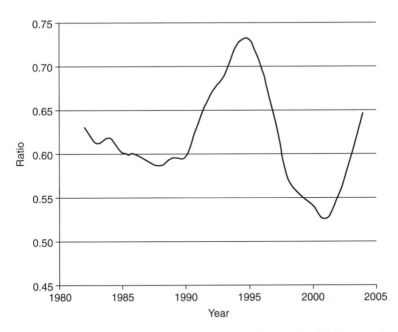

Figure 5.1. Food stamp accessibility ratio, 1982–2004. Source: For food stamps, U.S. Department of Agriculture, "Monthly Data—National Level, Food Stamp Program" (2005), http://www.fns.usda.gov/pd/fsmonthly.htm; for poverty data, U.S. Census Bureau, "Historical Poverty Tables—People," table 2, http://www.census.gov/hhes/www/poverty/histpov/hstpov2.html.

participation rate among recent welfare leavers increased from 49.6 percent in 1999 to 63.5 percent by 2002.[30]

These changes were accelerated by the Farm Bill of 2002. It not only expanded eligibility for legal immigrants but also allocated substantial funding for outreach programs and bonuses for states that demonstrated high or improved food stamp participation rates. These outreaches included the "Food Stamp Makes America Strong" campaign in both English and Spanish that led to more than a 50 percent increase in information requests to the program's toll-free number.[31] The bill also promoted coalitions with community organizations that served low-income populations. As a result, there was a 53 percent increase in the number of people receiving food stamps between October 2000 and October 2004, enabling the accessibility ratio to rebound to levels it reached in the early 1990s.[32]

LEAVERS STUDIES

Since not all leavers will find employment or retain food stamp allocations, it becomes important to assess the financial impact on those who left welfare rather than relying on table 5.2's simulations. Over a 30-month period ending in spring 2000, among a random sample of welfare recipients enrolled in New Jersey's WorkFirst program, three-quarters of the participants had left welfare. Almost two-thirds of those off welfare were working at the time of the last interview. Another 16 percent had worked in the past three months, were living with an employed partner or spouse, or were receiving Supplemental Security Income (SSI). In Massachusetts, three-quarters of welfare leavers who remained off welfare were still employed one year later, and fewer than 10 percent had not worked at all during that time period.[33] Based on these studies, we would expect to find the adversely affected families primarily among the 15–20 percent of leavers who experienced substantial employment difficulties but had not returned to welfare.

Similar results were found in national surveys. For example, a Michigan research team looked at a representative national sample of those who were on welfare in February 1997 to determine whether it pays to move from welfare to work. They concluded,

> We find that by the late 1990s, single mothers who had been welfare recipients are, on average, financially better off working or combining work and welfare than remaining as nonworking welfare recipients. Mothers who were working in fall 1999 had higher household incomes and lower poverty rates.[34]

Specifically, they found that the mean disposable income equaled $17,205 for wage-reliant leavers and only $8,244 for welfare-reliant mothers. Finally, in

contrast to studies that followed welfare leavers in the 1980s, the Michigan research team found that only a minority of welfare leavers faced severe employment difficulty.[35] Specifically, among leavers they followed, only 15 percent
worked in less than one-third of the months during a 55-month period from 1997
through 2001.[36]

Some critics reference other studies that support the Edin–Lein contention.
The majority of these studies, however, do not include the EITC, focusing solely
on wage earnings when assessing the well-being of welfare leavers.[37] This is
unfortunate, given the critical role that the EITC has played in reducing poverty.
Mark Levitan and Robin Gluck found that among working single mothers in
1999–2001, 36.5 percent did not earn enough to escape poverty through their
wages alone. Once government cash payments were included, however, only
14.2 percent had incomes below the official poverty threshold.[38]

My interviews with welfare leavers underscored the importance welfare leavers
place on the EITC. Julia's children no longer expect presents during the holiday
season. "For them," she laughed, "Christmas comes when I receive my tax return."
For Michelle and Devin, the tax refund was the only way that they were able to buy
the good used car they desperately needed to get to work. For Cynthia, it allowed
her to pay for tuition at the local college, and for Melinda it provided the down
payment for a first-time home buyers program in Milwaukee.

A few studies found that incomes did not increase even after including the
EITC. In these studies, however, welfare leavers had substantial wage income
while on welfare. Before welfare waivers began, federal regulations required
cash payments to be reduced by one dollar for each dollar of wage income. As a
result, single mothers had to choose to either be on welfare or to work. In order to
encourage work, the federal government began allowing states waivers to implement earning disregards: reduce cash payments only partially when recipients
gained wage income. By 1997, if a single mother earned as much as $9,000 an-
nually, in 10 states she would still qualify for at least $5,000 of cash benefits over
the first two years of employment, and between $3,000 and $5,000 in another 10
states.[39]

As a result of these provisions, at the point where recipients are about to earn
too much to be eligible for cash payments, they may have substantial total income. For example, Maria Cancian and colleagues studied women in Wisconsin
who left welfare in 1995. They estimated that just before moving off welfare, the
average leaver had total income of $12,000: $4,700 from earnings, $1,200 from
EITC, $2,100 in food stamps, and $4,000 in welfare payments. [40] Thus, it should
not be surprising that many of these individuals did not benefit further when they
finally left welfare.

For welfare-to-work advocates, the most compelling evidence is the dramatic reduction in official poverty rates, especially among children living in

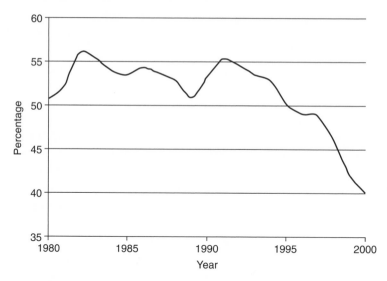

Figure 5.2. Child poverty rates among single-mother households, 1980–2000. Source: U.S. Census Bureau, "Historical Poverty Tables—People," table 10, http://www .census.gov/hhes/www/poverty/histpov/hstpov10.html.

female-headed households. After cycling between 50 and 55 percent, the share of all children living in female-headed households who were poor fell from 49.3 to 40.1 percent between 1996 and 2000 (figure 5.2). At the same time, their extreme poverty rates—income below 50 percent of the poverty threshold—fell from 25.8 to 18.7 percent. For black children living in female-headed households, poverty rates declined from 58.2 to 49.4 percent, while extreme poverty rates declined from 32.5 to 22.3 percent.[41] Among Hispanic children living in female-headed households, poverty rates declined from 67.4 to 48.3 percent, while extreme poverty rates declined from 33.6 to 25.1 percent. These dramatic declines in child poverty rates were persuasive enough to even convince Jencks to subtitle a 2004 article he co-wrote, "The critics of welfare reform were wrong."[42]

These declines in poverty rates also softened the daily struggle of simply obtaining food. One national survey found that among single noncohabitating mothers, food hardships lessened from 50.3 percent in 1997 to 46.8 percent in 1999.[43] In another national survey, food insecurity among native-born children declined from 16 percent in 1994 to 14 percent in 1998 to 9 percent in 2001. For children born to non-native-born mothers, it increased from 1994 to 1998, undoubtedly due to the 1996 welfare reform restrictions, but fell substantially after their elimination.[44] Using the Census Bureau's Food Security Survey, Scott Winship and Jencks found a significant decline in the share of single mothers who reported they had to stretch their food supply or who had a child that was not eating enough. They concluded that food problems among single mothers and their children declined consistently between 1995 and 2000, when the economy was expanding. In April 1995, for instance, 57 percent of single mothers reported having to stretch their food supply at some point during the previous year because their monthly budget came up short. By April 2001, this figure had fallen to 46 percent. The share of single mothers reporting that a child was not eating enough fell from 11 to 8 percent.[45]

Surveys also consistently show that the vast majority of single mothers believe that their lives have improved since leaving welfare. A Maine study found that 61 percent of leavers considered themselves better off than when they were on welfare, 23 percent believed their situation is about the same, and only 16 percent believed that their situation has worsened.[46] A New York study found that 71 percent of welfare leavers considered themselves better off and only 14 percent thought they were worse off than they had been on welfare.[47]

It was evidence like this that convinced even some of those who criticized Clinton for signing welfare reform legislation to admit that they were proved wrong. Most notably, Ellwood claimed that, as a result of the unexpected strength of the economy that forced employers to hire from an "at risk" population, welfare reform proved to be successful. Indeed, even after the economic slowdown, Winship and Jencks recommended that since "welfare reform has succeeded in its present form, in our view legislators should now leave it alone, rather than trying to fix what is not broken."[48]

Given the rising income of welfare leavers, the dramatic decline in official poverty rates among children living with single mothers, and welfare leavers' own perceptions of improvement, the remaining critics generally shifted to other issues. For example Peter Edelman, claimed in my interview that these employment successes and poverty reductions were due solely to the strong economy. Welfare reform, he insists, was responsible for those leavers who were adversely affected.

There is no direct method to measure accurately what share of welfare recipients would have left as a result of a more favorable labor market. Economists have attempted to separate the impact of welfare reform legislation and a strong labor market. Virtually all studies estimated that welfare reform was responsible for at least three times as much of the caseload decline as the growing economy.[49]

These results are consistent with changes in the labor force participation rate of never-married mothers, the group most sensitive to welfare policies. It remained fairly constant from 1978 through 1993, fluctuating between 50 and 55 percent. By contrast, between 1995 and 1998, it rose from 57 to 73 percent. This strongly suggests that the change in welfare policies, not simply the strong economy, provided a substantial impetus to leave TANF.[50]

Some welfare critics focused on the poverty rates of single *working* mothers, ignoring overall poverty trends. Kathryn Porter and Allen Dupree found that, in 1995 and 1999, the percentage of single *working* mothers being poor was unchanged.[51] These data have been widely quoted to support the claim that welfare reform did not significantly improve the economic well-being of families.[52] What is relevant, however, is to compare this percentage to the percentage of mothers on cash assistance who were poor. The Michigan research team found that 88 percent of welfare-reliant mothers were living in poverty but only 49 percent of work-reliant leavers were poor.[53]

Critics also claim that those who left welfare were much more work ready than those who remained, so studies that compare welfare leavers to those who remained on welfare are biased. Studies do find that the educational levels of those who remained on welfare were modestly lower than those who left.[54] The Michigan researchers found, however, that even after taking into account differences in the work readiness and barriers to employment of welfare leavers and welfare stayers, the shift to employment was financially beneficial. In particular, they estimated that monthly income (excluding the EITC) would have increased by almost $400 for leavers if they had the same work readiness and barriers to employment as those who remained on welfare.[55]

The welfare leaver population was not dramatically different than the welfare stayer population because states developed programs to aid hard-to-employ recipients. Washington's Community Jobs Program (CJP) was a particularly effective program. Its 1,132 participants faced many barriers: 32 percent had been victims of domestic violence, 35 percent had a chemical addiction, 35 percent had chronic medical problems, 57 percent lacked a high school degree, and close to 70 percent had less than a year of employment experience.

Participants entered a nine-month program during which they worked 20 hours weekly at community jobs. They spent another 20 hours weekly addressing the barriers that had kept them from working through a combination of mentoring, services, and targeted training. For their work time, participants were paid the Washington State minimum wage, received a 50 percent disregard on their regular TANF cash grant, and were eligible to receive the EITC.

Approximately 85 percent of participants completed the nine-month program, and of those who completed it, 84 percent attained gainful employment. This contrasted dramatically with their pre-CJP work experience. In the year before entering CJP, more than half of the participants did not work at all, and another 18 percent worked only for three months or less. Most rewarding, after two years of employment, the median monthly earnings of working post-CJP participants increased from $604 to $964—a 60 percent increase.[56]

These transitional programs even benefited those who were work ready. I talked with welfare leavers who valued the counseling that directed them to the correct employment path rather than into ineffective training programs. For Cutina it was the security field, something that she would never have considered without guidance. For Laura, it was a secretarial training program. For too many welfare recipients, the training policies they choose without guidance are, at best, ineffective and, at worst, a discouragement. For example, Laura didn't think it was wrong to have time limits, but she did think that the major impediment to a successful transition to work was the faulty services provided:

> What I think was unfair was the degree and level of services [recipients] received. I know that they have to have responsibility, but you could tell the difference when individuals received services that were in their benefit and presented in a way in which you could hear them; and I could tell the difference.... And many of the clients that failed, who could blame them, how they were treated.... Most of the time, work activities were meaningless, there wasn't anything that they were doing that would benefit them. Lots of providers of training were just in it for the money and it couldn't get them a job.

Not surprisingly, recipients sought out private-sector training positions, but many ended up with fields that were not in their long-term interest. Time and again, those I interviewed mentioned that they had a computer certificate or had completed a dental technician program only to realize that they had gained insufficient skills to enter these fields. In Florida, I interviewed Amber. Without any counseling or supervision, the welfare office allowed her to enroll in a new nursing assistant certification program at Remington College. There was a high turnover of teachers who often gave different instructions. Amber related how an administrator dismissed student complaints by claiming, "When you get out in the work field you're going to have different doctors going to show you different things." "That's a bunch of bullshit, I am paying you $10,000 and I want to learn something," Amber retorted. Not surprisingly, only 2 of the 34 students enrolled passed the state certification test that employers require. By contrast, when recipients received one-on-one counseling at programs like STRIVE or New Hope, they seemed much more likely to find fulfilling career paths.

Ongoing individual counseling is also crucial to leavers' success in their newfound employment. Leslie, a New Hope program director, told me about Jill, a recipient who was late for work two or three times at her job placement:

> We contacted Jill and found out her lateness was because she was having trouble getting her kids ready on time. I asked her, "Do you prepare their clothes the night before?" She responded, "I could do that." I asked her "How late do they stay up?" Jill thought for a moment and said, "I could get them to bed earlier." Her manager overheard this discussion and was in disbelief. He thought that these suggestions were common sense anyone should know. What he didn't realize, however, was that for some women, this is a new type of discipline and needs a new type of education. And Jill got better and better at it and no longer had a lateness problem.

IMPACT ON THE MOST VULNERABLE

While these success stories dominate, we should not ignore the impact of welfare reform on the most vulnerable mothers—those at the very bottom of the income distribution. Welfare critics suggest the following scenario. In the drive to reduce welfare rolls, many of these most vulnerable mothers left due to procedural harassment, unfair sanctions, or unreasonable workfare requirements. Even when unemployed, they resisted returning to welfare and fared even worse. Thus, welfare reform harmed the poorest families and must be condemned even if the vast majority of welfare leavers benefited financially.

Some statistical evidence seems to support these claims. Looking at the income of the poorest 20 percent of single mothers, Wendell Primus found that their average annual income, measured in 1999 dollars, declined from $8,532 in 1995 to $7,835 in 1999.[57] Similarly, an Institute for Women's Policy Research study found that the average monthly income of single-parent families living in extreme poverty declined from $402 in early 1996 to $352 in early 2000.[58] And Cynthia Miller found that while the welfare-to-work programs she analyzed reduced poverty rates, they increased extreme poverty rates.[59]

These figures seem alarming, but upon closer inspection, they often rest on faulty assumptions. First, using a slightly different data set, the decline in average annual income of the poorest quintile of single mothers between 1995 and 1999 was only $200, not the $700 Primus reported. More important, using this alternative data set, the 1999 income of the poorest quintile of single mothers was higher than in any previous year except 1995. Thus, if any other starting year is selected, even for the poorest quintile, average earnings increased.[60]

Second, lack of income does not necessarily mean lack of goods and services. The Census Bureau conducts surveys of consumer expenditures that show that, after adjusting for inflation, expenditures of the poorest single mothers increased continuously, rising by 11 percent between 1993 and 1998. Using a somewhat different measure, the Congressional Research Service found that consumer expenditures by the poorest single mothers increased by 18 percent between 1994 and 1997, the exact time period where Primus found that incomes declined the most.[61]

On assessing the disparity between income and consumption changes among the poorest single mothers, Bruce Meyer and James Sullivan concluded,

> First, consumption is probably a measure with less error than income for poor families, and is more strongly associated with other measures of well-being such as health and housing conditions. Second, there is overwhelming evidence that income is underreported by these mothers and that underreporting, especially of income from welfare and other transfer programs, has increased in recent years.[62]

Some studies assess the impact of welfare reform on only those who were disconnected: did not have a working spouse and were not receiving TANF or Supplemental Security Income (SSI). This group comprised 10–12 percent of welfare leavers between 1997 and 1999.[63] Though these single mothers have more economic hardships than do working welfare leavers, the differences were not dramatic. Thus, it appears that a substantial portion of nonworking leavers do not return to welfare because their well-being has not deteriorated substantially from what it had been when they were on welfare.

Finally, a number of researchers now find that any adverse income effects are concentrated in the poorest decile.[64] Reflecting on these studies, Jason DeParle noted:

> While reliable data on the very poor are scarce, the best guess is that about 7 percent of single mothers grew poorer in the second half of the 1990s. The worst of them . . . parceled out their kids, then trudged through the snow to sleep on church floors. Opponents of the bill sometimes cite such families as evidence of its failure. But a policy that fails the most marginalized few isn't necessarily a failure overall, especially if it brings significant improvement to the lives of most others.[65]

There are also important conceptual issues involved in judging the morality of welfare policies that will predictably adversely affect even a small group of the most vulnerable women and their children. This is most clear when time limits or sanctions terminate cash payments. Sanctions are not isolated but have affected a significant share of welfare recipients. While many of these sanctions are short term, there are certainly a large number that are permanent. In 1998, 5.21 percent of recipients were under some form of sanction, and 1.2 percent were under full family sanction.[66] For example, in 1999, 32 percent of welfare leavers who were disconnected from work said that they left welfare because of sanctions (only 7 percent of working former recipients gave this reason).[67]

Because sanctions can be arbitrary and sometimes are proven unfounded, many liberals recoil when considering them. Indeed, Ellwood remembers vividly the reaction of one liberal congressman. This legislator worried about the sanctions that were included in Ellwood's 1994 legislative proposal. He asked Ellwood, "Do you mean that if the recipient refuses to participate in any work or educational activities, she should be sanctioned?" To this, Ellwood replied in disbelief, "Of course!"

These adverse impacts on children can be mitigated somewhat by having only partial sanctions—still allowing the children to receive cash benefits. This is the situation in a number of states, including New York and California. Indeed, about 80,000 child-only cases nationally—about 10 percent of all child-only cases—reflect children receiving benefits because their mothers have been sanctioned.[68] Even in the most "justifiable" situations, however, partial sanctions of noncompliant recipients still put at jeopardy the economic well-being of children.

DeParle captures the inherent problem with judging sanctions. He notes that sometimes full sanctions are more effective than partial sanctions:

> At times, the tough sanctions were all for the best. In Oregon I met a methamphetamine addict who said losing her check helped save her life. "That was part of

the reason I went into treatment," Lori Furlow said. With weaker sanctions, New York found it harder to persuade troubled clients to get help. About a third of New York City's huge caseload was in the penalty process at any given time, and officials griped about the "happily sanctioned"; able to ignore the work rules and still collect three-quarters of their cash and food stamps, some people did just that.[69]

Time limits present another set of problems. At STRIVE, administrators found that they were accepting more women who were reaching their time limits. These women were required to attend STRIVE in order to maintain cash benefits. A significant share of these women remained on welfare because they did not believe that time limits would be enforced. Rather than adjusting their attitudes, many remained resistant to work, especially at the low wages they would obtain on their first jobs. More troubling, some chose not to show up for job interviews that had been arranged for them. As a result, some firms terminated their relationship with STRIVE, adversely affecting employment opportunities for other clients.

Similarly, Angie related to me how frustrated she was in her training program as a result of the actions of a bunch of welfare recipients from the Florida WAGES program. "These women were not focused on learning but were in the program in order to continue receiving cash payments," said Angie. "They would sit in the back, be rude and disruptive, and were always arguing with the teacher."

I do not reference these studies or conceptual issues to dismiss the hardships that many disconnected leavers faced. They certainly had lower cash incomes and had to rely on the goodwill of others, and their future was more uncertain than if they had remained on welfare. Most were not facing these adverse conditions because their attitudes and behavior justified sanctions or enforcement of time limits. Studies show that a significant share of this population suffer from health and emotion problems and are victims of domestic violence. Thus, there is no question that a small but significant share of the most vulnerable families were adversely affected.

IMPROVED WELL-BEING

Critics often refuse to look at changes based on official poverty rates. They note correctly that the government's measure substantially underestimates the income threshold necessary for families to escape poverty, especially once work-related expenses are included. For example, in 2000, the government estimates that for families of three—a mother and two children—$14,000 was sufficient for them to escape poverty. Even the government realizes that their income thresholds are unrealistic, allowing a number of government programs, including food stamps, child care and housing subsidies, and medical coverage, to provide benefits to families with incomes well above the official poverty thresholds. I wholeheartedly agree with many welfare critics that we must use alternative measures to judge poverty.

In the beginning of her book *Nickel and Dimed*, Barbara Ehrenreich used the Coalition for the Homeless's 1998 estimate of the poverty threshold ($18,491). The coalition's estimate posits that to escape poverty, a family must use only 30 percent of its income to pay for housing priced just below the local median rent. Ehrenreich then calculated the wage rate necessary for a year-round worker, employed 40 hours per week, to attain that income. Dividing the poverty threshold income by 2,080 hours yielded an hourly wage rate of $8.89. Ehrenreich claimed that "the odds against a typical welfare recipient landing a job at such a 'living wage' were about 97 to 1."[70]

Critics contend that welfare leavers are unlikely to attain this meager wage level since the jobs obtained will have little wage trajectory. This certainly was the image projected by Ehrenreich when she assessed her brief ventures into the low-wage labor market. At Wal-Mart, her starting salary was $7 an hour, and she projected that "if I had kept my mouth shut, I would have progressed in a year or two to a wage of $7.50 or more."[71]

What critics did not take fully into account was the impact of 20 million new jobs created during the Clinton administration. The Nobel Laureate Joseph Stiglitz was chair of the Council of Economic Advisors when welfare reform was passed. At the time, he went to a G-7 meeting where he spoke to economic advisors from the other major economies. At a talk given in New York City, he was boastful of the employment achievements of the Clinton administration compared to the many European countries that were experiencing double-digit unemployment rates. In disgust, a French advisor retorted, "You have only created crummy jobs. If we had created jobs, they would have been good jobs!" While Stiglitz claimed that there were many good jobs created, the crummy jobs were exactly the employment opportunities most suited to the majority of welfare leavers: jobs that required little work experience or skills.

As a result of the expansion of "nickel and dime" jobs, wage rates did not decline when welfare leavers entered the labor market. Indeed, this expanding labor demand fueled the first increases in the real earnings of less educated workers in two decades. So strong was this demand that wages increased at a faster pace for less educated workers than for the average worker during the period 1995–2000.[72] In New Jersey, the average wage of working welfare leavers equaled $8.15 per hour; only 18 percent were making $6 or less. The average hourly wage of employed Massachusetts leavers was almost $8.50 per hour, and based on their weekly hours, the average annual earnings would be almost $14,000 if they worked for 52 weeks.[73]

Moreover, Ehrenreich grossly overstates the image of former welfare recipients trapped in low-wage dead-end jobs. For those who were working at the end of the New Jersey study, their monthly earnings grew by 33 percent since their first job.[74] The wage gains were greatest for those who began with the lowest paid jobs; 40 percent of those workers whose first job paid less than $6 per hour had a wage increase of at least 50 percent. WorkFirst participants in Washington saw their average hourly wage rate increase from $7.50 to $8.91 two years later. At that point, the representative working leaver earned $13,324 annually.[75]

Katherine Newman and Chauncy Lennon also documented the ability of less educated workers to see their wages grow in a booming economy. They followed the lives of black and Latino minimum-wage workers, all of whom worked in fast-food restaurants in a poor neighborhood in New York City in 1993. Four years later, 81 percent were still working. For those employed in 1997, their average hourly wage, measured in 1997 dollars, increased from $4.85 to $8.04; 28 percent had a wage increase of at least $5 per hour.[76] Newman and Lennon also observed that, for most of those working in 1997, "the high flyers and low riders alike, expectations remain[ed] positive and a sense of personal responsibility for their fate strong, even in the face of recognized inequalities along the lines of race and gender," and even among women who "had *not* become astounding success stories . . . they still see themselves as moving toward a set of goals, not as stagnating in the face of impossible obstacle."[77]

Managing expectations became a priority for welfare-to-work program directors who saw their clients' unrealistic short-run goals as a major obstacle to their work readiness. STRIVE administrator Nydia Hernandez noted, "They would say that they had to make at least $10 per hour but when you looked at their lack of credentials—hadn't worked in six years and didn't even have a GED—you could see how unrealistic they were." When she was a caseworker at Goodwill Industries in Milwaukee, Leslie found the same attitude: "I was amazed at what they answered when I asked them how much they wanted to make. I thought that I would love to make that; I don't even make that at my job." The upward trajectory of wages during the economic boom period enabled program directors to convince many of their skeptical clients to look beyond the wages they might make at their first job.

But does this upward trajectory translate to the living wage Ehrenreich couldn't obtain? I have generally referenced studies from high-wage states since it is there that, thanks to the more generous welfare payments, there is the most concern that recipients might not benefit from moving into paid employment. Nationally, Pamela Loprest estimated that the average wage for welfare leavers equaled $7.15 per hour in 1999, and two-thirds worked at least 35 hours weekly, giving the representative welfare leaver annual wages of $13,000.[78] This figure, however, ignores the substantial income transfers available to working mothers. With this annual wage income, the representative welfare leaver would qualify for the following federal benefits in 2004: food stamps ($2848), refundable child credit ($250), and EITC ($4204). In addition, there are state financial support programs, including 28 state EITC programs.[79] For example, in Wisconsin our single mother would also receive a state EITC ($589) and a homestead credit ($844). After taking into account her payroll taxes, in Wisconsin she would have disposable income equal to $20,740. In addition, many leavers continue to receive child support payments and additional housing assistance. So once income supports are included, the representative *working* welfare leaver nationally has escaped poverty, even using the Coalition for the Homeless poverty threshold of $18,491.

These families are less likely than welfare stayers to experience material hardships: food insufficiencies and housing problems. Community Service Society surveys in New York City indicated that in both 2003 and 2004, 45 percent of poor families had experienced at least three hardships. By contrast, the rate among the near poor—families with incomes between approximately $15,000 and $30,000—was only 14 percent in 2003 and 21 percent in 2004.[80] In Maine, working welfare leavers were much less likely to go to food banks, to have their utilities shut off, or to skip meals.[81] And a national study of the mid-1990s found that 29 percent of poor families faced one critical hardship compared to 21 percent for near-poor families; 7 percent of poor families experienced at least two critical hardships compared to 4 percent for near poor households.[82]

CONCLUDING REMARKS

This chapter evaluated the conflicting assessments of the impact of welfare reform on material well-being during the economic boom. It highlighted the inherent problem policy analysts faced in having to extrapolate from past studies that may no longer be applicable. It also emphasized how an unforeseen occurrence—the unprecedented economic boom—had a decisive impact on the impact of welfare-to-work policies.

Some analysts, notably Christopher Jencks and Jason DeParle, reevaluated their earlier judgments when outcomes were much more favorable than they had thought possible. Other critics, however, were not dissuaded from their harsh early judgments. They relied on different measures of material success, minimized the impact of government income supplements like the EITC, or emphasized selective studies to sustain their early harsh judgments. In addition, some critics focused on the modest group of families that seemed to be worse off or the difficulties faced by poor families trying to access government benefits after leaving welfare.

What should not get lost in this controversy is the irrefutable evidence of a dramatic drop in poverty rates of children living in single-mother families and the consensus evidence that this would not have happened without welfare reform. These critics also ignore how the transition to work led to the undermining of negative stereotypes among employers that victimized all single mothers and to the more hopeful attitudes found among welfare leavers. Maybe most important in the long run, welfare-to-work shifted the emphasis from providing a safety net to nonworking mothers to providing support services that aided them in sustaining stable employment. Learning from these support policies can broaden our understanding of which policies can support effectively the needs of many working mothers, most of whom have never been nor never will be on welfare.

The economic benefits documented in this chapter and the social and psychological benefits detailed in chapters 3 and 4 demonstrate that, *when jobs are plentiful*, "Making Work Pay" policies enabled millions of women to lift one leg up—to improve their situation compared to what it would have been if they had remained on welfare. The persistence of material hardships among near-poor families, however, dampens any rejoicing. We cannot, and should not, be satisfied with lifting families into the near-poor income range. We must develop government policies to pull the second leg up, enabling welfare leavers to distance themselves and their families from material hardships. And, as chapter 6 demonstrates, we must demand that the government pursue high employment policies to further this goal.

6

Importance of a
High-Employment Economy

Chapter 5 demonstrated that in a high-employment economy, "Making Work Pay" policies moved millions of less educated single mothers into paid employment. Not only did these women have higher incomes, but they and their children benefited psychologically and socially. While a small share of mothers were harmed by the process, it is hard not to consider welfare reform a measured success when evaluating it at the top of the economic boom in 2000.

The problem emphasized by thoughtful critics of the 1996 reform, however, was that the policies enacted would fail miserably in the absence of a high-employment economy and generous work supports. They feared what would happen during the economic downturn, when jobs would be unavailable and states, strapped for funds, cut back on the work supports they provided.

The problems they predicted began to surface once the recent economic slowdown began. While its adverse effect was much less than initially feared, this experience still highlights the crucial role of high-employment policies. The economic slowdown of 2001–2004 also exposed the inadequacies of unemployment insurance. It was not an effective safety net for those welfare leavers who lost their jobs, and this has led to state policy changes that should be more widely implemented. Finally, economic growth may be moderated by the resistance to high-employment policies within the business community and the Federal Reserve.

THE ECONOMIC SLOWDOWN

The business press generally acted as though the economic downturn was relatively shallow and short-lived. Indeed, the question of poor economic performance was only faintly heard during the 2004 presidential election. Part of the reason that business and political commentators perceived this downturn as short and shallow reflected the way recessions are defined: periods in which *national production* declines continuously for at least six months. According to this definition, the recession lasted from February through November 2001. Since this was one of the shortest recessions on record, and the unemployment rate remained lower than during the previous two recessions, news reports suggested that it caused relatively little harm to the public.

If, instead, we use *unemployment* as a measure of economic performance, the economic slowdown would be judged much more severely. To just keep unemployment constant, the economy must grow at about 3 percent annually to compensate for increased labor productivity and new entrants into the labor force. For the three years following the official recession, annual growth averaged only 2 percent, so the official unemployment rate continued to grow, peaking at more than 6 percent during 2004. Measured from the beginning of the rise in the national unemployment rate to its peak, the economic downturn lasted 40 months rather than nine.[1]

Part of the press's complacency also stemmed from the attitude of business leaders. They had been dismissive of the weak employment recovery because profits had risen at a pace more robust than in previous recoveries. This helps explain why the Dow Jones Industrial Average and Standard & Poor's 500 Index were able to regain most of their losses three years into the recovery.

Finally, the damage during the recession and early recovery appeared by some measures to be smaller than in previous business cycles. For example, during the first 24 months after the onset of the 1990–1991 recession, the unemployment rate rose by 2.4 percentage points—from 5.2 to 7.6 percent. By contrast, during the 2001–2004 economic slowdown, the unemployment rate only increased by 1.7 percentage points—from 4.2 to 5.9 percent—over a similar two-year period (figure 6.1). The 2001–2004 economic slowdown, however, did not have growth as robust as the past recession during the third year, so only then did it become clear that the current economic slowdown was just as severe as the earlier one.

During the early stages of the 2001–2004 economic slowdown, analysts feared that welfare leavers would be disproportionately adversely affected because employment losses seemed to be concentrated in industries dominated by female employment. For example, employment in personal supply services and hotels and lodging saw heavy employment losses during the recession, and in the im-

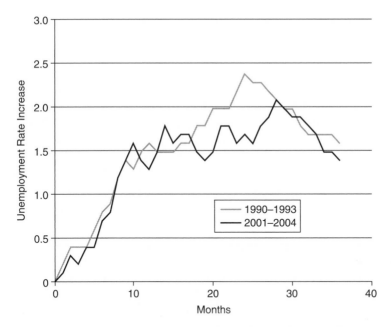

Figure 6.1. Unemployment rate increase since the onset of recession, 1990–1993 and 2001–2004. Source: Richard Freeman and William Rodgers, "The Fragility of the 1990s Economic Gains" (Allied Social Science Association, January 8, 2005).

mediate aftermath of 9/11, employment in the usually recession-proof bar and restaurant and general merchandising sectors fell substantially.[2]

The harsher employment experience of women during the *initial* stages of the 2001–2004 slowdown, however, was more than offset when the economy began to grow. Many of the private sectors in which female employment is high rebounded much more than the sectors in which male employment dominates. In addition, both the government and health care sectors—in which female employment is high—experienced steady growth. Thus, it was male, not female, workers that suffered the most during the recent economic slowdown.

One telling piece of evidence has been wage trends. Figure 6.2 plots female usual weekly wages as a percentage of male usual weekly wages for full-time workers. Notice that after a relatively continuous increase, the percentage remained fairly constant from the early 1990s through 2001. The lack of improvement during the mid-1990s is probably related to the substantial labor-market entry of welfare leavers. These mothers were overwhelmingly employed at low-wage jobs, so they would have dampened the upward trend in *average* female wages. And the decline in 2001 was undoubtedly related to the harsh experience of female workers in the initial stages of the 2001–2004 slowdown.

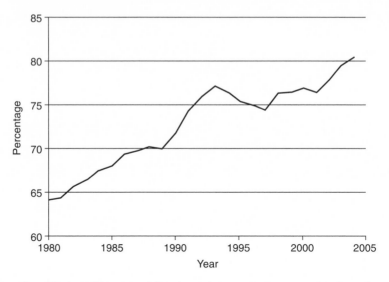

Figure 6.2. Usual weekly wage of female workers as a percentage of male workers' wages, 1980–2004. Source: U.S. Bureau of Labor Statistics, "Employment and Earnings," various years.

Since 2001, however, there has been a dramatic increase in female wages as a percentage of male wages—from 76.4 in 2001 to 80.4 in 2004—because female workers tend to fare better during economic slowdowns.[3]

Even if, on average, the job losses women experienced were not so severe, single mothers faced worse prospects. Recall that during the Clinton-era economic boom, their employment rate grew dramatically. Between 1996 and 2000, the number of working single moms rose by 1.1 million. As a result, the share of all single mothers who were employed increased from 65.9 to 75.5 percent.[4] Between 2000 and 2004, the female employment rate fell by only 1.1 percentage points. Most troubling, however, was the 4.3-percentage-point decline in employment for *single* mothers, from 75.5 to 71.2 percent.

Since they are the most vulnerable, welfare leavers might have fared even worse than the typical single mother. Heather Boushey and David Rosnick identified the nine industries in which 62 percent of welfare leavers were employed. In 2000, the share of welfare leavers employed in these industries was, for noneating retail, 17.6 percent; eating places, 14.4 percent; manufacturing, 7.4 percent; personnel supply services, 4.6 percent; hotels and lodgings, 3.7 percent; labs and home care, 3.6 percent; nursing and personal care facilities, 3.5 percent; elementary and primary schools, 3.5 percent; and child care services, 3.3 percent.[5] During the three-year period from the start of the recession in February 2001, private-sector employment declined by 3.1 percent while the estimated employment decline of welfare leavers employed in these nine industries was only 2.0 percent.[6] This strongly suggests that a favorable industrial concentration may have enabled welfare leavers to avoid as steep an employment loss as the overall economy.

POVERTY RATES AND WAGE GROWTH

For many advocates, the most troubling statistic has been the decline in the welfare rolls despite employment declines. One possible explanation is that unemployed recent leavers might have been eligible for unemployment insurance, so they would have no need to return to the welfare rolls. For example, during the previous period of weak economic performance, 1989–1992, the increase in number of children living in poor single-mother families was matched by the increase in the number of children living in single-mother families that received either welfare cash assistance or unemployment insurance. Thus, welfare and unemployment insurance together provided a significant safety net, moderating the hardships poor working families faced.

During the 2001–2004 economic slowdown, the number of children living in poor single-mother families that received either welfare cash assistance or unemployment insurance increased by 253,000. By contrast, the number of children living in these poor single-mother families increased by 845,000.[7] In addition, critics point out that the number of people living in extreme poverty (with less than half the income needed to escape poverty) increased by almost 2.5 million between 2000 and 2003. These data suggest that poverty and extreme poverty rates increased more than they should have because the government no longer provided the necessary safety net.

During the initial economic slowdown, child poverty rates among single-mother households held steady at about 40 percent from 2000 through 2002. However, as the weak job recovery persisted, the rate increased and stood at 42.76 percent in 2005 still, far below the 50–55 percent level that typified the pre-welfare reform era. More troubling has been changes in the extreme poverty rate (figure 6.3). During the 1980s, movement in the extreme poverty rate generally mirrored the movement in the child poverty rate, rising during economic slow-downs and declining during periods of robust economic growth. Things began to change after the 1990–1991 recession. While the child poverty rate fell, the extreme poverty rate increased. During a momentary pause in the economy in 1995–1996, the extreme poverty rate increased, and it did so again during the 2001–2004 economic slowdown. As a result, the share of people living in extreme poverty in 2005 was virtually the same as when welfare reform was enacted.

The persistence of extreme poverty rates is consistent with the structural problems that I emphasized in chapter 3.[8] The dangers threatening these individuals

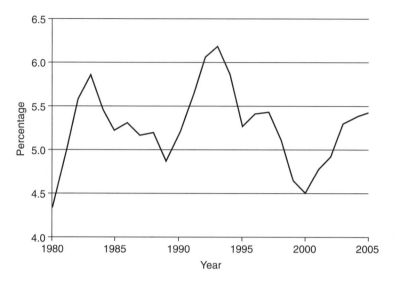

Figure 6.3. Extreme poverty rate, 1980–2005. Source: U.S. Census Bureau, "Historical Poverty Tables," http://www.census.gov/hhes/www/poverty/histpov/perindex.html.

on the edge are real, but it is not clear that a more generous safety net would rein in the extreme poverty rate during economic slowdowns. In particular, during the 1989–1992 economic slowdown, the extreme poverty rate rose by 1.2 percentage points despite the expansion of the welfare roles and unemployment insurance claimants. By contrast, during the the three-year period, 2001–2003, the extreme poverty rate increased by 0.8 percentage points. This evidence suggests that making welfare and unemployment insurance benefits more accessible, while clearly helpful, will not be sufficient to make a substantial difference for the most destitute families. More targeted programs are required.

Conservatives such as Douglas Besharov of the American Enterprise Institute point triumphantly to the continued decline of the welfare rolls while ignoring the underlying struggles that the poverty data suggest. He finds a positive interpretation for the decline in the welfare population during the economic slowdown, believing that many single mothers facing temporary difficulties no longer consider government their first option. Instead, they try to survive on their own or through the help of family, friends, and the private sector. As a result, their loss of wage income does not necessarily mean that these families are worse off. "Are you better off earning $15,000 but paying rent and all your bills, or are you better off earning $7,000 but living in someone else's house and having them pay the rent, utilities and phone?" he said. "This is not a clear picture."[9] For Besharov, avoiding reliance on government will strengthen personal responsibility and reliance on family and community ties.

Many policy analysts reject Besharov's complacency. Vicki Turetsky, lead policy analyst at the Center for Law and Social Policy, is appalled at this insensitivity. She stated,

> While it makes for good press to find women who have pieced together private support to overcome short-term disasters, for the vast majority there is much more value when the government guarantees a safety net, providing families with some certainty. Single mothers must expend enormous psychic energy to find alternative sources of food and shelter, robbing their children and themselves of the time and energy needed to move forward.

Boushey, economist at the Center for Economic and Policy Research, also recoiled at the notion that using individual initiatives to find alternative to government support is always uplifting. In my interview, she said, "While self reliance is an admirable trait, it should not be encouraged at the expense of a guaranteed safety net."

It is hard to believe that the caseload decline during the economic slowdown was due to an increasing self-reliant attitude. If self-reliance was so dominant a motivating factor for declining welfare caseloads, we should see the same dynamics in other safety net programs. Instead, virtually all other safety net programs expanded during the economic slowdown. Sharon Parrott, welfare analyst at the Center on Budget and Policy Priorities, believes that the divergent direction of welfare and food stamps reflects contrasting government attitudes, noting that "administrative agencies thought it was good thing for people to be on food stamps but a bad thing for people to go on cash assistance."

Whereas welfare administrators intensified diversionary tactics to dissuade families from applying for welfare, the U.S. Department of Agriculture supported food stamp expansion. As discussed in chapter 5, new procedures were developed and outreach encouraged increased participation rates. As a result, Parrott contends,

> The downturn in welfare caseloads while poverty rates were rising is an indictment of TANF [Temporary Assistance for Needy Families]. The program's name clearly suggests that it should aid people who are in temporary need during economic downturns. Instead, it turned its back on the recession's victims, robbing them of not only the cash assistance that they desperately needed but also of the program's mission to provide them with assistance to obtain future employment. Instead, politicians cheered because they thought it was a good thing that TANF was recession-proof.

These poverty and employment statistics suggest that while the recent economic slowdown put at risk the benefits of welfare reform, the reversal was not so dramatic.

Employment rates fell and poverty rates increased, but the vast majority of the financial benefits of welfare reform were sustained. Judging welfare reform, however, does not rely solely on employment and poverty rates. While exiting official poverty is important, there also should be some sense of upward mobility that would enable single mothers to distance themselves and their children from material hardships. And this requires that earnings continue to grow.

The 1990s economic boom made such growth possible for the first time. Despite the dramatic increase in their labor supply, the wages of single mothers rose substantially. After adjusting for inflation, their median hourly wage grew by 2.5 percent annually between 1996 and 2000. For those at the 25th percentile—more typical of welfare leavers—the real hourly wage increase was 3.5 percent annually. The booming economy provided not only jobs but also rising wages.[10]

During the 2001–2004 economic slowdown, female wages grew faster than male wages, reducing the gender earnings gap. After adjusting for inflation, the average real weekly wage of women working full time rose by 1.8 percent annually between 2000 and 2004. This wage growth, however, was highly unequal. For single mothers, real wages grew at only 1.2 percent annually during this time period. Most troubling, however, it appears that welfare leavers were employed in sectors that had particularly slow wage growth. Specifically, the average real wage growth was less than 0.5 percent annually for those who worked in the nine industries that dominate the employment of welfare leavers.

Robert Lerman, chief economist at the Urban Institute, has been following low-wage labor markets for more than 20 years. "Given that in the past economic slowdowns, wages for those at the bottom did not keep pace with inflation," he told me, "it is actually quite surprising how well the wages of welfare leavers have held up." He added, however, "This is still a pretty grim picture. For single mothers raising their families on $8 an hour in 2001, adjusting for inflation, they were able to earn $8.16 an hour in 2004."

This wage stagnation was particularly alarming for the directors at the New Hope and STRIVE programs when I interviewed them in November 2004. Both programs had been successful by impressing on welfare leavers the need to consider their first job as only the starting point in their employment trajectory. This worked well during the 1990s boom: work effort translated into promotions and substantial wage increases for many welfare leavers.

After three years of slow growth, however, these administrators could no longer instill such hope in the welfare leavers they were counseling. Without a strong business expansion, the number of promotions shrank along with the likelihood of a robust wage trajectory. Welfare leavers became frustrated with their flat paychecks, unable to secure a significant raise despite their best efforts. As a result, these administrators had to fight against the instinct of some welfare leavers to quit one job before they had another. Indeed, as STRIVE director Nydia Hernandez lamented, "We could no longer feel confident placing our clients in better jobs after they had gained work experience. We have to constantly tell them, 'Stay at your current job until you have been offered a better one.' " Gone was the substantial upward mobility, along with the belief that "work pays" that had marked the boom of the 1990s.

REFORMING UNEMPLOYMENT INSURANCE

As the economic slowdown highlighted, welfare reform left millions of families more vulnerable to economic fluctuations, particularly when it became difficult to move back onto welfare. As they became members of the workforce, leavers could potentially rely on unemployment insurance benefits rather than cash assistance. Indeed, since it offers more generous payments, unemployment insurance benefits are a more desirable safety net. Ideally, then, the employment losses leavers suffered during the 2001–2004 economic slowdown should have been moderated by the unemployment insurance they collected.

There have been justifiable concerns, however, that given their low wages and employment instability, unemployment insurance would not be a realistic option for most leavers if they lost their jobs. Indeed, there is ample evidence that unemployment insurance has become a weaker safety net for the typical worker. The share of the unemployed who received unemployment insurance benefits declined from almost 50 percent in the 1950s to 35 percent since the mid-1980s. When looking at periods of economic slowdown, when rates are higher, a similar picture emerged. Whereas during the 1975–1976 recession, almost 70 percent of the unemployed collected unemployment insurance, during the three subsequent recessionary periods—1980–1982, 1991–1992, and 2001–2002—only about 46 percent of the unemployed collected.

Evidence gathered before welfare reform indicated that the share of unemployed welfare leavers who collected unemployment insurance was much lower. This disparity was not because working welfare leavers were becoming ineligible by quitting their jobs. Instead, their employment instability disqualified them. In particular, eligibility requirements had been based on a male breadwinner model where applicants had been employed long term at decent wages. As a result, on the eve of welfare reform, state regulations were ill suited for a workforce that would be employed at low wages for short periods of time. Without a substantial adjustment of these regulations, unemployment insurance proved to be an inadequate safety net for welfare leavers.

One important set of eligibility requirements is earnings rules. In order to quantify the impact of earnings rules on the ability of welfare leavers to qualify for unemployment insurance payments, the consulting firm Mathematica studied five representative communities nationally. In each community, the study documented the earnings of mothers who were employed at the time they left welfare. Almost 90 percent of those mothers met earnings requirements *at some point* during the two-year period after exit. Only about 50 percent, however, met earnings rules throughout the entire eight-quarter period.[11]

Let us look at some of these earnings rules more closely. First, all states have a minimum total earnings threshold. Job losers who do not earn at least this amount over a one-year base period do not qualify for unemployment insurance payments. This earnings threshold varies substantially from state to state. The highest state earnings threshold is Florida's $3400 while the lowest is Hawaii's $130. Not surprisingly, an Institute for Women's Policy Research (IWPR) study found that, nationally, Florida has the third lowest share of unemployed workers collecting, more than 10 percentage points below the national average. Interestingly, just at the time of welfare reform in 1996, Florida increased its earnings requirement from $400 to $3,400. The IWPR study looked at unemployed Florida men and women who were not collecting unemployment insurance. It found that only 1 percent of the men but 17 percent of women earned at least $400 but less than the new higher threshold.[12]

The Mathematica study had similar findings. In particular, the study estimated the impact of changing the earnings threshold at its Maryland site from the current state level of $900 to $2,800—the average for the five states nationally that had the highest threshold. As a result of this change, 10 percent fewer welfare leavers would meet earnings requirements for unemployment insurance payments.[13]

A second earnings rule is the one-year period used to measure past earnings. The standard base period (SBP) uses the *first four* of the last five *completed* quarters. According to this procedure, if you are laid off on June 1, 2006, your last completed quarter would be January 1 through March 31, 2006, so total earnings would be calculated for your first four quarters: January 1 through December 31, 2005. As a result, your earnings during the *most recent* five months would not be included. Thus, those who lose their job within one year of employment would likely not qualify for unemployment insurance benefits even if they had substantial recent earnings.

As expected, the SBP limited the share of mothers who would meet the earnings threshold if they lost their employment during the first year after exiting welfare. For example, Mathematica found that only 45 percent of mothers met the earnings threshold if they lost their job six months after exiting welfare. If, instead, an alternative base period (ABP) was used that included the most recent months of employment, almost 80 percent of mothers would meet the earnings threshold. The IWPR study found that 28 percent of unemployed Florida women met the earnings threshold under the ABP but not under the SBP.

The final earnings rule that limits eligibility is the requirement that total earnings in the base period be at least 1.5 times the earnings in the highest earnings quarter. This rule required that unemployed workers have substantial earnings in at least two of the quarters in their base period. In Florida, the IWPR study found that this rule disqualified 5 percent of the unemployed who met earnings thresholds. The Mathematica study found that eliminating this rule would increase eligibility 15–20 percent nationally.

Of course, meeting earnings rules is only the first step in determining whether an unemployed worker qualifies for unemployment insurance benefits. The individual must also demonstrate a qualifying reason for leaving work. In Florida, almost 30 percent of the reasons women cited for leaving their jobs involved pregnancies, domestic violence, or the need to care for a sick family member. As the IWPR study reported,

> A child's or spouse's illness is not defined as a valid reason for quitting a job, even if there are no other family members available to provide care.... All too often, workers who experience these situations are forced either to quit their jobs or be fired for missing work, which leaves them with a poor employment record and also deprives them of [unemployment insurance] benefits....
>
> In Florida, survivors of domestic violence who leave work are denied unemployment benefits, even if the batterer intimidates or abuses the worker on the job. In a case brought before the Florida appeals court, a domestic violence survivor argued that she was entitled to unemployment benefits when her divorced husband repeatedly threatened her life and the safety of the children at the school where she was employed. The court ruled against her, finding her "decision to relocate to avoid conflict with her husband may have been a good personal reason, but it was not good cause attributable to her employer and disqualification was proper."[14]

Fortunately, advocacy groups such as the National Employment Law Project have convinced many states to adjust their unemployment insurance rules. By 2003, 27 states rejected Florida's approach and provide unemployment insurance benefits for victims of domestic violence who leave their jobs because of the abuse if they meet earnings requirements. Fifteen states have enacted provisions that allow for a broad range of compelling domestic circumstances, including child care and other situations that significantly impact women workers. In addition, 20 states allow workers to use an ABP so that their most recent earnings can be included in their base period. Finally, five states allow unemployed workers to qualify when they meet the earnings threshold through employment in only one three-month period.[15]

These efforts demonstrate that policy changes are possible and should be pursued in as many states as possible. Indeed, political pressure might even be eventually successful in Florida where a 2003 Senate bill proposing an ABP was passed unanimously.[16] Together with other improvements, including more help for part-time and immigrant workers, unemployment insurance can better serve the needs of all workers who suffer job loss.

TARGET UNEMPLOYMENT RATE

One of the most troubling things about government policies under the George W. Bush administration has been its eagerness to maintain a 5 percent unemployment rate. President Bush's chair of the Council of Economic Advisors, Harvey Rosen, defended this position during a June 2005 press briefing. After the White House released its updated economic forecasts, an interviewer asked: "I was wondering about your forecast. You have the unemployment rate going down to 5 percent, then remaining steady for a number of years after that. Is that standard practice, or you're just not forecasting in those future years, or what is that?"[17]

Rosen responded tellingly:

> That's our estimate of what a sustainable, long-term unemployment rate is. And I guess one point that's worth mentioning here is that we don't think of that long-term unemployment rate as a constant of nature like gravity. It's affected by public policy, and if we have policies that continue to enhance efficiency in our markets, then it could go lower. But we think that it is a sensible estimate of the long-term unemployment rate.[18]

No one questioned Rosen's judgment by pointing to the Clinton boom, when the unemployment rate was well below Rosen's 5 percent target for more than two years. Instead, the press conference quickly moved on to other economic issues, including the federal deficit and trade imbalances.

Part of the reason for this unquestioning acceptance is the broad consensus among economists that a significant share of those seeking jobs are just not employable, given their skills or geographic location. That is, those seeking employment do not have the skills necessary for the available jobs or do not live in the areas where jobs are being created. Recall that these structural explanations were the main reasons given for the joblessness of young black men who lived in central cities when manufacturing jobs were lost to suburban industrial sites and rural locations.

In addition, it is argued that a substantial share of those unemployed are simply searching until they find the best job available rather than taking their first job offer. These workers are characterized as "frictionally unemployed," in that they do not move smoothly and instantaneously from one job to the next. From this perspective, conservatives have argued that unemployment compensation has become an important barrier to rapid reemployment; those who collect become more selective in the jobs that they will accept. As a result, they remain unemployed for longer, raising the official unemployment rate. Indeed, it was just these arguments that led Congress in 1979 to begin taxing unemployment insurance and to restrict the number of weeks benefits could be collected during times of rising unemployment.[19]

Most economists believe that the sum of those who are unemployable because of skill or locational mismatches and those who are frictionally unemployed is 5 percent of the labor force, and hence this becomes the target rate. (Recall that Christopher Jencks projected this 5 percent rate as a reason why Clinton's reform would be unable to find sufficient employment for welfare leavers.) Economists such as Rosen use the term "sustainable" unemployment rate because they claim that the rise in inflation rates associated with lowering the unemployment further would be too costly. Firms and consumers would lose too much, weakening the economy until the unemployment rate rose back to its "sustainable" rate.

One of the least explored aspects of the Clinton economic team was that they were unwilling to accept this view of the benefits and costs of lower unemployment rates. When the unemployment rate fell below 5.5 percent in late 1994, the Federal Reserve began slowing down growth rates in the economy (just as they began doing in 2004). The Federal Reserve reduced the credit available to lenders at commercial banks because the majority of its members feared that maintaining the pace of economic expansion would accelerate inflation rates. It began reducing credit even before any direct signs of rising inflation rates to head off an upward spiral that might have started before it acted.

Rather than complacently accepting this approach, the Clinton economic team began criticizing the theory underpinning these policies. First, the head of Clinton's Council of Economic Advisors, Laura Tyson, wrote a widely circulated *New York Times* op-ed piece that questioned the link between lowering unemployment and rising inflation rates. Next, Clinton's appointee to the Federal Reserve, William Blinder, allowed his discussions at board meetings to leak to the press. Specifically, Blinder demanded that if the Federal Reserve adopted anti-inflationary policies, it must acknowledge that they would cause the unemployment rate to rise.[20]

Blinder's position was echoed by other economists who documented the production and employment costs to an economy if it sought to curtail inflation. These economists noted how difficult it was for firms to lower actual wage rates; they need the flexibility that rising prices gives them. As long as actual wage rate increases are below the inflation rate, firms facing financial difficulties can reduce their real labor costs. They concluded:

> The fortunes of firms continually change, and inflation greases the economy's wheels by allowing these firms to slowly escape from paying real wages that are too high without actually cutting the wage they pay. This adjustment mechanism allows the economy to avoid a large employment cost. At very low rates of inflation and productivity growth, such adjustments are short circuited, and employment suffers.[21]

Finally, Clinton floated the name of Felix Rohatyn as one of the individuals he might nominate for a vacancy on the Federal Reserve. Rohatyn was a New York investment banker whose took control of New York City's financial control board in the 1970s and instituted policies that headed off its own bankruptcy. Most important, Rohatyn was on record as opposing policies that would sacrifice employment in order to lower inflationary risks.

Clinton's actions made it clear to Federal Reserve chair Alan Greenspan that there would be a public battle if the Fed continued to weaken the economic expansion. As mentioned in chapter 5, Greenspan also likely understood that a robust expansion was necessary to absorb welfare leavers into the labor market. For these reasons, the Federal Reserve abandoned its contractionary policies in 1996. Indeed, it remained passive through 2000 despite the decline in the national unemployment rate to below 4 percent.

The experience of the late 1990s seemed to indicate that the economy could sustain much lower unemployment rates without generating substantial inflationary pressures. Moreover, a group of leading economists, including Tyson's successor as chair of the Council of Economic Advisors, Joseph Stiglitz, rejected the conventional wisdom that once inflation rates begin to increase, they would quickly accelerate to higher and higher levels.[22] These economists found that there were a number of reasons why even when low unemployment rates generate an excess demand for labor, wage increases do not generate ever-increasing production costs. They noted that for many workers, weekly wages begin to increase as they receive increasing hours of work: some shift from part-time to full-time employment, while full-time workers gain increased overtime. In addition, as the economic expansion enables firms to grow, they need not only more entry-level workers but are able to promote many of their present employees. Thus, promotions and increases in the work week enable many firms to raise the weekly wages of their workers without raising hourly wage rates.

The fear that hiring less skilled workers would be inflationary because it would substantially raise training and retention costs proved to be unfounded. As noted in earlier chapters, welfare leavers and others hired from "at-risk" labor pools during the late 1990s proved to be more productive than anticipated. As Ron Haskins told me, "These workers surprisingly mastered employment soft skills much better than we had anticipated." Thus, these economists claimed that there was no reason for the Federal Reserve to engage in *preemptive* behavior— restricting banking credit even before inflationary pressures appear.

Not only did the informed wisdom in the economics profession overestimate the costs from lowering unemployment rates below their 5 percent target, but also it did not anticipate the social benefits from these policies. As documented in chapter 5, very tight labor markets during the late 1990s forced employers to hire from at-risk populations: welfare leavers who had little recent work experience and young men with problematic backgrounds. Without these labor shortages, employers would never have hired from these labor pools. As a result, lower unemployment rates were centrally responsible for integrating into the economy many workers who had struggled on its periphery. Finally, the evidence of the past decade has demonstrated that wages for those at the bottom of the labor market rise substantially only when unemployment rates are low. Low unemployment rates, then, were shown to be crucial to racial and gender equity and reducing the size of a persistent underclass.

Rosen's interview, however, reflected a return to the old way of thinking. This, of course, troubles many policy analysts, including Jared Bernstein at the Economic Policy Institute, even as it's given short shrift in media accounts. Bernstein has written extensively on the benefits of full employment. He is frustrated, however, that the business press has been unwilling to build on the experience of the recent economic boom. He complained, "Whenever I bring up the positive labor market experiences of the late 1990s, they are dismissive, claiming that it was all the result of an unsustainable economic bubble."[23]

For many Federal Reserve critics, including myself, the reasons for the return to the old way of thinking go much deeper. The Federal Reserve looks at not only the benefits and costs of lower unemployment rates to the general public but also their effects on institutional investors. Institutional investors invariably have a substantial portion of their assets in government and corporate bonds. These bonds pay a fixed amount of interest, so their market price varies inversely with the interest rate. When interest rates decline, the market price of these bonds rises.[24] This is why bond funds were the highest earning assets at the beginning of the economic slowdown.

Bond holders face risks, however, from a robust economy. Workers may get large raises as firms compete for scarce labor, and firms are able to pass these higher costs onto consumers. In even a modestly inflationary environment, interest rates would rise, and this would lower the value of the bonds held. Moreover, higher interest rate on newly issued bonds might cause investors to shift funds to bonds and away from stocks, lowering stock prices. The experience of the 1990s suggests that this risk might be quite low. Bond holders and stockholders seem willing, however, to sacrifice the social benefits of low unemployment because it requires them to accept a (small) risk of losses on their financial assets. The disparate interests of workers and wealth holders is captured by an August 5, 2005, Associated Press story: "Stocks and Bonds Fell Friday after the Labor Department Reported Surprisingly Strong Gains in Jobs and Wages."

By contrast, most households own few stocks or bonds and instead are often in debt. For example, in 1998, the richest 1 percent held half of all individually held stock and mutual funds and two-thirds of all business equity, whereas one-quarter of all households had zero or negative net worth.[25] The only assets that are widely held by middle-class families are the homes they live in. A large share of these homeowners have fixed interest mortgages. How do lower unemployment rates affect them? The wage increases they receive would cause their debt burden—the ratio of mortgage interest payments to income—to decline. More generally, even if higher wages were inflationary, homeowners would benefit since they would be paying back their fixed mortgage loans with "cheaper" dollars. The Federal Reserve's willingness to sacrifice additional employment in order to limit the risk of accelerating inflation reflects the interests of stock and bond holders—not the general public.

Indeed, it was this resistance that James Tobin, head of the Council of Economic Advisors under President John F. Kennedy, had to fight when he desired to lower unemployment in order to reduce the racial employment gap during the 1960s. He feared that economic policies would be governed by the desires of the "vast comfortable white middle class, who are never touched by unemployment, and prefer to safeguard the purchasing power of their [financial assets] rather than to expand opportunities for the disadvantaged and unemployed."[26]

CONCLUDING REMARKS

While there has been a modest rise in child poverty rates and decline in employment rates, most of the gains from the economic boom period have been sustained. Not surprisingly, conservatives have trumpeted these findings as evidence of the long-term success of welfare reform. They contend that it demonstrated that those families adversely affected were able to piece together alternatives to government safety net programs and that these efforts will help these mothers gain long-term self-sufficiency. More tempered, Haskins stated, "Our strategy worked before the recession and is still working [during the economic slowdown] because of continued high levels of employment."

As this chapter highlights, however, these evaluations are overly generous if not mean spirited. Advocates for the poor see little to cheer about. Personal resiliency in the face of financial difficulties may have enabled many poor families to avoid severe material hardships, but it too often has been accompanied by social and psychological costs to these mothers and their children. Though it may be surprising that the wages of welfare leavers grew enough to cover price increases, the lack of a significant wage trajectory sapped many of hope that work effort will substantially improve their lives.

One way to create more stability in the lives of the working poor is to make it easier for mothers to use welfare cash payments as a safety net. This may mean modifying the five-year lifetime limits to take into account job market conditions. It certainly means suspending diversionary tactics when there is a weak job market.

An even better way to increase access to cash payments lies in improving the unemployment insurance system so that more low-paid workers qualify. Many states have been responsive and changed their method of determining eligibility by revising their earnings requirements and the qualifying reasons for leaving paid employment.

Support for further reforms at the state level can make the difference for many working families. These actions, however, cannot be a substitute for attempts to change national economic priorities. Without a national unemployment rate below 4.5 percent, many single moms with limited education will fail to move forward. Unfortunately, political leaders seem to have ignored the benefits for working families of high-employment policies in favor of corporate interests. The Federal Reserve has been willing to dampen economic growth by making credit more costly while the Bush administration is content with employment growth insufficient to create a high-employment economy. "The job market tells you that the economy is growing fast enough to keep people employed and to create jobs for people entering the work force," said James E. Glassman, senior domestic economist at JPMorgan Chase, "but it is not growing fast enough to restore the economy to full employment."[27] In commenting on the continued attempt by the Federal Reserve to raise interest rates, Maury Harris, chief U.S. economist at the financial firm of UBS, said, "Politically, they're not going to say 'We don't want to see unemployment come down any more.' But I think what they would like to see is an economy that grows just fast enough to keep unemployment stable."[28]

Maybe we will be fortunate enough to have robust job growth despite the indifference of government policy makers. Indeed, the national unemployment rate continued to decline, reaching a low of 4.4 percent in October 2006. This spurred the largest wage growth since the 1990s. Most notably, the average week earnings of full-time black workers increased 6.8 percent between the last quarter of 2005 and last quarter of 2006.[29] This wage growth led Federal Reserve chair Bernanke to worry about "harmful" inflation. Since then, he has been comforted by a slowdown of economic growth, causing the unemployment rate to inch up to 4.6 percent. It would be more comforting to working people, however, if there was a return to the economic policies that dominated the Clinton administration: high-employment policies that welfare leavers and other workers need.

PART III

Moving Forward

7

Federal and State Child Support Policies

Chapter 6 highlighted the central role of high-employment policies. A high-employment economy alone, however, is not sufficient to enable all welfare leavers to sustain full-time employment. Many leavers, especially those with preschool-age children, have difficulty working full time year-round without child care supports. And those families that need them most may have too much income to qualify, or their location may not be convenient.

Even if these supports are in place, some welfare reform critics worry that the rise in family income from paid work will come at the expense of the well-being of children. They fear that children will be placed in facilities that do not nourish their emotional and intellectual development. On the contrary, in this chapter I document that, in general, children of low-income single mothers are not harmed in any significant way by their child care placement and instead can benefit in a number of important ways.

Even if their children are eligible, the copayment might be sufficiently high that single mothers find alternative unsubsidized centers more advantageous. For these mothers, preschool and full-day kindergarten government programs and government tax credits to offset child care expenses are much more important. This chapter suggests ways in which the child care needs of working mothers can be met more effectively.

For welfare leavers, the most important of these government supports is child care slots provided through Temporary Assistance for Needy Families (TANF) legislation. Providing these supports to welfare leavers beyond a modest transition period, however, has been contentious. Indeed, the child care provision of TANF reauthorization has even caused a rift among conservatives. One group of conservatives believes that working mothers and states should have primary responsibility for child care expenses. By contrast, another group, siding with Democrats, believes that as long as the federal government is requiring single mothers to work full time year-round, it should provide them with necessary support services. These differences were largely responsible for a four-year delay in TANF reauthorization, the details of which I discuss below.

Even if single mothers have sufficient child care supports and wage trajectories, many still face an uphill battle in their attempt to distance their families from material hardships. The refundable earned income tax credit (EITC) has been effective in raising the purchasing power of working moms. One problem is that the EITC is means tested, so credits are reduced as wage income of single mothers rises above $15,000. At the same time, food stamps are reduced and copayments for government child care slots increase. In Chicago, when new government regulations enabled home health care attendants to receive an additional $2 per hour, it was estimated that their net income increased by only half as much because of the resulting reduction in the government subsidies that they were receiving.[1] This example highlights one important impediment to improving the material well-being of less educated working women: the extent to which wage gains are offset by reductions in aid from government support programs. This chapter details specific ways in which changes in government tax policies can moderate this problem, enabling working moms to gain more from wage increases.

CHILDREN OF WORKING SINGLE MOTHERS

Child care funding clearly eases the transition to work for many single mothers with young children. Rather than relying on informal arrangements that are often unstable, formal child care provides mothers and their children with a degree of certainty in their lives. Not surprisingly, studies consistently demonstrate improved work stability for single mothers. One such study was done by the economist Heather Boushey. She examined the employment stability of welfare leavers with children younger than six years who became employed in the late 1990s. Boushey found that those with formal daycare arrangements were nearly three times as likely to be employed after two years as those without formal daycare arrangements; those who had child care subsidies were 60 percent more likely to be employed after two years than those without subsidies.[2]

There is also evidence that the increased income enables single mothers to provide a better home environment. One study found that among unmarried mothers who remained unemployed, there was a sizable reduction in the quality of their home environment over a two-year period. The measure of home environment used included assessments of the home's physical safety and cleanliness, the amount of appropriate cognitive stimulation provided there, and the extent of interpersonal warmth shown by the parents to the child. By contrast, the home environment improved for working single mothers, except those who had jobs with the lowest wages and poorest working conditions.[3]

A better material home environment is only one impact of welfare-to-work policies. Many analysts worry that an absent mother can have adverse developmental effects on young children. These fears, however, have been discounted by several studies. In their summary of studies of low-income families done prior to the 1996 welfare reform legislation, Martha Zaslow and Carol Emig found that

> with a few notable exceptions . . . maternal employment among low-income families has generally had either positive or neutral implications for children's development. In a Head Start study, children who scored well on a verbal test were more likely than their peers to have mothers who were employed outside of the home.[4]

Zaslow and Emig also cite a study of inner-city children attending public schools who lived with single mothers. Those children whose mothers worked full time "had higher self-esteem and perceived that their families were more cohesive and organized" than those whose mothers were not employed. "Daughters of mothers employed full time had higher grade point averages than other children [in the study], and they described their families as placing a higher priority on independence and achievement."[5]

The two most widely funded public programs are Head Start and public pre-kindergarten (pre-K) programs. In 2002, $6.3 billion was distributed to local Head Start grantees, serving close to 10 percent of all three- and four-year-olds. With state expenditures of $2.5 billion, public school pre-K programs serve an additional 9 percent of all three- and four-year-olds.

Working mothers often find it difficult to enroll their children in traditional public school programs because they need all-day care for their three- and four-year-olds. Nationally, 45 percent of these children are in child care for at least 35 hours weekly; another 26 percent are in child care for between 15 and 34 hours weekly. In order to accommodate these needs, many states specify that a large proportion of pre-K slots must be full day, year-round. Since it is often difficult to make these arrangements in public school settings, most states offering pre-K programs specify that a certain percentage of slots must be in community-based settings. Indeed, in a number of states, including New York, New Jersey, Ohio, and Georgia, more than 50 percent of state-funded pre-K slots are in community-based centers. To guarantee a minimum level of quality, states regulate these facilities, including the salaries and qualifications of their teachers.[6]

These policies enabled pre-K programs to focus on low-income and minority children. Whereas pre-K programs are in 17 percent of elementary schools with an enrollment of no more than 6 percent minority children, they are in 45 percent of the elementary schools with more than half minority enrollment. Pre-K programs are in 23 percent of schools in which no more than 35 percent of their students receive subsidized lunches, while they are in more than half of the schools in which at least 75 percent of their students receive subsidized lunches. Overall, 61 percent of pre-K students come from low-income families.[7]

Surveying studies of these programs, sociologists Katherine Magnuson and Jane Waldfogel concluded, "Head Start appears to have beneficial cognitive and behavioral effects for the children it serves, though how large the effects are, how long they persist, and whether they vary by race and ethnic group remain unclear."[8] To answer some of these remaining questions, a comprehensive study of Head Start began in 2002.

Three- and four-year-olds were randomly assigned to either a Head Start group that had access to Head Start program services or to a non-Head Start group that could enroll in available community non-Head Start programs selected by their parents. The study found that for both groups of three- and four-year-olds, there were small to moderate statistically positive impacts on measures of pre-reading, prewriting, vocabulary, and parents' reports of children's literary skills. There was also evidence that Head Start improved parenting skills, as Head Start parents tended to read more often and use physical punishment less often than parents in the non-Head Start group.[9]

Studies of pre-K programs have been more limited but also show positive effects. In one Chicago study, enrollees in a pre-K program were compared to children from the same neighborhoods that were not. Results indicated that those enrolled in the pre-K program had significantly higher academic skills when they entered kindergarten and that "these benefits had a lasting impact on reading and math achievement, as well as high school graduation rates." In a Tulsa study, those enrolled in pre-K had improved language skills "compared to children who had just missed the age cutoff for the program."[10]

Recent research also finds that three- and four-year-olds enrolling at child care centers other than pre-K and Head Start had improved learning skills when compared to children who had either parental or informal child care. Magnuson and Waldfogel also cite a team study headed by Greg Duncan. After adjusting for family background variables, the research team concluded that there were significant gains in academic achievement among children attending child care centers compared to those children who did not. Magnuson and Waldfogel note, "And children whose cognitive ability was lowest gained the most."[11]

These benefits would be even more substantial if there were improvements in the quality of child care centers. Some studies rate the quality only a small fraction of these centers as good or better.[12] Improved quality would be particularly important for low-income single mothers. It is vitally important, then, that government policies provide sufficient funding for welfare leavers and other working families to have access to child care centers rather than the informal arrangements many choose when they are forced to rely on their own financial resources.

TANF REAUTHORIZATION

When welfare reform was passed in 1996, it committed the federal government to a funding formula and set of regulations that had to be followed for five years. After the five years, reauthorization would legislate new funding and regulations. In order to facilitate the reauthorization process, President George W. Bush appointed Ron Haskins as senior advisor on welfare policies in 2001.

TANF reauthorization, however, was stalled because of conflicts over the size of child care expenditures and work requirements of recipients. This was reflected most clearly in differences between the Senate and House bills. Every year the House passed a reauthorization bill that allotted no more than $1 billion in additional child care spending and required an increase in the work hours required of recipients from 30 to 40 hours weekly. By contrast, successive Senate reauthorization bills generally provided substantially more additional funding for child care and more flexible work requirements, especially for welfare recipients with younger children.

Advocates for additional child care expenditures note that if funding fails to keep pace with inflation, the number of child care slots available declines. They point to President Bush's own estimates that without additional child care funding, child care slots would decrease by 200,000–300,000 between 2005 and 2009.[13] Responding to these projections, the 2002 Senate finance committee sent a TANF reauthorization bill to the floor that contained an additional $7 billion for child care. It was up to Senate majority leader Democrat Tom Daschle whether to allow this bill to move forward for a vote.

Initially, Haskins was optimistic that a compromise could be reached with Senate Democrats since he had convinced President Bush to commit to a $3 billion child care increase. Haskins told me,

> The Republicans were never going to agree to $6 or $7 billion for additional child care—no way they would do it. Anyone who has spent 10 minutes in the House with Republican leaders, including Tom DeLay, would see that there was no way it could be done. I spoke with [leading welfare advocates] Mark Greenberg and Wendell Primus, hoping that they could convince Daschle this was the best offer that they would receive.

Rather than accept the compromise, Democrats decided to delay until after the midterm elections in hopes that they would regain control of the House, enabling them to fund a more generous bill.

Just as they had in 1994, the Democrats made a political miscalculation since Republicans not only retained control of the House but also took control of the Senate. As a result, the 2003 Senate bill offered by the Republicans was not as generous as the earlier offer made. When the new Senate finance committee chair Republican Senator Chuck Grassley did not include child care increases in the reauthorization bill, none of the Democrats was willing to vote it out of committee. At that point, Grassley needed all of the Republican committee members and made a deal with Republican Senator Olympia Snowe. In exchange for her committee vote, Snowe would be allowed to make the first amendment from the Senate floor—a $6 billion increase in child care funding.

When this amendment passed, new Republican Majority Leader Bill Frist pulled the legislation from the Senate floor and specified a number of conditions that the Democrats had to accept before he would allow the bill to move forward. He demanded that there be a limit on the number of amendments to the bill that the Democrats could offer and he excluded some specific amendments, including a proposed increase in the minimum wage that Senator Ted Kennedy was going to offer.

Once more, the Democrats had to carefully weigh their political tactics. As Sharon Parrott, welfare policy analyst at the Center on Budget and Policy Priorities, recalled,

> The Democrats decided that it was the right of the minority to offer as many amendments as they wished. They were particularly upset at their inability to offer a number of amendments that the majority of the Senate would have voted for. A line in the sand was drawn.

Without a resolution of this conflict, the reauthorization bill stalled, and another year passed without new legislation.

In 2004, Grassley made another attempt. This time he allowed child care to be included in the bill, so it came out of the finance committee with strong bipartisan support. The new problem was that, given the degree to which federal spending had been exceeding deficit reduction targets, the Republican leadership had already decided that in fall 2005 that there would be a budget reconciliation. Under reconciliation, each committee would be assigned a required spending reduction on all nonlegislated appropriations. Grassley's finance committee would have to come up with $10 billion (over five years) of spending reductions. If, however, the Senate passed a TANF reauthorization bill, it would not be subject to cuts under the reconciliation process.

TANF reauthorization had some unavoidable cost increases that had nothing to do with increased benefits for current or former welfare recipients. Prior to 1996, children in families who left welfare were allowed to continue receiving Medicaid for one year even if their families' income made them ineligible. This transitional medical aid was continued in a supplemental bill when welfare re-form was passed. It has been part of a supplemental spending package each year since then, pending the reauthorization of welfare. According to the budget-office procedures, however, its *inclusion* in TANF reauthorization is scored as a net increase of $5 billion over five years. Similarly, the $1.2 billion continuation of the supplemental grants that were given to a dozen states as part of the original TANF legislation is also scored as a net increase. As a result, just continuing the same policies of the original TANF legislation is considered a $6.2 billion in-crease according to the method the Congressional Budget Office used to score the cost of legislation. When child care increases are included, the Senate's re-authorization bill was scored as more than a $10 billion increase.

With such a large spending increase, many Senate Republicans perceived Grassley's efforts to pass a reauthorization bill separately as an end run around the reconciliation process. In response, budget committee chair Senator Judd Gregg requested a hold on the reauthorization bill, and Frist pulled it. Grassley continued to attempt to convince Frist to let the Senate vote. As Parrott indicated when I interviewed her in June 2005:

> Grassley wants, if at all possible, to avoid having to include TANF reauthorization in reconciliation. His committee has to come up with $10 billion in cuts from all its ap-propriations including Medicare and Medicaid. These looming medical cutbacks are upsetting to a number of Republican committee members: Olympia Snowe, Gordon Smith, and Oren Hatch. So it will be hard enough for him to gain a Republican consensus on the $10 billion cuts without adding TANF reauthorization to the mix.

By contrast, House Republicans were eager to add TANF reauthorization in the reconciliation process, which would have virtually guaranteed that there would be no additional child care expenditures. The reconciliation process was not just a bitter partisan battle; it also forced moderate Republicans to withdraw support from some legislative proposals in order to protect other appropriations. As Parrott noted, "Republican moderates will have many battles to fight in the reconciliation process, and it is unlikely that protecting additional TANF child care expenditures will be a priority."

Some Democrats have tried to find a silver lining in their defeat. While having TANF resolved as part of the reconciliation process virtually guarantees no additional child care funding, it potentially constrains the ability of House Re-publicans to institute changes in work rule requirements. As part of the 1996 welfare bill, cash recipients without paid employment could be required to be engaged in a work activity for up to 30 hours weekly. The House bill ups that to 40 hours and raises the share of recipients who must be in such activities, dra-matically increasing the number of welfare recipients in workfare programs. Margy Waller, a research scholar at the Brookings Institution, feared that the additional child care and administrative costs to implement these work rule changes would adversely affect working families' access to child care funding and other services. She asked,

> Where will the money come from to pay these additional costs? States are not likely to raise taxes to spend more on these programs, so they would have to reduce spending on the support services to low-income working families that they have created and expanded with caseload reduction savings.[14]

Liberal Democrats hoped that the work rule changes would be excluded because they did not have a sufficient fiscal impact. Under what is called the "Byrd Rule," once a bill is in reconciliation, legislators cannot change policies that do not have a financial impact. Parrott was not very optimistic. "Republicans have already begun working on language that would allow new work rule requirements to meet the Byrd Rule hurdle," she lamented, certain that they would find a way to include changes in work rule requirements in the reauthorization bill.

Haskins was not overly sympathetic to the complaints of liberal Democrats. He pointed to the doubling of child care funding since 1995 and how it should be more a state responsibility. More generally, he noted, "In 1984, the federal government expended about $6 billion annually on programs for the poor, while by 1999 these expenditures had grown to $55 billion." He then pointed to evidence of these policies on child poverty rates. As far as Haskins and fellow Republicans were concerned, the federal government was already doing more than enough to aid the poor.

The fate of child care spending and work rule changes was certainly important. A major shortcoming of the reauthorization debate, however, was the lack of recognition that TANF funds were being diverted away from direct aid to families. As a result of the dramatic drop in welfare families, in recent years only about half of the funding has gone for core activities: cash assistance and job-related expenditures. One of the major uses of the additional funds has been an expansion in child protective services. "There was growing awareness [in the 1990s] that these children really need it," said Parrott. "TANF funds didn't replace state funding but enabled states to meet their growing needs while limiting their financial exposure." An increasing share of the expanded services to these children, particularly helping those most "at risk," began to lock in a sizable portion of the TANF block grant and reduce the direct assistance for which it was intended. Whether it's child protective services, Bush's marriage proposal initiatives, or aid to the victims of Hurricane Katrina, Republican legislators have been successful in limiting the overall funding of social spending. Rather than rescind tax cuts to the wealthy, they have forced trade-offs where the cuts in one social program fund the increases in others.

With states increasingly strapped for funds during the economic slowdown, they could ill afford an expansion of the welfare rolls, which would have put strains on activities that they were funding through the TANF block grant. This led states to reduce access to child care funds and the subsidies received by eligible families. For example, in 2004 a single mother with two children earning 150 percent of the poverty line ($23,500 in 2004) would be ineligible for child care assistance in nine states, up from six states in 2001. And in 10 states that maintained eligibility, the annual copayment for this family increased by at least $500.[15]

In addition, states had financial incentives to use sanction and diversionary policies to limit the ability of poor families to access TANF during this time period. This also explains why states have been against the work rule changes that are included in the House reauthorization bill. Indeed, Waller believes that these work rule changes are included precisely because it would put added strain on states that will have to reduce further the eligibility of nonwelfare families. Waller stated,

> It's my bet that there are some conservatives who have noted the increase in spending for work supports and want to put a stop to it before the pressure to more adequately fund these popular services becomes a political problem. That's why they're promoting an expensive addition to the cost of running a program of temporary cash assistance.[16]

Democrats are also partly to blame for the lack of expansion of federal spending on child care slots. Just as with the original TANF legislation, they rejected a compromise in the hopes that election results would put them in a better bargaining position. On closer inspection, however, I believe there is a deeper explanation for their uncompromising stance. If illusions concerning upcoming election results were the primary reason, Democrats could always first accept the compromise and then enhance spending after the election. After the 1996 elections, President Bill Clinton was able to make a number of adjustments to welfare legislation, including reinstating some benefits for legal immigrants. Deeper political motives no doubt clouded Democrats' willingness to compromise early on.

Most of these Democrats have a strong liberal constituency. If they had accepted the $3 billion child care expansion that Bush offered in 2002, these Democrats would have been criticized by their political base as selling out poor women. They probably would not have regained that trust even if a Democratic victory in the 2002 elections would have led to enhanced child care funding. After all, few welfare reform critics even acknowledge the enhancements President Clinton brokered after the 1996 elections. Democrats also realized that when the Republicans froze child care funding in the 2005 reconciliation legislation, they can keep blaming Republicans and conveniently forget their fateful hesitation in 2002. These political calculations may explain why we live in a very polarized political environment where partisan politics reign.

FUNDING-CENTER-BASED CHILD CARE PROGRAMS

Federal and state child care spending increased dramatically after welfare reform was legislated, from $4.1 billion in 1997 to $12.3 billion by 2003.[17] This reflected a temporary bipartisan commitment to aid welfare leavers as part of the make-work-pay strategy. These additional funds, however, were not enough to keep pace with the growing demand. Despite the benefits of center-based child care for three- and four-year-olds, only about half the children of this age group who are cared for outside the home enrolled in these programs. Indeed, critics contend that child care subsidies go only to a small share of those who are financial eligible.[18]

During the economic slowdown, federal bipartisan support collapsed. Moreover, states responded by increasing eligibility requirements and reducing subsidies for qualifying children. Despite the continued increase in the number of working single mothers, these policies led to a 5 percent decline in the number of children served between 2001 and 2004.[19]

One obvious solution is for communities to expand their pre-K programs, programs that currently reach only about one in five children who are in child care outside the home. There are two obstacles, however, to expanding universal pre-K programs. First, the U.S. public continues to be ambivalent about having mothers with young children work full time in the paid workforce. This is especially reflected in the attitudes and behavior of some married women with family incomes about the national average. These women are less likely to be working full time when their children are younger than six years, and less likely to have their children in a full-day child care setting, than either single mothers or married women with low income. These are also the women whose vote shifts often determine elections, so politicians are very sensitive to their concerns. Without stronger support from these so-called "soccer moms," it is unlikely that states will expend funds in order to universalize pre-K full-day programs.

In addition, any substantial expansion of pre-K programs within the public schools would require communities to make significant investments. Parrott offered her personal experience in Montgomery County, Maryland: "Though the third richest county in the United States," she lamented, "it took years before Montgomery was willing to fund full-day kindergarten." Given the ideological ambivalence and financial costs, Parrott favored current efforts to target expansions for low-income families rather than attempts to universalize pre-K programs.

GOVERNMENT TAX SUPPORTS

Without further expansion of pre-K and all-day kindergarten programs, many near-poor families have substantial out-of-pocket costs, creating significant financial burdens. One measure of the impact of these financial burdens on the working poor is the share of children in any center-based care as a function of family income. Nearly 36 percent of young children of employed mothers who have earnings below the poverty line are enrolled in a center-based program. This share declines to 30 percent for mothers with earnings of between the poverty line and double the poverty line, and then rises to 39 percent for mothers with earnings more than double the poverty line.[20]

This U-shaped relationship between enrollment in center-based programs and family income was also reflected in the work of David Ellwood and Jeffrey Liebman. When analyzing the whole range of federal child-related benefit programs, they identified a "middle-class parent penalty": these working families have too much income to qualify for need-based child-related programs such as the earning income tax credit (EITC) and subsidized child care, but too little income to reap as much in tax benefits from the dependent child care tax credit (DCTC) or their dependent allowance as higher income families.[21]

One reason for this "penalty" is how the DCTC works. As part of the federal tax code, the DCTC allows families to obtain tax credits if they have qualifying child care expenses. Depending upon their earnings, families can receive a tax credit for a sliding percentage of their qualifying child care expenses. In 2006, with earnings of $15,000, families can receive a tax credit of 35 percent of their qualifying expenses. This percentage declines to 20 percent as their earnings increase to $43,000. Families with one child can have qualifying child care expenses of up to $3,000, while those with two children can have qualifying expenses of up to $6,000.

In theory, the working poor can use these tax credits to offset their child care costs. However, the DCTC is a *non-refundable* credit. Once federal income tax liabilities are zero, families do not benefit from this provision of the tax code. Since many near-poor families have little or no federal income tax liabilities, they are unable to gain the full benefits from this provision of the tax code. For example, a single mother with two dependent children having wage income of $23,000 and $5,000 of child care expenses has a *potential* tax credit of 30 percent of qualifying child care expenses equal to $1500. She would be able to obtain the total tax savings, however, only if her federal income tax liability was as high. Since she has a federal tax liability of only $965, this is all the DCTC is worth to her. More generally, Ellwood and Liebman found that families with incomes between $25,000 and $45,000 gain much less from the child care provisions of the federal tax code than do families with earnings of $75,000.[22]

Some advocates have campaigned for allowing the tax credit schedule to be adjusted annually for inflation rates. This change, however, would have little benefit for working poor and near-poor mothers since, as the numerical example illustrated, their *actual* tax savings are already capped by their limited income tax liability. A more promising approach is for states to institute their own DCTC programs. In 2004, 27 states provided child care tax credits, though this list did not include some of the largest states: Illinois, Michigan, Pennsylvania, Texas, or Florida. In 12 states, the tax credits were refundable, so the potential benefits are not capped by income tax liabilities. Any excess credit over tax liabilities would be paid out as a tax refund. In the most generous states—California, New York, Louisiana, and Vermont—these refundable credits could total more than $1,000 for a single mother with two children.[23]

Another possibility is for many single mothers with incomes of at least $20,000 to switch from DCTC to the Dependent Care Assistance Program (DCAP). This alternative program allows families with qualifying child care expenses to use an employee account of up to $5,000. The account requires the employer to subtract a specific amount from each pay check during the year. This amount is specified by the employee at the beginning of each calendar year. The funds collected by the employer are placed in an account that can be used only to pay for qualifying child care expenses during the calendar year. Only under a specific set of circumstances can the employer stop contributing to the account during the year. At the end of the year, any remaining funds in the account go to the federal government.

These families gain because DCAP accounts lower their reported earned income by the size of the account. With lower reported income, families will be able to keep more of the EITCs and pay less payroll and personal income taxes. Once state benefits are taken into account, many single mothers can gain more than $1,000 if they switch to the DCAP from the DCTC. The problem is that these potential benefits from switching to the DCAP are very dependent on the ability of workers to accurately estimate their qualifying child care expenses and the full tax implications. In addition, employers may balk at doing the necessary paperwork to set up these accounts. Not surprisingly, few working single mothers take this option.

IMPROVING THE EITC

The federal EITC has been crucial to the success of welfare-to-work policies. In 2005, it provided $4,300 to single mothers with two children with earnings between $10,500 and $14,000. If they are lucky enough to live in the 13 states (or the District of Columbia) that have refundable EITC programs, they gain even more. The six most generous localities provide an EITC equal to at least 20 percent of the federal EITC. As a result, working single mothers with two children in these areas receive an additional $860 or more.[24]

These credits have enabled welfare leavers to purchase automobiles and make other large expenditures that allow them to move forward. The EITC, however, has some shortcomings. In particular, it is a means-tested program targeted to low-income families. As a result, benefits are phased out as incomes rise above a certain level. Together with the phasing out of other benefits, including food stamps and child care subsidies, the net gains from additional earnings might be too modest to truly move out of poverty. Therefore, let us look more closely at the structure of the EITC program and explore ways to overcome its current short-comings.

The EITC is a credit against federal income tax liabilities. The EITC is re-fundable: if the credit exceeds tax liabilities, the taxpayer receives the difference in cash from the Internal Revenue Service. While available to a limited number of childless workers, its benefits are overwhelmingly to families with children. In the phase-in range, the EITC is a wage subsidy; additional earnings increase the EITC received. Once the taxpayer's earnings push benefits up to the legal maxi-mum, they remain constant over a range of income called the "plateau." Finally, at a certain point, credits decrease until eligibility ends.

The specific parameters that determine the EITC received depend upon the worker's marital status and number of qualifying children. However, the struc-ture of the credit remains the same: a phase-in range, a plateau, and a phase-out range. The program costs more than $30 billion annually, making it the largest entitlement program in the federal budget aside from health programs and Social Security.

For a single mother with two (or more) qualifying children, the phase-in rate is 41 percent. In other words, for each $100 of wages in the phase-in range, the taxpayer is entitled to a $41 credit. For 2005, the phase-in range extended to $10,500, at which point the maximum credit was $4,300. Between $10,500 and $14,000, the credit remained constant. Between $14,000 and $34,500, the credit phased out at a 21 percent rate. At incomes above $34,500, households were ineligible for credits. The EITC is indexed for inflation, so the maximum credit and the cutoff points for each range increase automatically each year.

The EITC is more effective in moving families over the poverty line than any other governmental program. Participation rates are high, compared to other income support programs; more than 85 percent of those who are eligible for the credit apply for it. A major motive for preferring a tax credit such as the EITC to traditional public assistance is the boost to work incentives. From 1984 to 1996, employment rates for single mothers with children increased significantly, and researchers attribute a significant share of this increase to repeated expansions of the EITC. Indeed, in the pre-1994 environment, the EITC acted as an effective "carrot" to prod some recipients to choose work rather than welfare.[25]

While the EITC has very positive antipoverty effects, it has three major weaknesses. Many households in the phase-out range face a high implicit tax rate. They also face a severe marriage penalty. Finally, the EITC helps create the middle-class parent penalty that was documented by Ellwood and Liebman.

The implicit tax rate is the proportion of any earnings increase that goes to the government as either additional taxes or a reduction in benefits from government programs. In the phase-out range, for each additional $100, credits fall by $21 for a single mother with two children. Though she has neither federal nor state income tax liabilities, she will have to pay additional social security and Medicare taxes of $7.65. In addition, she is probably receiving benefits from other means-tested programs. In each of these programs, benefits are also reduced as income rises. For each additional $100 of income, food stamp benefits decline by $24 and rent payments in public housing projects or section 8 housing increase by $30. As a result, working mothers who collect food stamps and have housing subsidies would net only $17.35 from the additional $100 of earnings, so they would be facing an implicit tax rate of 82.65 percent. The implicit tax rate is even higher—and the net gains to working mothers still lower—if they also are eligible for medical or child care subsidies. Indeed, for some working mothers who are receiving all of these subsidies and credits, additional earnings might actually cause net income to decline! In 1998, the House Ways and Means Committee estimated that for a female head of household with two dependent children, if her gross income rose from $15,000 to $20,000, after taking into account the additional taxes, lost benefits, and additional child care and commuting expenses, the family would gain only an additional $861 of net income.[26]

For households with a bit more income, the implicit tax rate is also high. Their incomes are too high for food stamps or housing subsidies, so they no longer have these losses if they earn additional income. However, now when they earn an additional $100, they must pay federal and state income taxes. Together with the social security and Medicare taxes, and the lost EITCs, the increase in disposable income would still only be $50 to $55.

The high implicit tax rate makes it difficult for these families to rise above near poverty because extra work adds so little to net income. Indeed, from a social standpoint, it may be best for these households to *reduce* market labor time, especially if children are young. Studies have shown, however, that few EITC recipients understand the relationship of earnings to their implicit tax rate. Almost all families receive the EITC as a lump sum at the end of the tax year and are generally unaware of how the credits are calculated. As a result, the EITC probably has only a modest effect on labor supply decisions for households in the phase-out range.[27] Our main concern, however, should not be whether the EITC distorts employment decisions. Instead, we should be concerned with the inappropriateness of having low-income families facing higher implicit tax rates than millionaires and how this can trap them in near poverty.

The EITC can substantially increase the marriage penalty a single mother faces. If she marries, both partners' incomes *must* be combined to determine eligibility and benefits. In general, if the single mother has earnings of at least $8,000 and marries a partner earning at least that amount, the couple will receive

a smaller EITC. The marriage penalty rises as the income of the childless partner increases. For example, if a single mother with two dependent children and
earnings of $12,000 marries a childless partner with earnings of $25,000, they
would lose all of the EITC ($4,300) that the single mother was entitled to. The
penalty can be even more severe if both partners have qualifying children.

Finally, the combination of the EITC and other child-related tax benefits
families receive creates additional inequities. In order to judge equity of treatment of families with children, we must aggregate benefits from the three child-
related provisions of the tax code that affect all families: EITC, child credit, and
dependent allowance. In 2005, the federal tax code exempted $3,000 from tax-
ation for each dependent child. The higher one's tax bracket, the more an ex-
emption is worth. Exempting $3,000 for a family in the 26 percent tax bracket,
reduces their tax liability by (0.26)($3,000) or $780. For a majority of taxpayers
who are in the 15 percent bracket, the savings are (0.15)($3,000) or $450 per
child. In 1998, the federal government enacted a child credit of $500 per child. In
2003, it was raised to $1,000 per child and made partially refundable.

The solid line in figure 7.1 indicates the tax benefits from these three tax
provisions for single mothers with two children as a function of their earnings.
At low earnings, these mothers receive no benefits from either child credits or
dependent allowances. As a result, in this income range, the only child-related
benefits they receive are from the EITC, and it grows with income because this is
the phase-in range. When the refundable child credit begins to phase in at
$11,000, this adds further to the benefits received as earnings rise.

The growth of credits as earnings rise ends when the family enters the phase-
out range of the EITC. Now families experience a loss of credits as their earnings

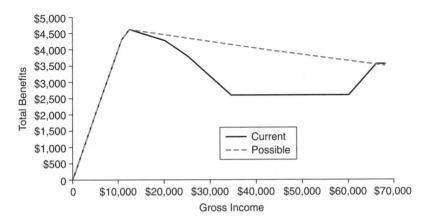

Figure 7.1. Total child-related tax benefits to single mothers with two children: EITC,
child credit, and dependent allowance.

increase. For some income range, the loss of credits is partially offset by the continued phasing in of the child credit. It is also offset by the phasing in of income tax savings due to the dependent allowance. After the household receives the full benefits from the child credit and dependent allowance, the EITC continues to be phased out and the combined benefits decline sharply. At $34,850, households no longer qualify for the EITC, so tax benefits are reduced to $2,600—the value of the child credits and dependent allowances.

Benefits of $2,600 continue as income rises. At some point the next dollar would have been taxed at a higher 26 percent rate. Now the dependent allowances are worth more, so once the household gains its full effect, combined benefits equal $3,560. This combined benefit schedule indicates that poor and some near-poor households gain substantially due to the EITC, and those earning more than $60,000 gain substantially because the dependent allowance is worth more to them than to households in the 10 or 15 percent tax brackets. Recall that the benefits of government child and dependent care tax credits also followed the same pattern. Unfortunately, the current structure provides lower middle-class households with less combined child-related benefits than either their wealthier or poorer counterparts.

Together with an economist at the Economic Policy Institute, Max Sawicky, I have developed a tax proposal to reduce these inadequacies of the current tax system.[28] Initially, it was endorsed by Ohio Democrat congressman Dennis Kucinich and Wisconsin Republican congressman Thomas Petri. The 2000 election led, however, to more partisan politics. While sympathetic to tax simplification reforms that would provide more equitable child-related benefits, Republican legislators, including Petri and Utah Senator Orrin Hatch, came under tremendous pressure to instead support the Bush tax cuts. As a result, the tax proposal became associated exclusively with the Democrats, especially with Illinois Democratic congressman Rahm Emanuel, who had been a senior staff member in the Clinton administration.[29] He continues to support our policy initiative. Called the Simplified Family Credit (SFC), it combines these three universal child-related benefit programs.

The SFC benefits for households earning up through $12,500 could be equivalent to the amount currently being received from the EITC and refundable child credit. These benefits could then be reduced continuously—the dashed line in figure 7.1—until benefits are phased down to $3,560, which is the amount that wealthier households are currently receiving from their child credits and dependent allowances. A similar SFC can be done for households with one child.

The SFC lowers the phase-out rates, creating a more balanced benefits structure that removes the penalties for families gradually moving out of poverty. With a smaller phase-out rate, single mothers do not lose significant credits if they earn additional income or if they marry. This lowers the implicit tax rate, especially when households are currently subject to both the phase-out rate and federal taxation. In these situations, the SFC would lower the implicit tax rate by more than 10 percent.

In the example above, when a single mother with two children and income of $12,000 marries a childless partner with income of $25,000, $4,300 in credits disappears. With the new phase-out rate, the family loses only $450 in credits. Our actual SFC proposal reduces the marriage penalty by more than $1,000 for a wide variety of potential marriage partners. If we are to make any serious attempt to reform the way benefits are distributed, we must begin by removing the tax penalties looming over those families on the edge of poverty.

CONCLUDING REMARKS

The benefits from center-based child care are substantial, and efforts should be made to expand access to them. This funding should increase not only the number of slots so that more of the working poor can be served but also the quality of centers by strengthening teacher requirements and improving the teacher-to-child ratio. Unfortunately, federal spending on child care for the working poor is not likely to be enhanced in the near future unless the constituency for these programs expands. Efforts should be made to universalize the appeal for these pre-K programs among middle-class families who currently face substantial out-of-pocket costs when they choose private child care programs.

In California, Rob Reiner organized a broad coalition that in 1998 successfully sponsored a state initiative, "First Five," that funds an array of services to children from birth through five years old. A significant portion of that funding has gone to preschool programs. Building on these successes, Reiner has again organized a broad coalition to place a universal preschool initiative on the ballot in 2006. If approved, every four-year-old will have access to a fully funded half-day preschool program.[30]

This chapter also explores the ways that the government aids parents through child care tax benefits and the EITC. Unable to calculate the relative merits of alternatives because of the complexity of the tax system, parents may lose out on benefits to which they are entitled. For example, in order to determine whether to use DCAP accounts, a near-poor family must judge how it would affect the federal child tax credits and EITC they receive. If that is not enough, parents must also judge the impact of DCAP accounts on state income taxes, EITC, and child care credits. These complexities often stump experts.[31] As a result of these problems, millions of working families are either unaware or ill informed about the benefits that they could receive from opening up DCAP accounts.

Due to the complexities of the tax system, working families have limited knowledge of the high implicit tax rates they face. Unlike a number of countries, the child-related benefits of the federal tax system are fragmented.[32] Families receive child-related benefits from the EITC, the child tax credit, the dependent allowance, and either the DCAP or the DCTC. If we add to that the benefits from other means-tested programs, it becomes quite difficult to calculate precisely the implicit tax rate they face. And without this calculation, it is impossible for them to rationally determine many important employment decisions. It is for this reason that reforms that would simplify the tax system, such as the SFC, are important to working families.

8

Vocational Training that Works

Welfare reform has moved many single mothers from poverty to near poverty once government income supports are included. Absent a four-year college degree, however, only a very small proportion of single mothers can attain family incomes of $30,000, the income necessary to completely avoid basic material hardships. As a result, if the objective is to allow single mothers to be independently self-sufficient, it seems imperative that they must have four-year college degrees. A college-for-all perspective, however, often sets students up for failure. It also disregards the value of vocational training, maligned by critics but a much more effective stepping stone to meaningful employment for many mothers.

There are problems with "college for all" that even some of its advocates admit. Most welfare recipients performed poorly in high school and are constrained by family and work responsibilities. For this group, access to college does not guarantee success, especially in the attainment of the prized four-year degree. High failure rates in the community colleges indicate that weakly prepared students will not always be able to take full advantage of educational opportunities provided. And sometimes even the four-year degree does not guarantee financial rewards for these students.

For example, after Belinda pulled her life together, she enrolled at a private four-year college. Working two low-wage jobs over a six-year period, she obtained a bachelor's degree in human resource management, accumulating a sizable student debt along the way. While her debt was more than $7,000, Belinda had not had one interview since receiving her degree six months before I interviewed her, and the school has been less than helpful. Belinda complained,

> I have tried to see a placement counselor a number of times since I finished the program but she is always busy with something or not around when I come. The staff was helpful when I was in their program but now that I have finished, and they're not getting any money from me, it doesn't seem like they care if I get a job.

As a result of what I learned from my interviews, I am troubled by the perspective of the LIFETIME program I visited in Oakland. This program had substantial success in helping women, *who were already in college* when they applied for welfare, to complete their four-year degrees.[1] In an attempt to expand their program, LIFETIME began accepting welfare recipients who have not already attended college. In our discussion, the program director, Anita Rees, mentioned one of the new women in the program who had failed her GED degree exam twice but was still determined to gain a four-year degree. When I questioned the soundness of this goal, given the difficulty in first obtaining her GED (and that she just had a fourth child), the director told me that the program refuses to be judgmental. As long as their clients desire to pursue a four-year college degree, LIFETIME is obligated to do all that is possible to help them achieve their goal.

For many of these mothers, vocational programs that prepare them to successfully pass certification exams or are linked directly to employment may be much more effective. Though this approach might not provide financial independence, it might be the best choice for many of these students, especially if government programs and financial support from fathers can supplement the modest wages attained.

If we want to provide welfare leavers with meaningful educational opportunities, I believe there should be more emphasis on improving the vocational programs offered by the public sector. Half of the leavers I interviewed enrolled in private, for-profit schools in an attempt to obtain vocational credentials that would improve their earnings. Virtually all had unpleasant experiences. Few felt they had gained much from these programs, and almost all were saddled with student loans that they were unable to pay. This strongly suggested to me that the community colleges and continuing education programs at public colleges should play a much greater role in providing vocational education.

THE ROLE OF COMMUNITY COLLEGES

Welfare leavers are part of a larger group of individuals who did poorly in high schools, either dropping out or graduating with low grades. Most college-for-all advocates reject attempts to funnel these students into narrow vocational programs. The educational theorist Joe Kincheloe sees vocational programs as a fundamentally racist enterprise. He dismisses them as a tool to oppress blacks and Latinos, noting that "education has been used as a hegemonic force, a means to control the poor and dispossessed. . . . "[2] He vilifies their pro-business ideology that "efficiently educated workers will be prompt and loyal; social unrest will be a distant memory."[3] Moreover, vocational programs doom students to a job with low pay and low respect.

But counselors do little to dissuade even the weakest skilled students from plans to attend colleges with the expectations that they have a reasonable chance of attaining four-year college degrees. Indeed, the college-for-all norm makes Kincheloe's claims of racist victimization out of touch with the realities of most contemporary urban high schools.

Moreover, the lower educational attainment of black and Latino students is not the product of institutional racism. James Rosenbaum looked at the educational attainment of individuals in 1992, 10 years after they graduated high school. As expected, black and Latino students had lower educational attainment. Once other factors were incorporated into the analysis, however, the racial gaps were reversed. Among students of the same socioeconomic status, blacks and Latinos had higher educational attainment than whites with the same test scores, high school average, and time spent on homework.[4] While class background remained a significant determinant of educational attainment, the data refute any claims of systematic racist educational tracking. In fact, he reported that in the early 1990s, following the college-for-all vision, the superintendent of schools in Chicago "urged all high schools to stress college goals and closed or reduced resources to many vocational schools."[5]

The main point of Kincheloe's work is not, however, to give reasoned assessments of the barriers faced by poor black and Latino students or the role of vocational programs. It is to discourage any serious debate over educational policy for groups that have fared poorly in high schools. By characterizing vocational tracks as racist enterprises, he demonizes anyone who would argue that expanding them might improve the life chances of many poorly performing students.[6]

A much less politicized but just as deeply flawed defense of the college-for-all perspective is laid out by W. Norton Grubb and Norman Lazerson, two of the most influential educational theorists nationally. Unlike Kincheloe, they do not criticize vocationalism and, indeed, note correctly that virtually all education at the comprehensive four-year colleges can be considered vocationalism. By this they mean "an educational system whose purposes are dominated by preparation for economic roles, and respond to external demands—in this case, the demands for the essential skills employers want and the skills of the twenty-first century."[7]

This is certainly the situation at my school, Brooklyn College, where the vast majority of students are majoring in accounting, business management, health science, computer science, film, television and radio, physical education, and general education. While we have a core curriculum that requires students to take a set of humanities and pure science courses, these traditional academic areas have few majors, and the overwhelming majority of students perceive these courses as hurdles they must endure.

Grubb and Lazerson support the educational shift to vocationalism because they believe that it better prepares students for lifelong learning. It is the extremely narrow skill-based programs that limit occupation mobility and intellectual growth that they reject. They also reject any attempt to restrict access to higher learning by enforcing entrance requirements tied to prior academic achievement.

When criticizing narrow vocational tracking, Grubb and Lazerson raise the possibility that community colleges may undermine the educational attainment of working class students. A number of times they refer to the risk that

> community colleges operated to divert or "cool out" unprepared students into low-status occupations away from academic programs leading to baccalaureate degrees... similar to the critique of high school vocational education as a dumping ground for students unable to do academic work.[8]

Grubb and Lazerson are not dismissive of this viewpoint, especially when they discuss vocational programs in the community colleges.[9]

In their college-for-all zeal, however, they downplay a key fact: weakly prepared students entering a community or four-year college simply do not succeed at the same rates that better prepared students do. There is a strong correlation between high school grades and college completion rates. Fewer than 15 percent of A and B high school seniors who planned to attend college did not earn college credits, while 32 percent of C students did not. These students either dropped out before completing a semester or never got beyond remediation courses. As a result, Rosenbaum believes that "the greatest benefit in educational attainment would come from an improvement in [high school] grades, and this is true for both blacks and whites."[10]

An Ohio study looked at the educational progress of students five years after they had enrolled full time in one of the state's community colleges. Among those who did not have to take a math remediation course, 29 percent had completed a two-year associate degree and 16 percent either were still enrolled in or had completed a four-year college degree program. By contrast, among those full-timers who had to take a remediation math course, fewer than 18 percent had completed their associate degree and only 9 percent either were still enrolled in or had completed a four-year college degree program.[11] Comparable results were found for students who were required to take a remedial English course.[12]

Success rates are particularly low for those students who need remediation in a number of areas. In Miami-Dade Community College, fewer than 25 percent of students who were deficient in three areas successfully completed remediation, and only 4 percent had completed an associate degree within five years. By contrast, almost two-thirds of all students deficient in only one area successfully completed remediation, and 20 percent had completed their associate degree within five years.[13] In another study funded by the Community College Association, Robert McCabe found that only 5 percent of seriously deficient entering students completed at least 20 college credits.[14]

Similar findings come from the Southern Regional Educational Board and the 18 southern states it follows. The board estimated that among first-year community college students in 2001, only 64 percent were enrolled the next year at the same or another college, and that after three years, only 43 percent either had obtained a degree or certificate or were still enrolled in a postsecondary school.[15] Even if we extend the period for completion to five years or more, only about half of those who enter associate programs are successful.[16]

Rosenbaum also found a strong relationship between grades and earnings when analyzing data of students who completed high school but did not enter college. He stated, "Although grades do not improve wages for new high school graduates in the High School and Beyond 1982 cohort, grades have a strong payoff for their earnings ten year later."[17] These data also indicated that achievement test scores had a strong influence on later earnings.[18]

Many economists include results from the basic skills Armed Forces Qualifying Test (AFQT) in their analysis of earnings differences. Racial differences on this test are substantial; only 14 percent of black men score at the fiftieth percentile or better. Studies consistently find that at least half of the earnings gap among equally educated black and white men is explained by racial differences in performance on the AFQT.[19] For example, June O'Neill found that if black men had the same AFQT scores as white men, the black–white earnings gap would be reduced by 12.4 percentage points among male college graduates and by 5.4 percentage points among men with less than a college degree.[20] These results suggest that, independent of years of school completed, basic academic skills have a significant impact on lifetime earnings.

Low success rates trouble Grubb. He laments, "These open-access institutions for nontraditional students have replicated a traditional pattern whereby students who are poorly prepared, including many low-income and minority students, fail to make much educational progress."[21] He blames these failure rates, however, on the inadequate teaching they receive. Grubb states, "For those students who arrive underprepared, the vast amount of dismal remediation following skills-centered approaches is unlikely to engage their attention, and high rates of failure to complete remediation programs result."[22] As a result, Grubb strongly recommends that schools expand the support services that they provide.

When California expanded the services to welfare participants at its community colleges, however, failure rates were essentially unchanged. Almost one-third of welfare participants leaving California community colleges had completed no college credits, and another 30 percent fewer than 12 credits both before and after the service expansion.[23] Similar to Grubb and Lazerson, McCabe placed part of the blame on unnecessary academic standards. In response to the low mathematics pass rate, he suggested, "Either adjustments in expectations or major improvements in high school preparation are needed—perhaps both."[24]

The reason for these particularly low success rates might appear to be the inability of students to complete their remediation in a timely fashion. Evidence, however, seems to indicate that the problem goes much deeper. For example, Nancy Ritze reports that at Bronx Community College in New York City, a special program was set up to help the least prepared students navigate through their remediation courses. Expending substantially more resources on support services and small classes, this Freshman Initiative Program (FIP) was able to substantially increase pass rates on all three remediation exams, by about 20 percentage points.

While this program enabled more students to continue at the community college, it did not have that significant effect on overall retention rates and other measures of progress. Since the college instituted the FIP, the rate of passing credit-bearing courses increased by only 2 percent, while the rate of course withdrawals decreased by 3 percent and the number of students on probation dropped by only 1 percent. Even after this program was instituted, the six-year graduation rate increased only slightly, remaining well below 30 percent.[25]

Why do higher pass rates have only a modest effect on six-year graduation rates? One reason is that the vast majority of these students are still weakly skilled since very few have improved dramatically. For example, for many years, Brooklyn College ran an intense summer program to aid students who had failed the skills assessment exams. The passing score on the math exam was 25 out of a possible 40. The summer program had an almost 90 percent success rate, but very few of the students attained a passing score greater than 30. Thus, effective programs might be successful in getting most students through remediation, but these students still have very weak academic skills, so they remain vulnerable to subsequent failures in their credit-bearing courses.

Even those students who are most successful and transfer to four-year colleges have persistent difficulties. Ritze found that though these transfer students were able to sustain enrollment at four-year colleges, they performed poorly. In their first year after transferring, these students attained a grade point average of only 2.52, well below the four-year college norm.[26]

Because of the hurdles most weakly prepared high school graduates face, Rosenbaum believes the college-for-all vision is like a con game where students with deficient cognitive abilities are the victims. He states,

> [S]tudents are promised college for very little effort. Just as some high schools implicitly offer students an undemanding curriculum in return for nondisruptive behavior, many high schools enlist students' cooperation by telling them college is the only

respectable goal and is easily attainable for all.... The "college for all" norm...
encourages youth to retain ambitions of advancement as long as possible, but ignores
the barriers that limit their careers.[27]

POSTSECONDARY VOCATIONAL PROGRAMS

Ignoring the substantial basic skill deficiencies of many welfare leavers, Grubb
and Lazerson claim, "What counts in the labor market is the quantity of education an individual has completed, not the quality of learning."[28] Furious with the
work-first policies of welfare reform, they accused states of barring welfare recipients from education and training that would insulate them from the low-wage,
unskilled positions most vulnerable to economic business cycles.

Their criticisms of work-first policies are misplaced. The Manpower Demonstration Research Corporation was hired to study the effects of welfare-to-
work policies. At 11 sites nationally between 1991 and 1994, welfare recipients
were randomly selected for a welfare-to-work program or a control group that
remained in the general welfare population. Welfare-to-work programs were divided into those that emphasized work-first activities (WFA) and those that
emphasized a human capital development (HCD) approach. Each participant was
followed for five years, with the WFA programs increasing earnings by $1,500–
2,500 and increased the number of quarters employed from 0.7 to 1.1. By contrast, the two HCD programs with low enforcement failed to raise employment,
and the other five HCD programs increased earnings by $800–2,000 and increased
the number of quarters employed by 0.3–0.8.[29] Instead of referencing these data,
Grubb and Lazerson simply assert that work-first policies extended inequality
by forcing participants to take "transient, low-paid jobs"[30] and "abandon those
most in need of the second-chance opportunities that job training is suppose to
provide."[31]

As the data indicated, work-first programs were effective when compared to
the short-term skill-enhancing HCD programs.[32] Many welfare leavers consider
steady employment and basic skill development as best serving their *immediate*
needs. At Brooklyn College, the literacy program aided many welfare leavers
who lacked the basic skills to pass the GED examination. Its director, Lillian
O'Reilly, believed that for this population, promoting the goal of four-year degrees would be "grooming them for failure." She felt that direct employment was
crucial to "getting their lives in order" and was glad that the program had received funding for a job placement counselor. O'Reilly also noted that a modest
number of the students who passed the GED examination enrolled in community
colleges but overwhelming in vocational programs there.

Effective vocational programs do have the potential of being even more beneficial in the long run. Welfare leavers that I interviewed sought out vocational

programs that would provide them with credentials that would enhance their earnings. Most of these leavers chose programs offered by private, for-profit post-secondary institutions—known as proprietary schools—rather than enrolling at community colleges. In 1996, one-quarter of students enrolled at proprietary schools were single mothers—almost double their share at public two-year colleges.

Proprietary schools do not attract less educated, poor, minority students simply because of the value of their programs. Proprietary schools are viable only because their students receive substantial government funding, particularly Pell Grants and student loans. This is most striking when we look at independent full-time students with annual incomes of less than $25,000. At proprietary schools, 73 percent of these students have grants with loans, compared to only 29 percent at public two-year colleges.[33]

Until the early 1990s, there was little to constrain proprietary schools from recruiting unqualified students and obtaining generous federal and state funding. Federal officials became concerned when the default rate on student loans reached more than 30 percent. In response, the federal government began in 1992 to limit Pell grants and student loans to only those proprietary schools in which at least 15 percent of students—later reduced to 10 percent—received no federal aid. The federal government reasoned that for a program to have value, a modest share of students must be willing to pay for it. Immediately after this rule took effect, many proprietary schools closed, and the default rate on student loans dropped dramatically, eventually falling to less than 10 percent.

After industry reorganization, proprietary schools responded to growing demand for vocational programs. Between 1995 and 2002, enrollment in proprietary schools grew by 147 percent while the enrollment grew by only 18 percent at two-year colleges. In New York, enrollment in colleges and universities grew by 15 percent while in proprietary schools, it grew by 46 percent. In California alone, more than 100,000 students attend proprietary schools annually. As a result, by 2002, two-thirds of the students enrolled in vocational nondegree programs attended proprietary schools.

Though still enrolling only about 6 percent as many students as two-year colleges, certificate programs disproportionately attract poorer, less educated, minority students. Whereas 28 percent of those enrolled in less than two-year programs had either a GED or no high school equivalent, this was true of fewer than 8 percent of those enrolled in public community colleges.[34] More than 39 percent of those enrolled in certificate programs were black or Latino, and 58 percent of independent students at these schools had annual incomes of less than $20,000. By contrast, only 28 percent of community college students were black or Latino, and fewer than 38 percent of independent students enrolled there had annual incomes of less than $20,000.

While the 1992 regulation eliminated the most egregious abuses, federal and state funding continued to provide generous incentives for educational entrepreneurs. Stephanie Cellini estimated that, in California, a "$1000 increase in the maximum personal student award sparks a 22 percent increase in the net number of proprietary schools.... The effect is stronger in [areas] with higher poverty rates, where more students qualify for these grants."[35] In New York, needy students can receive $4,050 in Pell Grants and another $5,000 from the state's tuition assistance program. "That is a pretty good recipe for making money," said Brian Pusser, an assistant professor at the University of Virginia's Curry School of Education, who studies profit-making higher education.[36]

Unfortunately, educational entrepreneurs do not always serve the best interests of their students. At a 2005 Congressional Hearing on Enforcement of Anti-Fraud Laws in For-Profit Education, Congresswoman Maxine Waters highlighted some of these abuses. She stated,

> I had GED courses conducted in my office so that my constituents could pass the math portion of the GED to get into the construction training programs.... Many of these students...had defaulted on previous student loans used to attend a trade school, and thus did not qualify for any current financial aid including Pell Grants which they needed to support themselves while attending Community College to obtain training. At one graduation ceremony at the Employment Preparation Center, I asked how many of the graduates had been ripped off by a trade school, and all hands but one went up.[37]

When Drake Business School in New York City closed, LaGuardia Community College attempted to help its students. "We found it impossible," said Gail Mellow, president at LaGuardia, "Even though some of these students were at the end of their sophomore year, their level of preparation was so low that they were not passing our basic skills tests."[38]

The director of continuing education at LaGuardia, Sandra Watson, highlighted the importance of providing an alternative to proprietary schools. She described her division as a "proprietary school with integrity." By this she meant that, thanks to extensive funding grants, LaGuardia students were provided with the necessary support services, such as counseling, child care, and smaller classes, that are crucial to their success. Just as important, LaGuardia's programs provide career ladders so that there can be lifelong learning within chosen career paths. These career ladders are most clearly defined in the health field. Students with the weakest skill preparation begin in "Bridge to the Health Sciences." After completing this entry program that has employment links, they might choose to continue to the licensed practical nurse program. And after completing that program, they might choose to extend their education further through a registered nurse program.

Watson was also proud of the placement activities built into their continuing education programs. This included career fairs for a broad range of programs, career nights for specific programs, and placements through federally funded workforce career centers. She also noted how partnerships can be particularly effective.

Watson explained how only through a partnership with a group of hospitals was it possible to develop a successful radiology technician program. While the university was willing to fund instructional staff, the program stalled because funding for the training equipment was not forthcoming. LaGuardia had developed a working relationship with a number of hospitals through its other medical programs. When these hospitals learned that the radiology program was being held up for a lack of funding, they voluntarily contributed the necessary equipment.

Rather than relying on the proprietary schools, New York City instituted a College Opportunity to Prepare for Employment (COPE) program at the community colleges in the early 1990s to facilitate the educational advancement of welfare mothers. The stated goal of COPE is to increase the number of public assistance recipients who graduate from college and enable them to move toward long-term economic self-sufficiency. For many welfare advocates, this has been interpreted as providing the ability of mothers to complete a four-year degree while on welfare—the goal of the LIFETIME program discussed at the beginning of this chapter.

By contrast, for practitioners, the goal of COPE primarily involved vocational programs at the community colleges. This became clear when I interviewed the former director the COPE program at LaGuardia Community College, Audrey Harrigan. Now assistant to the president at LaGuardia, she was quite proud of the success of the COPE program there.

Much had been made by activists that initial Temporary Assistance for Needy Families rules made it impossible for welfare mothers to enroll in two-year associate degree programs. In response, however, states increased access for welfare recipients.[39] In 2002, almost 40 states allowed recipients to attend for two full years, up substantially from three years earlier.[40] As Thomas Brock and colleagues noted,

> Many welfare agencies currently allow welfare recipients to participate in ten or more hours of educational training per week provided that they work at least twenty hours. Some community colleges have developed work-study options to help welfare recipients meet their work obligations while going to school. Ideally, work-study positions can be structured to reinforce clients' career goals through placements in the college's administrative offices, student services, library, and other facilities, or even off-campus with local public or nonprofit employers.[41]

LaGuardia takes this approach. As a result, the college can always justify the continuation of recipients in their two-year programs, and their decline in number of students served reflected the decline in the size of the welfare population.

The COPE program accepted all recipients who were high school graduates and, through expanded support services, had a completion rate of 50 percent.

Harrigan gave me a copy of the program for an event celebrating the 10th anniversary of the first COPE graduates at LaGuardia, which featured the postcollege experience of 28 students who had responded to a mailing. From this group of successful students, only one attained an associate degree outside of a vocational program. Ten of the students graduated with an associate degree in human resources with a specialization in child development, while another five were in areas that prepared them to work in the technical end of the computer field. Only five were either still in a four-year program or had graduated one. Most were working full time in a field related to their associate degree program. Even among these success stories, fewer than 20 percent went to a four-year program within a short time of receiving their associate degree.

The experience at LaGuardia demonstrates that the fears vocational programs will consign students to low-end jobs with no chance for educational or career advancements are vastly overstated. These vocational programs provide entry into careers that do not foreclose further education and career ladders. For many adults, this makes far more sense than enrolling in academic programs at the community college.

Charles Outcalt and James Schimer are optimistic that the 1992 federal regulations caused a "sea change" and that a more recent attempt by a significant share of proprietary schools to seek accreditation limits the abuses students might suffer. They point to the greater focus at proprietary schools on practical skills without the general education requirements that create hurdles for students. They also emphasize the greater student support services and job placement found at proprietary schools.[42] Tony Zeiss, president of Central Piedmont Community College claims,

> Recent success of proprietary schools has meant that community colleges must adapt quickly or risk losing a substantial portion of their students.... Students and employers now demand skills that proprietary schools can perhaps provide more easily and effectively than the community colleges, and that there is a "serious mismatch between education policies and market need [and so] there is no certainty that community colleges can dominate those new roles."[43]

Just like LaGuardia, many community colleges have responded effectively. In Florida, there are

> lines at both ends of some Pinellas Tech programs: Students wait for class slots, and companies wait to hire them. Two-thirds of Pinellas Tech students complete requirements for professional certification or state licensing, and 82 percent end up employed in their fields of study.[44]

Columbus State Community College in Ohio provides customized training for more than 4,000 employees at almost 60 different companies. The Hagerstown

Community College Advanced Technology Center in Maryland has delivered training to more than 650 companies and 29,000 employees since 1990. Spartanburg Technical College in South Carolina has a corporate program in which more than 80 percent of graduates have accepted employment with their sponsoring company after graduation.

The Advanced Technology Program at Oakland Community College in Michigan has strong industry partnerships and career opportunities for participants. Oakland Community College developed this advanced technology program to train welfare recipients in high-skill areas. It has enrolled more than 250 participants, 98 percent of them women, with a completion rate of more than 80 percent. More than 90 percent of the participants who completed the program have acquired full-time jobs in the area in which they were trained, with starting salaries averaging $20,000 and annual salary increases averaging $2,000.[45]

In Kansas City, Metropolitan Community College's Business and Technology Center responded to corporate needs for customer service representatives in the growing call centers located there. With seed money from AT&T, Lucent Technology, Gateway, and Sprint, the college developed a curriculum that has a 92 percent graduation rate. Almost three-quarters of graduates obtained employment, and 85 percent remained on the job for at least three months. The average pay for graduates is typically between $9 and $11 per hour.[46]

Unfortunately, there continues to be a reluctance to strengthen and expand these programs at many community colleges. Vocational programs are often not perceived to be a core function at community colleges so vulnerable to cutbacks. As one administrator lamented, vocational programs "fight for funding, yet they have track records business leaders and legislators should admire."[47]

This attitude has adverse consequences for students in vocational programs. According to researchers at the Community College Research Center at Columbia University,

> Occupational students pursuing an associate's degree complete their degree goals less often than their academic counterparts. Part of this difference can be explained by differences in student characteristics and expectations, but the gap remains after controlling for these factors. We conclude that community colleges have yet to figure out and implement the optimal approach to provide occupational preparation within an institutional structure that *continues to rest on a foundation oriented towards academic education.*[48]

Due to shared governance between educators and administrators, community colleges often do not quickly respond to changing business needs, especially when it is perceived to infringe on faculty prerogatives. College may balk at having courses at work sites or at times most suitable for a company's employees. Many faculty members are less enthusiastic about these relations because they often must modify traditional or unique academic courses in order to meet industry needs.

Administrators and faculty members also may view contract training or specialized skill preparation as a distraction from the more fundamental missions of the community colleges, such as access or transfer. This is one contributing factor in the inability of vocational programs to have permanent job placement positions paid through general university funding. Instead, program directors have to write grants and find outside funding sources for this crucial link between training and employment. Facing this funding problem, the continuing education director at Brooklyn Colleges is exploring the possibility of negotiating partnership agreements with proprietary schools to take advantage of their job placement services.

CONCLUDING REMARKS

While it may make advocates feel comfortable, promoting the college-for-all philosophy to the detriment of vocational programs harms many weakly prepared single mothers in two ways: failure in their academic coursework without gaining employable skills, and being forced to seek certification programs at problematic proprietary schools. There is certainly a risk that some students who could have been successful in four-year programs end up in less lucrative vocational careers. And black and Latino students may be particularly vulnerable, so it is possible that encouraging vocational programs may contribute to the persistence of racial educational disparities.

But for many students, enrolling in vocational programs *increases* options rather than constraining them. Vocational students have enhanced employment possibilities that they would not have if they had enrolled in the general education programs that are recommended for students hoping to transfer to four-year colleges. As the success stories demonstrate, while some welfare leavers continued their education beyond the community college, this became an option, not a necessity.

Encouraging students with weak academic skills and family responsibilities to focus on a four-year degree is increasingly problematic. The vast majority of the limited number who do attain four-year degrees will graduate from less prestigious colleges with below-average grade point averages. These students will be at a disadvantage in the job market, especially with a growing oversupply of college graduates. In 2002, the Bureau of Labor Statistics found that 17 percent of the nation's office clerks had bachelor degrees or higher. So did 12 percent of derrick operators; 19 percent of theater ushers, lobby attendants, and ticket takers; 13 percent of bank tellers; 14 percent of typists and word processors; and 37 percent of flight attendants.[49]

In 2006, the lowest-paid one-quarter of women with four-year degrees had weekly earnings of $450 or less. Among women with only some college or a two-year degree, almost half had weekly earnings of at least that much.[50] Thus, as the evidence from LaGuardia and elsewhere indicated, for many women attaining an associates degree or professional certificate will be more valuable than those pursuing a four-year degree.

While program administrators, the business community, and students understand the value of vocational programs, many college faculty members continue to resist expanding and improving these programs. In particular, there is a continued reluctance to hire qualified full-time instructors, a reluctance to hire permanent job placement personnel because it detracts from educational activities, and a reluctance to embrace partnerships with industry because of a fear that academic integrity will be compromised. We must overcome these shortcomings so that community colleges can better offer meaningful vocational training to welfare leavers, single mothers, and students who did not excel in school but seek to maximize their opportunities in the workforce.

9

Strengthening Partner Relationships and Child Support

In 2004, nearly one out of every three children was born out of wedlock, and many of these single mothers have difficulty earning enough to support their families. Indeed, a child born to a never-married mother is seven times as likely to be poor as one born to a married couple. Children living with a single mother often have more psychological and learning problems than do children living in a two-parent family. For these reasons, many policy analysts across the political spectrum believe that strengthening the relationships between a child's parents, as well as the child support received from noncustodial fathers, should be important components of the policy mix.

Starting in 2001, President George W. Bush proposed $750 million to fund programs that would promote healthy relationships leading to marriage. Many critics of President Bill Clinton's welfare reform policies balked at these new initiatives. They particularly questioned the focus on marriage rather than women's earnings and feared that these new programs would trap poor women in inequitable, if not abusive, relationships without providing the real independence that only decent employment could.

Welfare reform critics also rejected the view held by many policy makers that noncustodial fathers are "deadbeat dads" who must be coerced and threatened to provide child support. Instead, many reform critics suggest that these men are victims of an uncaring system and have little income to provide for the support of their children. These critics contend that the best way to improve parental relationships in poor communities is to improve the employment opportunities and earnings of these men.

HEALTHY MARRIAGE PROPOSALS

With much fanfare, the Bush administration has made government funding of marriage initiatives one of its priorities. While these initiatives are linked financially to government Temporary Assistance for Needy Families (TANF) funding, advocates contend that its focus is the general population of young adults. This objective is spelled out by Robert Rector, senior researcher at the conservative Heritage Foundation:

> There is now a broad bipartisan recognition that healthy marriage is a healthy protective institution that, in most cases, promotes the well-being of men, women, and children: It is the foundation of a healthy society. Yet, for decades, government policy has remained indifferent if not hostile to marriage. Government programs merely sought to pick up the pieces as marriages failed or worse—actively undermined marriage.
>
> President Bush seeks to change the policy of indifference and hostility. There is no group that will gain more from this change than low-income single women, most of whom hope for a healthy, happy marriage in the future. President Bush hopes to provide young couples with the knowledge and skills to accomplish their dreams.[1]

This rhetoric did not sway most welfare reform critics. Director of the National Organization for Women's Legal Defense and Educational Fund in New York, Jennifer Brown, claimed, "This is a ruse by the White House to make the social experiment of getting poor people married more palatable."[2] Others see it as a political strategy. John Green, a political scientist who studies voting behavior, suggested that the marriage initiative could have symbolic and real results. "The White House perceives married people as a key GOP constituency," he explained. "To that end, it pays both to have more people married and to affirm the values and commitment of people who already are married."[3]

Still others are concerned by the willingness of Bush to link his marriage promotion initiatives to his Christian values. Sharon Parrott, senior staffer at the liberal Center on Budget and Policy Priorities, noted that "one of the real dangers of marriage money is it could lead to extremely ideological grant making." She feared "small organizations are in a position to get relatively large grants that could potentially be intensely religious."

Many critics are troubled by proposals that will force poor black women to enter undesirable marriages, proposals such as those of Republican Senator Sam Brownback of Kansas to provide marriage bonuses of up to $9,000 to poor District of Columbia mothers who choose marriage.[4] It is troubling that the Bush administration has signaled its support for such proposals. In particular, critics cite Wade Horn, Assistant Secretary for Children and Families at the U.S. Department of Health and Human Services (HHS), who publicly supported a similar West Virginia proposal, and Rector's proposal that women at high risk of bearing a child out of wedlock should be given up to $5,000 if they bear their first child within marriage.[5]

Rector scoffs at the idea that Bush's marriage initiatives primarily seek to increase marriage among TANF recipients. He notes that welfare mothers have poor relationships with their children's fathers and that relationships disintegrated long ago. Rector contends, "Attempting to promote healthy relationships in these situations is a bit like attempting to glue Humpty Dumpty together after he has fallen off the wall."[6] Instead, these initiatives would target young, single adults and seek to strengthen existing marriages. Rector concluded,

> The primary focus of marriage programs would be preventative—not reparative. The programs would seek to prevent the isolation and poverty of welfare mothers by intervening at an early point before a pattern of broken relationships and welfare dependence has emerged. By fostering better life decisions and stronger relationships skills marriage programs can increase child well-being and adult happiness, and reduce child poverty and welfare dependence.[7]

Critics are also troubled by funding priorities. As Parrott complained,

> Wade Horn has honed his message to a tee arguing that poor families should have access to counseling just as higher income households do. I don't begrudge low-income couples having access to counseling and relationship services. But I don't think it is at the top of the list of the problems facing low-income families. What Wade doesn't step up to the plate on is there is a whole host of things that high-income families have access to that low-income families don't. If these marriage promotion funds had been put instead into child care, these low-income families would have benefited a lot more.

Vicki Turetsky pointed to another way that marriage promotion initiatives shifted priorities:

> By 2000 fatherhood programs had just started to be institutionalized and gain acceptability for the mission of these programs. Proponents were very optimistic that the funding spigot could be sustained. But now [2005] most of these programs have gone out of business. Part of the reason was that energy around them dissipated and foundation funding priorities changed. Most important, however, the political agenda got hijacked by marriage proposals.

Despite these concerns, many in the liberal advocacy community have some guarded optimism concerning the healthy marriage initiatives. Indeed, Urban Institute director Robert Lerman suggested, "People should get behind the marriage program and use it." He noted that because of its infancy, "HHS is really going out of its way to make the package of services allowable far richer than anyone could have anticipated, and it includes a lot of male employment-related activities."

More generally, advocacy groups support the marriage and relationship education (MRE) services provided. They point to research findings that MRE programs are generally effective in producing immediate gains in communication processes, conflict management skills, and overall relationship quality. In particular, controlled studies have found that the Prevention and Relationship Enhancement Program (PREP), one of the more successful programs, has been effective in enhancing long-term relationship satisfaction and reducing spousal physical violence.

Advocacy groups are also hopeful because so far federal funding has included efforts to adapt and expand upon the design of existing successful MRE programs to meet the needs of low-income and specific populations, such as unwed parents and particular racial and ethnic groups. Some state demonstration projects, for example, are being developed with input from the domestic violence community to address unhealthy behavior and to identify the signs of abusive relationships.

In a comprehensive review of state programs, Center for Law and Social Policy researchers Mary Parke and Theodora Ooms found that most initiatives are adopting proven programs such as PREP, so fears that these programs would be thinly disguised attempts by Christian conservatives to promote traditional patriarchal relationships are vastly overstated.[8] This concern spurred one noted critic of welfare reform, Katherine Boo, to interview women who participated in an Oklahoma program run by Pastor George Young at the Holy Temple Baptist Church. A voluntary program, it did recruit woman from low-income neighborhoods such as the Sooner Park housing project, but none of its participants was currently on cash assistance.

Young did not romanticize marriage. Boo pointed out,

> The data [presented] was bleak by design; the social scientists on whom Oklahoma relied believe that a crucial part of making and keeping a marriage is disabusing oneself of sentimental notions. Marriage is not sexual or emotional bliss between soul mates, they contend; it is a job requiring as much patience, self-sacrifice, and discipline as any other.[9]

Instead, Young focused on conflict management. Boo reported, "Pairing off for role-playing, the students learned to refrain from saying to a man who disappointed them, 'You're an oily, two-timing toad,' and to say instead, 'When you did x, in situation y, I felt z.'" Boo emphasized that "they practiced swallowing their rage, articulating their grievances specifically and respectfully, recognizing when a fight might turn violent, and listening with open minds to imaginary mates."[10]

Boo noted that the women involved enjoyed the honest, intimate conversations they engaged in during their marriage classes. They did not believe, however, that their efforts alone would translate into successful relationships. "My thing is: how do you get a man to talk about marriage when you're pretty sure he's still sleeping with his baby's mother?" a nurse's aide asked, expressing a problem so familiar at Sooner Haven that it is known by the term "baby-mama drama."

Indeed, Boo felt that these marriage promotion efforts were doomed because of the history that these women have had with men. She reported,

> All but one of the women in the room had grown up without a father in the home. At least two had been sexually abused in the first ten years of their lives. Those who had children had been left by their children's fathers. Three had been beaten by men they had loved, and two had been involved with violent criminals. In short, it required an imaginative leap to believe that a committed relationship with a man would rescue a woman from poverty.[11]

RACIAL DISPARITIES AND THE PRICE OF MARRIAGE

Boo suggests that the irresponsible male behavior she documented is the direct cause of the persistent low marriage rates among black women. In 2001, 69 percent of white children but only 27 percent of black children were currently residing with both their biological parents. Most troubling for many analysts, 63 percent of black children but only 20 percent of white children were living in households headed by a noncohabiting single parent or adults other than their biological parents. Among white single parents, only 18 percent had never been married. By contrast, 59 percent of black single parents had never been married.[12]

Much has been written attempting to explain these disparate racial histories. The most widely held explanation was developed by the sociologist William Julius Wilson. Rather than their social behavior, Wilson argued that the persistent joblessness of a large share of black men has reduced dramatically the number of black men considered by black women suitable for marriage.[13] Most recently, many of the critics of President Bush's marriage promotion initiatives have embraced Wilson's thesis to argue that providing more access for black men to stable, decent-paying jobs would be the single most important means of increasing the share of black children raised in married households.

Based on their early 1990s interviews, Kathryn Edin and Laura Lein reached a different conclusion.[14] As Edin related,

> Though many of our respondents have given up on marriage altogether, this is more because of their low view of the men they know than because they reject the institution of marriage itself. Among the low-income couples we observed, the battle

between the sexes often looks more like outright war, and many women say that they regard men simply as "children," "no good," or "low-down dirty dogs." Women tend to believe . . . that the men will not (or cannot, in some women's view) be sexually faithful.[15]

Edin did not dismiss the need to improve the employment and earnings of low-skilled (black) men. She concluded, however, that black marriage rates would remain low as long as male behavior toward women was unchanged.

While irresponsible behavior of many black men may be the proximate cause of the low marriage rate, this may be the result of their relative scarcity rather than any inherent cultural norm. Scarcity could be measured by the number of men in the noninstitutionalized population for every 100 women in the noninstitutionalized population. In 2004, among the noninstitutionalized population 20–35 years of age, there were 97 white women for every 100 white men. In the Asian and Latino communities, there were 104 and 85 women, respectively, for every 100 men. By contrast, as a result of high incarceration rates of black men, there were 119 black women for every 100 black men in the noninstitutionalized population.[16] This relative scarcity can explain both low marriage rates and the high levels of irresponsible behavior among black men.[17]

Not surprisingly, black welfare recipients realized that they must be more willing to privilege their partners. As one recipient told Edin, "There's a shortage of men so that they think, 'I can have more than one woman. I'm gonna go around this one or that one, and I'm gonna have two or three of them.' "[18] Many of these women feared that they would become their partner's personal slave, cooking his meals, cleaning his house, and doing his laundry. These women expected that their partners would feel free to spend money on personal leisure activities rather than on family necessities. As one respondent recounted, "I gave my child's father the money to go buy my son's Pampers. He went on some street with his cousin and they were down there partying, drinking, everything. He spent my son's Pamper money on partying."[19] Thus, the irresponsible behavior toward women that many black men exhibited in the 1980s may have had much more to do with structural factors, including increased incarceration, than with any intergenerational cultural norms.

EMPLOYMENT AND RELATIONSHIP STABILITY

Infidelity as a cause of relationship breakups was found in the larger, more systematic government-funded Fragile Families and Child Wellbeing Study begun in 1998. The study collected data on about 4,700 couples with a child born between 1998 and 2000. One of the first reports of the findings was by the Institute for Research on Poverty. A 2002 article looked at results from Oakland.[20] It indicated that at the time of birth of their child, 50 percent were cohabitating and another 35 percent were romantically involved, virtually the same figures as in the entire Fragile Families study.

At time of birth, one-third of all mothers believed strongly that they would marry, as did half of all fathers. White mothers were twice as likely and Hispanic mothers were 1.5 times as likely to have a strong expectation of marriage as black mothers. The authors suggested that these differences may be related to demographics: 46 percent of black mothers but only 30 percent of nonblack mothers have children with more than one partner; 20 percent of black mothers had at least two children by someone other than the father of their newborn. (In the Fragile Families study, more than half of the couples included parents who had had a child with another partner.[21])

One year later, the share of couples cohabitating remained at about 50 percent, but the share of couples not cohabitating but romantically involved shrank from 35 to 7 percent. In addition, among those cohabitating at the time of birth, despite their avowed commitment to marriage, only 7 percent had married within the next 12 months. Among the breakups of those romantically involved at the time of birth, fewer than 10 percent were due to violent abuse, alcoholism, or drug use. The dominant reasons cited were trust, fidelity, and commitment.

These patterns were also found among TLC3 parents: couples from the Fragile Family Study who were selected for more extensive interviews. While the vast majority of TLC3 romantically involved couples said there was a good or certain chance of marriage, 30 months after the child's birth, almost half of the couples had broken up. In studying these couples, Edin, Paula England, and Kathryn Linnenberg found a "pervasive theme of distrust about sexual infidelity.... Nearly four in ten mothers (39%) said they believed or feared that the father of their children had been unfaithful.... For [about half of] these mothers, these beliefs and fears were the result of actual past cheating . . . but only 13% of fathers admitted to it."[22]

Similar to Boo's mothers, TLC3 interviewees indicated that when a father had outside children, the mother's distrust of the father's relationship with the other child's mother often poisoned the relationship. More generally, Edin, England, and Linnenberg stated,

> For one-third of couples who have broken up since baseline, cheating figures in many of their stories of relational dissolution. Nevertheless, roughly one in four couples say they are still together despite an episode of cheating . . . and another quarter are together despite fears that their partner may be sexually unfaithful.[23]

These researchers, however, did not take the defeatist view that this is a hopeless situation where nothing can be done to improve relationships. Instead, they claimed that the irresponsible male behavior was a result of their low self-esteem due to their inability to sustain stable decent-paying employment. This viewpoint comes out most clearly in a series of interviews Edin conducted with noncustodial fathers Virtually all of the men who chose to take part in her study evinced fatherly rhetoric. In a section titled "I Can't Imagine Life without My Children," the research team highlighted one man's transformation:

> Before I became a father I didn't really see no future. . . . I had no concept of what the future was even to bring or what the future was about. But after he was born, my first son, I began to look . . . and say, "Well, I want more out of life because there are more things that I want to do for him as well as myself."[24]

And the research team emphasized how fatherhood gave meaning to life: "Once you have children, then you got to live for them. It ain't just about you no more, it's about them." In a telling statement, the research team noted, "Regardless of the actual level of involvement with their children (and many of the men in the sample had only sporadic involvement), the symbolic meaning of fatherhood resonated."[25]

Why didn't the men have more contact with their children? According to the researchers,

> The level of involvement with their children was profoundly affected by the father's relationship with the child's mother. For fathers who were still romantically involved with the mother, their involvement was quite high. Once separated from the mother, however, ongoing involvement dwindled. Issues of control and authority over the child's upbringing, the ability to provide financially for the child, imprisonment, drug and alcohol addiction, and the relationship with the children's maternal grandmother all influenced contact and involvement.[26]

Most important, according to these researchers, "When fathers could not provide for their children, mothers were often less supportive of their contact with the children, and fathers often separated themselves from the families out of shame and a sense of degradation."[27]

Notice that these researchers ignored any personal responsibility on the part of the fathers, though this was emphasized by *mothers* in the earlier interviews done by Edin and Lein.[28] Instead, the emphasis in the most recent interviews with *fathers* is on the economic system for not providing these "caring" men with access to decent, steady employment. Avoiding holding fathers responsible for their lack of support comes out most clearly in the discussion of why they are largely absent in their children's lives. The research team concluded,

> Children did a lot for the fathers in these studies. However, fathers sometimes did very little for their children in return, particularly as the children aged. . . . They were often ashamed of their inability to contribute more and, consequently, they

decided to withdraw from their children's lives. . . . The qualitative data in the papers reported here offer insight into how low-income African American fathers construct their parental role and strive to fulfill the duties that they associate with such a role in the face of tremendous barriers.[29]

David Pate presented an even more sympathetic view of noncustodial fathers from his interviews in Milwaukee during the late 1990s. Just more than 60 percent of the men interviewed had fathered children by more than one partner. Pate found that "all but two have had contact with at least one of their kids in the last three months," and he defined regular relationships as seeing at least one of their kids in the last month. Even for the seven fathers who did not meet this very generous threshold, Pate did not believe it was their fault: some had children older than 18 who no longer lived with them, and others had poor and hostile relations with the mothers of their children. To highlight the victimization of these men, Pate told the (unconfirmed) story of one man who

> dreamed of being a truck driver but the dream was destroyed when he came to police attention as a result of an accident in which he was found to be driving with only a permit. Over the years, he was not able to attend to the traffic violation and accumulated substantial financial penalties that he could not pay. He had recently put out ten job applications, for "any kind" of a job but received no calls. So mostly he sells marijuana.[30]

There is no question that many young black men cannot overcome youthful indiscretions. Spotty employment records and limited schooling are often sufficient for employers to reject black applicants. As documented in chapter 3—the Pager study in Milwaukee—it has become very difficult for young black men with a criminal record to gain entry-level employment. This is particularly troublesome because for every eight black men 20–39 years old in the noninstitutionalized population, there is another black man in jail or prison.[31]

Not only would solving these employment difficulties benefit these men, but also there is evidence that it would improve relationship stability. In a Baltimore study, 135 black mothers were interviewed, all of whom were younger than 25 at the time of their child's birth. Just as the national data indicated, many fathers had little ongoing contact with their children. Half of fathers were virtually uninvolved at the time of birth, and the percentage was the same three years later. This study did find, however, that the employment of fathers had a significant impact: "Employed fathers were nearly seven times as likely as unemployed fathers to have moved from low to high involvement or to have always been highly involved."[32]

Based on his ongoing research, Lerman is particularly sanguine in his assessment of the relationship between employment and marriage. In my interview, he stressed, "Having stable employment increases the number of marriages and reduces the number of divorces. In addition, being marriage has a settling effect on men, increasing their employment stability."

MARRIAGE VERSUS COHABITATION

National data verify the uphill battle faced by those who seek to increase marriage rates, especially within the black community. Between 1997 and 2002, there was little change in the black marriage rate, though it did increase for Hispanics and whites. Blacks did move a bit toward cohabitating, but given how few black mothers maintained relationships with biological fathers, it didn't amount to much.[33]

Given the persistence of low marriage rates, some researchers have argued that a single-minded emphasis on promoting marriage has little to gain. "Current proposals to promote marriage," suggested Urban Institute researchers Laura Wherry and Kenneth Finegold, "may be too narrow to benefit most low-income black children, the group of children least likely to be living with two married parents."[34] Instead, many researchers believe that initiatives should be developed to strengthen the stability of cohabitating relationships by focusing on male employment issues and interpersonal skills.

Horn has been most outspoken against this perspective. He stated, "Congress should make clear that the intent of the 1996 law was to promote marriage, not cohabitation or visits by nonresident parents. When it comes to improving the well-being of children, neither cohabitation nor visitation is the equivalent of marriage." With Isabel Sawhill, Horn noted the reluctance of Fragile Family researchers to focus on marriage and instead sought to simply strengthening existing relationships. However, Sawhill and Horn claimed, "There is little empirical evidence to support the idea that it is possible to keep fragile families together absent marriage."[35] To the contrary, they cited research that as many as three-fourths of children born to cohabitating parents will see their parents split up before they reach age 16, compared to only one-third for married parents. And this research finds that once fathers cease to cohabitate, they become disconnected. Sawhill and Horn reported that in one study, 40 percent of children with nonresident fathers have not seen their father in more than a year. Of the remaining 60 percent, only one in five sleeps even one night a month in the father's home.

While employment seemed to strengthen cohabitation somewhat, these Fragile Families interviews gave little support to those who stress providing fathers with stable, decent jobs would *substantially* increase marriage rates. Most cohabitating couples did not view a job for the man "as sufficient for marriage, even if it was stable and above the legal minimum" and "were often eager to list a long set of criteria that had to be met before a marriage should occur."[36] As another Institute for Poverty Research report stated,

Couples seem to be demanding that their expectations be met *before* they marry, rather than seeing them as common goals toward which the couple will work after they marry. TLC3 parents in particular expressed unusually high expectations about the level of financial security (living standards) they would need to achieve before they marry.[37]

Summing up this situation, Edin, England, and Linnenberg concluded, "Clearly, in the moral hierarchy these couples have adopted, it is better to have children together and not marry than to get married and then divorce."[38]

Finally, some marriage promotion supporters emphasize its potential anti-poverty effects. Data indicate that married couples are generally much better off than cohabiting couples. For example, children of cohabiting couples have almost three times the poverty rate as children of married couples. Whereas half of children of cohabiting couples suffer food insecurity, this is true of only one-fifth of children of married couples.[39] Evidence also suggests that cohabiting relationships tend to be more violent than marriages.[40]

These figures, however, tell us little about what would happen if *currently* cohabiting couples married, for they differ in important ways from current married couples. Cohabiting couples tend to be younger and have less schooling and predictably lower levels of employment and earnings than married couples. We must therefore disentangle the reasons that married couples on average have better outcomes for children than do cohabiting couples. Urban Institute researchers Gregory Acs and Sandi Nelson found that differences in these personal characteristics explained 70 percent of the differences in poverty and food insecurity rates. Thus, if all cohabiting couples married, the poverty would still be twice that of other married couples, and 40 percent would still suffer from food insecurity.[41]

While marriage does not dramatically reduce poverty or food insecurity, Ron Haskins and Sawhill contend that marriage promotion still has a potentially greater antipoverty effect than many other policies. In particular, they claim, "While education is commonly cited as a prime source of poverty, it . . . is less important than . . . marriage."[42] They estimated that if all single mothers had a high school degree and earned as much, the poverty rate for female-headed families with children would drop by two percentage points. By contrast, Haskins and Sawhill estimated that if the marriage rate was increased—after adjusting for the earnings and availability of men—the poverty rate would be reduced by 3.6 percentage points.

CHILD SUPPORT ENFORCEMENT

Better policies can strengthen relationships and increase the number of two-parent households among the working poor and near poor. In the best of circumstances, however, there still will be a large number of unattached single mothers. For this reason, many analysts have focused attention on increasing child support payments from nonresident fathers.

In 1994, only 18 percent of families in the child support program received any child support. This was the result of inadequate funding for caseworkers and a lack of state priorities. As a result, in most states, fathers had to simply change jobs or cross county lines to avoid payment. When members of the Clinton administration argued that federal and state policies should place higher priorities on child support enforcement, there was little support from many of the liberal advocacy groups. The main criticism was that absent fathers of children on welfare had such unstable and limited incomes that child support orders would generate little additional revenue and put many mothers in physical danger by needlessly creating more antagonistic relationships. Still others claimed that a focus on child support enforcement was a form of "blaming the victim"—these fathers were victims of a racist system that denied them decent jobs. Therefore, it was the government, not the fathers, who should be responsible for providing financial support to their families.

Despite this resistance, changes in state policies and federal welfare reform led to more aggressive approaches to child support enforcement. As a condition for receiving cash payments, states began to require mothers to name the fathers of their children and cooperate with efforts to obtain child support from these men. As a result, paternity establishment rates more than tripled.[43]

Child support enforcement got a further boost from the 1996 welfare legislation. The Internal Revenue Service was required to intercept tax refunds, and state governments could garnish wages in order to pay for child support orders. In addition, states could suspend drivers' licenses and licenses for recreational activities, including hunting, if court child support orders were not being fulfilled. Just as important, the federal government more substantially underwrote the hiring of caseworkers and also provided financial incentives to states that increased their collection rates.

By 2004, the collection rate had risen to 51 percent among mothers seeking support. Once a court order had been issued, the rate rose to 69 percent. Whereas court orders represented 30–40 percent of welfare caseloads in 1995–1996, it rose to 70 percent by 2001. And once an order was in place, payments were usually steady. In 2004, the total state administrative costs of child support enforcement was $5.4 billion, three-quarters of which is paid for by the federal government. In return, collection totaled $21.9 billion.[44]

Researchers have quantified the link between child support enforcement and the payments received. For each addition $100 a state spends on enforcement, mothers can expect to receive, on average, an additional $4 in child support payments. The increase in child support payments provides an impetus for some mothers to leave welfare, with many obtaining paid employment. As a result, for each additional dollar of child support received, family incomes increase by $1.89 after taking into account these labor market effects.[45]

Because the caseload reductions are so substantial, it is estimated that welfare cash payments are reduced by more than the administrative costs of additional child support enforcement. That is, for each additional federal dollar spent on enforcement, federal welfare expenditures would be reduced by more than one dollar as higher collection induces some mothers to leave the cash payment system.[46] These income increases have reduced the number of children living in poverty by between one-half million and one million.[47] Thus, there seems to be substantial financial benefits to both the federal government and mothers from expenditures that strengthen child support enforcement.

These figures reflect the overall impact of child support enforcement, outcomes that are not necessarily representative of its impact on the poorest mothers. Despite the prediction of critics, child support enforcement was financially beneficial to women living in poverty. Between 1996 and 2001, the share of single mothers with incomes below the poverty line receiving child support rose from 35 to 40 percent. Among those mothers with court orders, 66 percent received some payment in 2001. Not only did the share receiving payments increase, so too did the size of these payments, from $2,280 to $2,550 after adjusting for inflation. In 2001, the $2,550 child support payment represents 30 percent of the total income of poor mothers, up from 27 percent in 1996.[41] Realizing the benefits gained, 78 percent of former TANF mothers indicated that child support payments made a "very big difference" in their lives.[49]

Studies also indicate societal benefits beyond financial gains. According to economist Irwin Garfinkel and associates, "There is also an emerging body of research that finds that stringent support enforcement reduces marital disruptions and out-of-wedlock childbearing."[50] In particular, researchers found that the reduction in nonmarital births was strongest within the black community, especially among women at least 20 years old.[51] In these communities, adolescent males who were aware of paternity establishment modified their sexual behavior, especially if their peers were doing so. Thus, policies aimed at making unmarried fatherhood more costly had the effect of not only preventing nonmarital births but also benefiting children who are already born.

Evidence does find that increased violence is a potential downside of stricter child support enforcement. In the Fragile Families study, mothers with nonresident fathers were interviewed 12–18 months after the birth of their child. More than 40 percent of these absent fathers had spent some time in jail. These interviews indicate that the incidence of violence did rise when child support enforcement increased.[52] Increases, however, were only among mothers who did not have a child support court order. This suggests that there are threats and intimidation *prior* to obtaining court orders, and thus the risk may be temporary and decrease once orders are issued. In addition, the mothers that did not seek court orders may have former partners who are particularly violence prone, making these threats even more likely.

This fear of abuse limits the willingness of mothers to seek child support orders. In a Massachusetts study, 28 percent of mothers who were recent victims of abuse said that they did not want to pursue child support. Thus, caseworkers must demonstrate some flexibility to limit the future violence that a significant share of TANF mothers could experience if child support enforcement is initiated.[53]

PUBLIC POLICY APPROACHES

As discussed in this chapter, there are two distinct approaches to improving the situation for mothers and their children: improving child support enforcement policies and improving the employment and earnings of fathers. Focusing on the first approach, the Center for Law and Social Policy has stressed proposals to increase the pass-through formula to enable mothers to receive a larger share of the child support payments made by fathers. The 1996 legislation gave the states the right to keep all payments they collected from nonresident fathers through Internal Revenue Service tax refund interceptions. These confiscated funds could be used to defray the cash payments provided to current recipients or even to pay back previous cash payments received by former recipients. In 2001, 50 percent of all funds collected for current welfare recipients but only 14 percent of funds collected for former recipients went to the government. Before reauthorization, few states had a pass-through of more than $50 monthly for current TANF recipients. To some extent, this created an incentive for absent fathers to pay voluntarily and for mothers to leave TANF.

Those who advocated a greater pass-through point to the results of a Wisconsin experiment. Wisconsin divided fathers into two groups. In the experimental group, child support payments were completely passed through to mothers, while in the control group, only $50 was passed through monthly. The study found that the collection rate was 10 percentage points higher for the fathers in the experimental group than those in the control group. The study also found that the experimental group fathers had decreased parental conflict and increased contact with their children compared to fathers in the control group.[54]

These results are consistent with the attitude of the Milwaukee men that Pate interviewed. He concluded,

> They would have been willing to engage in the child support system if they could have been assured that their engagement would have a direct and positive impact on their children's lives. In the absence of such assurance, the fathers and their families tried to negotiate their lives outside the formal legal and administrative structures of government.[55]

Based on the results, Wisconsin decided to pass through all cash payments to mothers.[56]

Other advocacy groups, including the Urban Institute, have stressed reforms that would be more sensitive to the plight of poor nonresident fathers. Minimally, these advocates argue that further increasing enforcement levels would be unproductive. Given the levels of payments currently received from poor nonresident fathers, they doubt that further enforcement would yield much additional revenue. If all court orders were fulfilled, they estimated that the typical poor mother would receive no more than an additional $100 monthly.[57]

These advocates look more closely at the 2.5 million poor nonresident fathers who make no child support payments. Forty-one percent of these men are black, 40 percent white, and 14 percent Latino.[58] For these men, child support requirements are often unrealistic. For example, among one-quarter of poor fathers who pay support, payments comprise more than half of their incomes.

One reason for these unrealistic burdens is the dynamics that occur when fathers do not show up for child support hearings and default orders are issued. In California, regardless of the father's circumstances, default orders are set at $423 monthly. If the father had appeared, however, and had a net disposable income of $1,000 monthly, he would have had to pay child support of at most $250 monthly.[59]

These advocates recommend that states adopt more realistic child support schedules. As a model, they cite recent changes in Colorado. The new schedule there doubled the share of support orders for $150 or less, which led to a 31 percent increase in the actual payments by this group. They also advocate some forgiveness for support arrears. For example, instead of retroactively determining past child support arrears back to the child's birth, court orders should go back no more than four years. In addition, Medicaid should not be suspended for nonresident fathers if they have arrears as long as they are making current payments. Advocates also recommend that food stamps be available to absent fathers on the same basis as they are to custodial mothers if the men are meeting their child support requirements.[60]

Many advocacy groups stress that more funds should be allocated to these men for improved employment. While nonresidential fathers are eligible for welfare-to-work programs, the criteria have been so restrictive that these men fill only 10 percent of these slots, though administrators had set a goal of 20 percent.[61] Some groups suggest that child support administrative funding should be used to provide job training and job placement to absent fathers. In particular, they advocate that some of the $454 million incentive funds states annually receive for meeting federal collection goals could be used, and cite three states that are already doing so, including Missouri, where unemployed delinquent fathers are required to enroll in a 30-hour weekly program that includes job readiness, job search, and career assessment components.[62]

Interestingly, the views of these advocates seem to reflect the views of HHS director Horn. With Sawhill, he has argued,

> Too strong a focus on child support enforcement may lead these already marginally employed men to drop out of the paid labor force in favor of participation in the underground economy and make it even more difficult for them to be involved fathers. Moreover, an exclusive focus on child support enforcement ignores the many noneconomic contributions that fathers make to the well-being of their children. If we want fathers to be more than cash machines for their children, we need public policies that support their work as nurturers, disciplinarians, mentors, moral instructors, and skill coaches, not just economic providers.[63]

They strongly support father support initiatives, including the Parents' Fair Share program. This program was designed to help noncustodial fathers of children on welfare who owe child support to (1) find more stable and better paying jobs, (2) pay child support more consistently, and (3) assume a fuller and more responsible fathering role.

CONCLUDING REMARKS

This chapter focuses on the issues surrounding recent initiatives to increase marriage rates, especially within the black community. While fears that these marriage initiatives would force poor women into unhealthy marriages appear to be unwarranted, it is doubtful that these initiatives would do much to increase black marriage rates. Research seems to indicate that, compared to that of the white community, black marriage rates are low primarily because of the irresponsible behavior of a large portion of black men and an unrealistic perception of the conditions that must be met before there is a willingness to marry.

There are a number of explanations for this irresponsible behavior. My own work suggests that one reason is the relative scarcity of black men, an indirect outcome of the decision to arrest a large proportion of young black men for non-violent crimes related to illegal drug sales. Their scarcity forces young black women who desire social companionship to accommodate to the irresponsible behavior of the available black men.

Other researchers link the irresponsible behavior to the lack of self-esteem of many black men created by their inability to obtain stable, decent-paying employment. Whether or not employment will induce more responsible behavior, it does seem to strengthen the stability of the parental relationship, especially among cohabiting couples. And given how unlikely marriage appears, many advocates suggest that a focus on improving the employment and incomes of black men might be the most effective policy to build two-parent households. Thus, they advocate "marriage plus" policies rather than a single-minded focus on increasing marriage rates.

My own assessment is that initiatives should focus more on the benefits of marriage than on simply strengthening existing relationships. This is especially the case where the reluctance to marry is at least partially due to an unrealistic assessment of marriage requirements. While it is upsetting that many of the conservative proponents of marriage do not extend this approach to gay and lesbian couples, this should not cloud our judgment.

10

TANF Reauthorization

Where Do We Go from Here?

After four years of heated debate, reauthorization of the Temporary
Assistance for Needy Families (TANF) program was accomplished
as part of the 2005 budget reconciliation bill. In some ways, the final
bill was harsher than the earlier House proposals that were rejected by
Democrats and some Senate Republicans, causing the prolonged legislative stalemate. Some work requirements were increased beyond
previous proposals, and these provisions increased the likelihood that
support services for welfare leavers and the working near-poor would be
slashed. This gloomy assessment suggests that the "Making Work Pay"
approach has been undermined. Indeed, reform critics would argue
that this outcome was the inevitable consequence of President Bill
Clinton's capitulation to reactionary forces.

The TANF reauthorization outcome certainly weakens the prospects
for single mothers and their families. It should not, however, cause a
reassessment of the basic make-work-pay strategy—a strategy that
should continue to provide a foundation to move families forward. This
hopeful perspective reflects an evaluation of the reauthorization process and the policies that can further improve the lives of working
women.

THE TANF REAUTHORIZATION OUTCOME

Some liberal policy advocates continue to believe that their strategy
at the beginning of the reauthorization debate was appropriate. Explaining

his organization's refusal to support the initial deal offered by the George W. Bush administration (through Ron Haskins), Mark Greenberg, a policy analyst for the Center for Law and Social Policy, pointed to the seemingly broad bi-partisan support for welfare-to-work support policies. He explained, "There was expectation that there would be more effort to expand supports for the working poor and to focus on poverty reduction." At the time, there was virtually no discussion of participation rates in work-related activities, so there was no reason to assume that if a deal was not struck then, there would be such adverse con-sequences. "There was a paradigm shift overnight," he lamented.[1]

By contrast, Urban Institute policy analyst Robert Lerman was surprised that reauthorization had to be done through the reconciliation process. The Bush administration had made clear from the beginning that it was prepared for level TANF funding and some additional funds for child care. Rejection of the Bush proposal was unexpected given that in 2001 Lerman remembered "a senior Senate Democrat staffer indicating that if the Bush administration would maintain the current funding level, a deal could be made." For Lerman, "This was another example of advocates miscalculating that if they just delayed, they could get a better deal later."

Economic Policy Institute analyst Max Sawicky was more philosophical about the reluctance of the advocacy community to accept the Bush administration offer. He explained,

> In difficult times, it is hard to judge what direction to take politically. Some favor narrow, marginal legislative initiatives that have a chance of gaining a few more benefits while others favor more comprehensive, structural changes that provide a vision of where we have to go. One unfortunate problem is we can "go too far in either direction."

After the 2002 election, the House bill proposed to increase work-related requirements substantially: from 24 to 30 hours per week for single mothers with children younger than six years, and from 30 for 40 hours per week for other single mothers. The final legislation, however, left unchanged the requirements for single mothers, raising it only for the small number of two-parent families receiving cash assistance.

Similarly, the actual legislation left largely in tact the kinds of activities that could be counted, whereas the proposed legislation threatened to make them much more restrictive. In particular, the ability of those mothers receiving cash assis-tance to enroll in vocational and community college programs changed very little. While this did not please advocates who hoped for a substantial expansion of access, it abandoned more restrictive proposals that were present in earlier leg-islative proposals.

The one fundamental change was the share of those on cash assistance who must be in work-related programs. Over the first decade, TANF required that

50 percent of those on cash assistance be enrolled in work-related activities. It allowed states, however, to count the decline in welfare caseloads since 1995 in assessing their work participation rate. As a result, if a state had a 40 percent caseload decline, to meet federal guidelines it only needed to have 10 percent of its current caseload in approved work-related activities. If a state had a 50 percent or more drop in its welfare caseload, it automatically fulfilled the federal requirement.

This policy allowed most states to have full discretion as to the share of its caseload in work-related activities. As a result, in 2005 states had, on average, 32.4 percent of their eligible caseload in these activities.[2] TANF reauthorization kept the 50 percent rule for single mothers but changed the base year from 1995 to 2005. Thus, states could no longer rely on the dramatic decline in welfare caseloads over the last decade to satisfy their federal requirements.

With the substantial leveling off of welfare caseloads in the last few years, there is little reason to believe that caseloads can fall more than 10 percent from their 2005 levels in the future. Even if a state had such a decline, it still must have 40 percent of its caseload in work-related activities, a substantial increase over the current work participation rate for most states.

The Congressional Budget Office (CBO) estimated that the new work participation rate formula will have a substantial cost impact: more than $8.4 billion over the five-year period 2007–2012. This reflects the staffing and other direct costs of setting up and maintaining these additional activities. The fear is that in order to meet these new expenditure requirements, states would undertake harmful strategies. The CBO expects "that states are more likely to meet the requirements by applying a combination of approaches including . . . imposing tighter up front requirements and adopting stricter sanctioning policies."[3] There seemed to be a trend in this direction before reauthorization, so there is a reasonable likelihood that it will be accelerated as states face these additional costs and work participation requirements. States could also meet these additional costs by shifting funds away from work supports, making it more difficult for welfare leavers to sustain employment.

The CBO projects that a number of states will be penalized for not meeting the new work participation rate requirements. This projection was crucial since it enabled the legislation to get around the "Byrd Rule," a requirement that policy changes can be included in reconciliation bills only if they have a budgetary impact. Sharon Parrott suggests, "Thus, these provisions may have been designed not as good policy, but to secure a budget impact 'score' from the CBO."[4]

We should keep in mind that the penalty for falling short of the 50 percent participation requirement is quite moderate. The maximum penalty is 5 percent of the state's federal allotment. The penalty, however, is reduced substantially as long as the state is moving toward the requirement. For example, suppose a state currently has a 25 percent work participation rate and a 5 percent caseload reduction since 2005. If its work participation rate increased to 30 percent, two-thirds of the penalty would be eliminated.[5] Thus, the full work participation requirement must be met only after a number of years of gradual increases.

Sawicky was not overly alarmed by the new requirements. "While some of the formal requirements in reauthorization seem especially onerous, there is a difference between the requirements in federal laws and enforcement by states," he noted.

> Federal oversight is not a particularly sexy enterprise so that lawmakers often have little appetite to provide the necessary funds to make it even modestly effective. States have the resources to get out from under things they don't like, and Washington has few resources to counter these efforts.

Haskins agreed with Sawicky that states have substantial latitude and can circumvent rules that they don't like. However, he cautioned, "It might not be as easy since reauthorization gave additional enforcement powers to [the Department of Health and Human Services], including the ability to dictate what numbers states must produce."

One response a number of states are considering is to adopt "up-front" programs for TANF applicants. Rather than all eligible applicants immediately enrolling in the TANF program, those not deemed ready for work-related activities would enroll in a state program for a short period of time where they would receive cash payments and support services. As Lisa Schott explains,

> An up-front precursor program can be designed to assess families' circumstances, develop an appropriate employment plan, help families in securing child care, engage parents in work activities, and help job-ready parents find jobs quickly. By engaging in these "up front," a state can increase the likelihood that families will be engaged in work activities when or soon after they enter the ongoing TANF/MOE cash assistance caseload.[6]

Schott highlights two states that have already implemented these kinds of programs: Minnesota's Diversionary Work Program and Pennsylvania's Work Support Component.[7]

A second response reflects changes in rules governing transitional jobs (TJ) programs. These programs serve as a bridge to unsubsidized employment since they combine subsidized employment with services in order to help participants overcome personal barriers to steady employment by building work-related skills. Before TANF reauthorization, all hours in TJ programs counted as work-related activities. According to the new guidelines, however, a state can only count hours spent in education, training, barrier removal activities, job search, and job readiness activities as subsidized employment when those hours are paid.

Some advocates have recommended that states try to fund as much as possible to these skill-building areas rather than to on-site employment subsidies when states are unable to fund all activities. In addition, they suggest that states count education and training activities as either vocational education training or job skill training directly related to employment. In particular, Abby Frank recommends,

> If the participants work at least 20 hours a week, states should report any training activities as job skills training (a non-core activity) rather than using up the 12 months individual lifetime limit on time that participation in vocational educational training may be counted toward participation rates. Barrier removal activities may also be counted as job search and job readiness assistance, subject to the time limits on counting of such activities.[8]

The most dramatic change affected two-parent families. For this group, the required participation rate increased from 50 to 90 percent, and there was also an increase in weekly work requirement. No one seems to believe that this is remotely feasible, and Haskins was quite confident that it would be corrected before implementation. After all, these families represented less than 0.2 percent of the TANF caseload. Haskins envisioned that there will be a "bipartisan move to 'suspend the rules,' and it will be done in the middle of the night" without the need for a formal roll-call vote.

The CBO also estimated that in order to meet the child care needs of all families in work-related activities over the five-year period, as well as the needs of nonwelfare families currently enrolled, an additional $12 billion of funding would be required. The TANF reauthorization legislation, however, allocated only an additional $1 billion for additional child care expenditures. As a result, the CBO estimated that there would be 255,000 fewer children from low-income working families receiving child care assistance in 2010 compared to 2004. Accounting for all children served, the Center on Budget and Policy Priorities estimated that there will be 645,000 fewer children served in 2011 than a decade earlier—a 25-percent decline.[9]

This has come at a time when states have also been restricting child care access. In 2004, government child care spending nationally fell for the first time since the passage of welfare reform in 1996. Thirty states cut spending on child care assistance in 2004. To ration these diminished child care slots, the majority of states made their income eligibility criteria more restrictive.[10] In addition, an increase the share of recipients in work-related activities will put even more pressure on states to reduce the number of nonrecipients receiving child care subsidies. While somewhat smaller, there were further child care funding cutbacks so that, in 2005, federal and state child care funding was down to $11.7 billion from its peak at $12.3 billion in 2003.[11]

Reauthorization also made some important changes in child support enforcement policies. It held constant the matching rate: for each one dollar of state funds allocated, the federal government has two dollars of matching funds. There was, however, one crucial change: states receive federal incentive funds for good performance in five areas—establishing paternity, establishing support orders, collecting current support, collecting arrears, and cost-effectiveness. These incentive funds were considered state money, so they were able to qualify for federal matching funds. Under the reauthorization bill, these incentive funds no longer qualify for matching funds. Thus, unless the state puts up more of its own funds, there will be a substantial cutback in federal funding of child support policies.

The CBO estimates that even if states made up one-half of the losses, the total federal funds for child support enforcement would decline by $4.9 billion over the next 10 years. These cuts were estimated to cost families at least $8.4 billion in uncollected child support. Most troubling for some, the CBO estimated that 90 percent of the child support that would go uncollected because of the cuts in funding would have gone to families not receiving TANF income assistance.[12] Thus, as with child care funding shortfalls, the harm done is likely to be felt most by the working poor and near poor.

TANF reauthorization did, however, legislate that more of the funds collected would go to mothers and their families. It limits how much support funds states can keep and how much they must share with the federal government. In particular, if a state chooses to pass along collected support to TANF families, the federal share is waived, up to $100 monthly for one child and $200 monthly for two or more children. It also strengthened collection from fathers who have moved out of state and the ability to use passport denial as a means of forcing payments.

Finally, as part of the Deficit Reduction Act of 2005, $750 million was allocated over the next five years for marriage promotion, with up to one-third of the funds capable of being spent on fatherhood programs. "One surprise was that initially the marriage proposals were quite controversial with some advocacy groups," Lerman noted, "But by the time it was legislated, there was little conflict or bitterness."

Lerman was particularly hopeful that a substantial portion of the funds would be used to improve employment of young black men with limited schooling. He pointed out, "The gap between men and women is growing among the less educated, and especially within the black population. Black women are seeing a lot more success than black men."

POLICIES TO MOVE FORWARD

Initially, TANF reauthorization led me to be quite pessimistic. Conservative Republicans had successfully defeated virtually all federal efforts to aid welfare leavers and other working families. Not surprisingly, limited legislative opportunities at the federal level had led many progressives to focus on state-level initiatives. I initially believed that these state efforts would weaken pressure on future effects to enact federal legislation.

For example, since 1996 there has been no legislation to increase the minimum wage. In response, labor coalitions led successful campaigns to enact state minimum wages increases in 14 states. I feared that congressional representatives from these states would no longer have as strong an incentive to pass federal minimum wage legislation, further weakening its likelihood. Similarly, state child care and educational initiatives could weaken the movement for national legislative initiatives in these areas.

My fears led me to underestimate the importance of these state initiatives. These initiatives have been substantial and have benefited many working families. They have also built organizational coalitions that can be quite effective in pressuring congressional representatives to pursue national legislation. It is the power of these grassroots organizations—energized by their state victories—that will overcome any congressional complacency.

State waivers after 1993 were crucial to the success of national welfare legislation. They provided evidence of which welfare-to-work policies were effective and which were not. Similarly, the success of state educational and child care initiatives will provide evidence that might be crucial to the success of future federal legislation. With this more positive outlook, let me focus on the four policy areas that can provide benefits for working families: government tax and labor policies, educational enhancements, work supports, and healthy relationship initiatives.

The most important federal labor policy cited is the goal of tight labor markets. In particular, very low unemployment rates were crucial for the integration of young black men and women into the mainstream of the labor market and for fostering robust wage growth for those at the lowest rung of the economic ladder. Unfortunately, there has been a tendency among policy makers to be dismissive of the ability of the economy to function effectively with national unemployment rates at 4 percent or lower.

Sadly, I believe that this is one area in which advocacy groups have been negligent. Some advocacy groups continue to minimize the positive impact of the Clinton-era economic boom on the economic well-being of low-wage workers. In addition, they are reluctant to admit the importance of labor demand and supply factors in determining wages in low-wage labor markets. Instead, they focus on the importance of government or union policies in determining wages: living and minimum wage policies and unionization efforts.

Most recently, these advocates have ignored the potential adverse impact of immigration on the wages of native-born less educated workers. In particular, they often minimize and marginalize evidence that immigration has adversely affected both the employment and wage rate of young black men with no more than a high school degree, and ignore the burden that immigration places on urban schools.[13] Instead, most immigration advocates suggest that if the black and immigrant communities unite, they both can benefit. Once again, political power rather than supply and demand are thought to determine wages and employment.

A second important federal policy would be an increase in the national minimum wage. In 2006, six state referendums to raise the minimum wage were passed. The success of these state initiatives raised the Democratic Party's commitment to raise the federal hourly minimum wage from $5.15 to $7.25. In addition, the widespread implementation of higher state rates over the last number of years has provided evidence that minimum wage hikes have virtually no adverse effects on businesses. For example, comparing businesses in Idaho, which has the lowest minimum wage in the nation, and Washington, which has the highest, provides a real-life laboratory. Many Idaho residents living near the border with Washington seek jobs there, creating problems for Idaho businesses seeking new employees; they have been forced to offer more than minimum wage to attract new workers. Indeed, small-business owners in Washington say they have prospered while counterparts in neighboring Idaho have not.[14]

This minimum-wage increase would disproportionately benefit younger workers: 30 percent of teenagers and more than 8 percent of workers 20–24 years old. It would also immediately benefit 16 percent of workers with less than a high school diploma and about 6 percent of black and Latino workers. Thus, a minimum wage increase would benefit many lower income working families, helping them distance themselves from poverty and material hardships.[15]

In addition, the minimum wage increase will dramatically affect the share of worker living in poverty. In 2006, a single mother with two children working 2000 hours had a net income of $18,948 after including the federal EITC, child credit, food stamps, and tax liabilities. With the new minimum wage, however, her income will be $23,115 once the full increase to $7.25 is implemented by 2009.[16] (In addition, state income transfers, including the EITC and refundable dependent care credits, add to this total.)

The struggle over a minimum wage increase illustrates an important political lesson. Whenever legislation to raise the minimum wage has come up for a congressional vote, it has overwhelmingly passed. Few politicians wish to defend a vote against raising the minimum wage. The consistent problem that advocates face, then, is getting the legislation through committees so that there can be a congressional vote. In recent years, this legislation has been locked up because of Republican control of the relevant committees.

In addition, the majority party also has control of whom to select for reconciliation committees when Senate and House bills differ. The pattern during the first six years of the Bush administration has been that when a Senate bill has much more generous provisions than the House bill, the leadership make sure that "independent" Republicans are not on the reconciliation committees so that the final bill looks much more like the House than the Senate bill. Often it becomes difficult to vote against the reconciliation bill since it would mean that legislation would be effectively killed.

This illustrates an important issue when considering the role of independent, sometimes progressive Republican members of Congress. These "independents" often cite the instances when they break with the Republican majority on congressional votes. What is almost always ignored, however, is how their numbers enable the Republican Party to have majorities on congressional committees. To take one example, Republican congressman Christopher Shays of Connecticut has a long history of splitting with the Republican majority when legislation is voted on. He no doubt would support an increased minimum wage if it came up for a vote. Shays is not, however, on the House Labor Committee, so Republican members, by voting together, continue to stifle minimum wage legislation. If instead, "independent" Republicans were replaced by Democrats, it might not change their individual votes on pending legislation. It would, however, change the legislation that would come up for congressional votes by enabling Democrats to have a majority on legislative and reconciliation committees. This is exactly why the Democratic victory in the 2006 elections enabled minimum wage legislation to be passed by both House and Senate by early February 2007.

The final piece of federal labor legislation that will aid working families is a reduction of the high implicit tax rate they face. At lower incomes, these families receive substantial means-tested supports: food stamps, child care and housing subsidies, and the earned income tax credit. Unfortunately, when their wage income rises into the $15,000 to $25,000 income range, these families receive reduced subsidies and transfer payments from these programs. As a result, their disposable income does not rise nearly as much as their gross pay does. Unless this problem is moderated substantially, many single mothers will be trapped in near poverty despite their work efforts that enable them to gain modest wage increases.

One way to moderate this problem described in chapter 7 is the Simplified Family Credit, which would reduce substantially the phasing out of credits families would receive as their wage income rises. This would extend program benefits to a much larger group of working families, families that have historically been ignored by public policies because they had too much income to benefit from means-tested programs and too little income to take advantage of many of the tax breaks available to wealthier households. Of course, there are alternative proposals, some calling for more comprehensive changes in the tax system, but they all require a slower phasing out so that these benefits would be extended to a larger section of working families.[17]

The second area that must move forward is expanding the education enhancements provided to working families. Haskins does not believe that the federal government has been primarily responsible for the limited use of educational programs. He noted that no state is even close to a federal cap on the share of its recipients in educational programs.

Haskins believes that we still don't have a very good idea of how to improve the lot of the vast majority of young people who have ended their education prematurely. He contends that the work-first approach was adopted by default because federal programs have had "so little success except for mandatory work." For this reason, he is hopeful that as data from the community colleges show consistent evidence of improving the earnings, the federal government would be willing to make a bigger investment.

Haskins is correct that states have the ability to expand dramatically the share of recipients in educational activities. Whereas federal regulations would allow 15 percent of recipients to be in educational activities, nationally only about 5 percent of recipients are in those programs. However, I do not agree with Haskins's contention that this low utilization rate is due to a dearth of evidence on how to run successful programs. Over the last decade, many community colleges have developed effective programs that can be replicated elsewhere.

I continue to be impressed with the efforts of community colleges to develop programs that serving populations that have limited basic educational skills and substantial constraints on their time. In February 2006, I visited one such site, Union Community College in New Jersey, the largest provider of welfare-to-work and vocational programs available to recipients in the state.

The director of the college's welfare-to-work programs noted that placements have become more difficult, to some degree, because "in the last few years there has been a noticeable decline in the skill and motivational levels of recipients." The college, however, has become more creative by, for example, outfitting a "job van" to more efficiently link students with interviews with prospective employers. The college has also expanded its job fairs, enabling the college to maintain its 40 percent placement rate.

One of Union Community College's most effective innovations has been to "develop a flexible and customized system that addresses the lifelong learning and skill training needs of existing and potential workers in concert with the skills demanded by employers."[18] As the Work for Development director at the Rutgers Labor Center, Mary Gatta, notes,

> The lack of access to transportation, childcare, and disability services, along with one's work schedule itself, can make it difficult to attain employment and training services. The workforce development system must encompass a holistic approach that not only provides services but also creates and institutionalizes a structure that is flexible and amenable enough so that all workers can avail themselves of these services.[19]

Gatta evaluated an online learning program provided to low-earning single mothers in five New Jersey counties. A similar program was administered at

Union Community College, where mothers were provided with computers and enrolled in courses that combined home computer-simulated training with once weekly in-class instruction. This program has been enormously successful, with job placement rates of more than 60 percent.

Union Community College also takes seriously the additional barriers working women face. Realizing that welfare leavers may be managing their finances for the first time, director Paul Gemo noted, "We are considering methods of providing more finance and life management skills into our programs. Our clients certainly need it."

The college also knows concretely how transportation barriers can undermine stable employment. Gemo cited the experience of an onsite training program it has at a large mall just outside Elizabeth, New Jersey. The college uses some vacant space to train service workers employed in the mall's stores. The stories have found this successful in attracting and retaining their service personnel. One problem, however, has been that most of the workers lack their own transportation. In response, the college and mall executives lobbied successfully for Elizabeth to run its bus service between downtown and the mall late enough that workers could us it for transportation. While this still requires workers to make transportation arrangements from the town center to their homes, it has substantially reduced the problems workers face.

Welfare-to-work programs have also been a catalyst for expanding "state and local government partnerships with business and industry to train low wage workers and help them advance."[20] These partnerships involve customized training to incumbent workers or new hires, career ladders that fill gaps in education and training services, and state skills certificates that give individuals occupational credentials. A research team at the Center for Law and Social Policy assessed five initiatives in four states—Georgia, Kentucky, Louisiana, and Massachusetts—that illustrated the broad potential for government–business partnerships.

What links all of these initiatives is the realization that realistic vocational education is the most effective set of educational enhancements for many working mothers, especially those who are older and have not previously been very successful in school. While four-year degrees should not be foreclosed, evidence strongly indicates that it should not be the first option provided and that financial support and creative energies should be shifted to making vocational programs as effective as they can be.

The third area of public policy is child care programs. Heather Boushey, an economist at the Center for Economic and Policy Research, was surprised that there were not "more work supports, especially since many conservative states, including Texas, Oklahoma, and Georgia, are moving towards providing universal pre-K." In these states, 46 (Texas) to 64 percent (Oklahoma) of four-year-olds are enrolled in state-funded prekindergarten (pre-K) programs.[21]

One of the crucial aspects of the movement to universal pre-K has been the ability of states to utilize community-based child care providers rather than simply using only the public school system. Community settings have more experience providing the eight hours or more that a working mother typically requires. State funding of community settings also provides a means by which the state can raise the standards of these facilities.

While a few states are well on their way to universal pre-K, the vast majority of states currently (2006) serve only a modest share of four-year-olds. The states that serve the fewest children generally restrict access to only low-income families and have the vast majority of the children in public schools. While almost all the states that serve a greater share of children give priority to those from poorer families, they extend access to middle-income families and make greater use of community-based settings.[22]

There is certainly a clear trend toward more universal provisions of pre-K in most states, and political effort should be expended to accelerate this movement. By having such a broad range of policies, states can learn from each other and build on best practices. It would be a mistake, however, to focus solely on pre-K policies. For many working mothers, child care resources are required for their children prior to pre-K, and the major source for these funds currently is the federal government. This is why it is most important that advocacy groups continue to encourage states to shift more of their TANF funds toward child care.

With the Democratic election victory, there is more hope that the federal government will make it financially easier for working families to access child care. Montana Democratic Senator John Tester is one of the sponsors of The Middle Class Opportunity Act of 2007. This bill proposes doubling the child tax credit in the first year of a child's life in order to help defray the additional costs associated with a newborn. The bill would also expand the dependent care tax credit. For families earning between $43,000 and $75,000, the maximum credit would rise from $1,200 to $2,100.[23]

The final area of public policy reflects the Bush healthy marriage initiative. The new funding offers to improve the stability of parental relationships, which have substantial positive effects on children. While the demonstration programs have proven effective, many advocates, such as Greenberg, worry what will happen with the dramatic expansion of ongoing programs. In particular, a substantial amount of funding will be given to small organizations, and it is not clear that they have the experience and expertise to handle an unprecedented scale of operation.

Many advocacy groups are concerned that programs will not be supportive of sustained cohabitation outside of marriage. Advocacy groups also hope that substantial funding will aid the employment of fathers, especially those reentering society from prison. Thanks to foundation grants, these fatherhood programs flourished in the late 1990s and developed an expertise among a group of professionals. These programs waned as foundations changed their priorities and the economic recession curtailed state funding but can be expanded quickly given the trained personnel available.

I also hope that a significant amount of the healthy relationship funding will go to reestablish and expand reentry programs and am confident that they will be effective given the professional expertise available. My only concern is that unless, the job market tightens considerably, these programs will be severely limited in their ability to successful transform the lives of these men. My conversations with welfare-to-work administrators in Chicago, Milwaukee, and New Jersey all tell the same story: a slackening job market has made it impossible for them to shift most men with criminal records to stable employment. For no other group are high-employment policies as crucial as for these men.

One hopeful sign has been the realization that the separate programs that focus on responsible fatherhood, domestic violence, and healthy marriages must find ways to coordinate their efforts. All too often, each area has an antagonist attitude towards one of the other areas. For example, many marriage proponents are against divorce, whereas members of the domestic violence movement often don't believe men can change and so actively encourage battered women to immediately leave their husbands. Similarly, many responsible fatherhood professionals make excuses for bad-acting dads and are exclusively interested in fathers' rights.

Tensions are particularly strong when each partner is counseled by a different area. For example, conflict exists when a responsible-fathers program encourages a father to visit his child more frequently, while at the same time a domestic violence advocate, aware of the father's abusive history, is working with the mother to restrict his visits. In order to clear up misunderstandings and tensions, the Johnson Foundation organized a Building Bridges Conference, held in May 2006.

The conference participants developed a set of suggestions to improve coordination. For example, participants explored cross-training of professions and the development of protocols for sharing information, making referrals in ways that respect client confidentiality, co-locating staff to better integrate activities, producing educational and promotional material that emphasize shared goals, and participating in common-ground dialogues.[24]

CONCLUDING REMARKS

Beyond the specific policy recommendations, let me end with a summary of the most important themes presented. I have emphasized how the Clinton administration's position on welfare reform was built around the make-work-pay philosophy. An integral part of any welfare-to-work transition is providing a sufficient income floor and set of work supports so that mothers can sustain full-time employment and escape official poverty. In addition, evidence suggested that the move toward welfare reform in the 1990s was not so much a capitulation to conservative demands as a concern that transfer programs were growing too rapidly, as was the share of families that were becoming welfare dependent. In this book I have also emphasized that the need for reform reflected the damaging effects of employment losses and the crack cocaine epidemic that victimized the postmigration generation of African-Americans rather than any deeply rooted set of cultural norms.

During the late 1990s, a robust job expansion enabled most leavers to find stable employment and obtain modest wage increases. The benefits from work were enhanced by the earned income tax credit, and leavers gained significant nonfinancial benefits, as well. States flush with money from the booming economy and the declining welfare caseloads expanded substantially the work supports available. While there were instances of insensitive policies by local welfare administrators, including inappropriate sanction policies that caused undue hardships, there was an unprecedented drop in poverty rates for children living with single mothers.

The recent Bush years have not been as kind to welfare leavers. The slower job growth led to a small decline in employment rates and, just as important, a substantial reduction in wage growth. Mothers trapped at low wages became a more prevalent phenomena. In addition, there was a breakdown of a bipartisan consensus that embraced the provision of work supports for welfare leavers.

With this book, however, I hope to provide more than a necessary corrective to the more publicized negative views of the Clinton administration's welfare policies and their impact on single mothers and their children. Today, adults on welfare represent a dwindling share of those needing government supports. By 2005, there were only about 1.9 million *families* receiving cash assistance, down from the 5.1 million in 1994. These figures, however, understate the decline in adults served. Specifically, in both years there were approximately 800,000 child-only cases, so the number of *adults* receiving cash assistance declined from 4.3 to 1.1 million.

Some policy groups point to statistics indicating the share of families that qualify for cash assistance who actually receive it has fallen from 84 percent in 1994 to just below 48 percent by 2002.[25] They contrast this with other safety net programs, including food stamps and health care, where the take-up rate has increased. For this reason, they believe that energies should be directed to correcting the hostile approach in welfare offices, enabling more families to gain these benefits.

My own sense of the situation is that a substantial reason for the decline in qualifying families receiving cash assistance is the possibility of work requirements. In my interviews, a number of women avoided going back on welfare because they rejected the work requirement. They viewed these requirements as forcing them to "work for nothing." This suggested that they perceived the welfare check as an entitlement and believed that if they had to work, they might as well seek paid employment. This was certainly the attitude of Jason DeParle's women, as discussed in chapter 3. Rather than entering a workfare program, they decided to keep paid employment. Since many of these mothers will have cash income below the government's poverty measure (which excludes the earned income tax credit), it is not surprising that the take-up rate has declined dramatically.

Most important, while we should not be insensitive to current recipients, and states should end many of the diversionary tactics used to discourage enrollment in cash assistance programs, it would be a mistake to focus on this set of issues. By 2005, the two million families receiving cash assistance was dwarfed by the other 35 million poor individuals not receiving TANF and the additional 54 million people who are members of the near poor—families with incomes between the poverty line and twice the poverty line. We should focus more on how welfare-to-work initiatives have created an opportunity to build on best practices. Learning from these experiences, we can create policies that serve all working families who remain vulnerable, families that are one paycheck away from significant material hardships. This book has highlighted those practices that can be reproduced nationally and it is my hope that the next few years will bring them to fruition.

Notes

PREFACE

1. Robert D. Cherry, *Discrimination: Its Economic Impact on Women, Blacks, and Jews* (Lexington, 1989).

CHAPTER 1

1. Marian Wright Edelman, "Protect Children from Unjust Policies" *Washington Post* (Nov 3, 1995).

2. E.g., see Randy Albelda and Chris Tilly, *Glass Ceiling and Bottomless Pits: Women's Work Women's Poverty* (South End Press, 1997); Randy Albelda and Ann Withorn (eds.), *Lost Ground: Welfare Reform, Poverty, and Beyond* (South End Press, 2002); and Barbara Ehrenreich, *Nickel and Dimed: On (Not) Getting By in America* (Metropolitan, 2000).

3. Ehrenreich, *Nickel and Dimed*, 1.

4. Ehrenreich came to each city with no ties and no knowledge and required to find jobs and housing within a few days. One of the central features of the low-wage labor market is networking. In her study of 300 fast-food workers in Harlem (N.Y.), Katherine Newman wrote:

> [A] job-seeker's greatest asset is the chain of friends and acquaintances who are already working somewhere, people who can provide a personal connection to an employer. . . . Everyone in the labor force, working or searching for work, is aware that these connections spell the difference between having a serious shot at a job and wasting your time. Young people in the inner city, even those who

have grown up in "welfare households," know the value of networking, of meeting new people in order to extend their reach. (*No Shame in My Game: The Working Poor in the Inner City* [Russell Sage Foundation, 1999], 78)

Thus, it is quite likely that a typical job seeker who had a network would have found better paying jobs than Ehrenreich did.

5. This was the main reason given for Henry Ford's decision to double hourly wages on his assembly line in 1913, virtually eliminating labor turnover. More generally, efficiency wage theory asserts that firms can lower their total costs by paying their workers more than the going wage. The savings in turnover and training costs are greater than the additional wages paid. See Daniel Raff and Lawrence Summers, "Did Henry Ford Pay Efficiency Wages?" *Journal of Labor Economics* (October 1987); and Lawrence Katz, "Efficiency Wage Theories: A Partial Evaluation," in *Macroeconomics Annual, 1986,* ed. Stanley Fischer (MIT Press, 1986).

6. For examples of current situations where adverse conditions dominate, see Kim Moody, *Workers in a Lean World* (Verso, 1997); and C. D. Cook, "Plucking Workers: Tyson Foods Looks to the Welfare Rolls for a Captive Labor Force," *The Progressive* (August 28, 1998).

7. Ehrenreich, *Nickel and Dimed,* 221.

8. "African Americans and the Social Benefits of Tight Labor Markets," *WorkingUSA* 5 (fall 2001): 106–118; "When Is a Soft Landing Too Hard?" (with Jared Bernstein), *Viewpoints* (January 2001), http://www.epinet.org/webfeatures/viewpoints; *Prosperity for All? African Americans and the Economic Boom* (co-edited with William Rodgers; Russell Sage, 2000).

9. "And Now for Something Completely Different: Progressive Tax Cuts That Republicans Can Support" (with Max B. Sawicky), *Challenge* 44 (May/June 2001): 43–60; "Improving the Equity and Efficiency of Child-Related Federal Tax Policies," *Eastern Economic Journal* 27 (summer 2001): 309–322; and "Giving Tax Credit Where Credit Is Due: A Universal Unified Child Credit," Public Policy Brief (with Max Sawicky; Economic Policy Institute, 2000).

10. For a positive academic support, see David Ellwood and Jeffrey Liebman, "The Middle Class Parent Penalty," Working Paper 8031 (National Bureau of Economic Research, December 2000); for political support, see Rahm Emanuel, "The Democrats Can Win on Taxes," *Wall Street Journal* (October 15, 2003).

11. Gina Adams and Monica Rohacek, "Child Care and Welfare Reform," in *Welfare Reform: The Next Act,* ed. Alan Weil and Kenneth Finegold (Urban Institute Press, 2004), 121–141.

12. See Valerie Polakow et al., eds., *Shut Out* (SUNY Press, 2004).

CHAPTER 2

1. Shulchan Arukh YD 247:1.

2. Babylonian Talmud Pesachim 113A.

3. Richard Coe, "Welfare Dependency: Fact or Myth?" *Challenge* 25 (1982): 43–49. These figures somewhat understate the extent of long-term use prior to the 1990s.

Mary Jo Bane and David Ellwood (*Welfare Realities* [Harvard University Press, 1994], table 2.3) estimated that during the period 1968–1988, 29 percent of women first entering the welfare system would be expected to spend at least eight years on welfare, while 36 percent will spend no more than two years on welfare during their lifetime.

4. U.S. Bureau of Labor Statistics, *Employment and Earnings: Employment Rates for Women with Children Six to Seventeen Years Old, by Marital Status, 1980–1995* (January 2000).

5. U.S. Census Bureau, *Statistical Abstract of the United States* (1999), tables 93 and 94. http://www.census.gov/prod/99pubs/99statab/sec02.pdf.

6. Rebecca Blank, "Evaluating Welfare Reform in the United States," *Journal of Economic Literature* 90 (December 2002): 1115.

7. Bruce Reed, *All Too Human: A Political Education* (Little Brown, 1999), 357.

8. Mikhailina Karina, "Shalala Gives Straight Answers," *American (University) Weekly* (February 29, 2000), http://veracity.univpubs.american.edu/weeklypast/022900/story_2.html.

9. The concept was first publicized in David Ellwood, *Poor Support* (Basic Books, 1988).

10. University of Maryland Women's Studies Database, "Women and Family Issues in Congress," *Congressional Updates* 14, no. 5 (July/Aug 1994), http://www.mith2 .umd.edu/WomensStudies/GovernmentPolitics/CaucusUpdates/.

11. University of Maryland, "Women and Family Issues."

12. University of Maryland, "Women and Family Issues."

13. White House Press Release (March 17, 1995), http://clinton6.nara.gov/1995/03/1995-03-17-shalala-briefing-on-the-record.html.

14. Department of Health and Human Services, "GOP Plan Leaves Poor Children and States without Support," Press Release (December 29, 1994), http://www.os.dhhs .gov/news/press/pre1995pres/941229.txt.

15. Quoted in Ross London, "The 1994 Orphanage Debate," in *Rethinking Orphanages for the 21st Century*, ed. Richard McKenzie (Sage, 1998) 86.

16. Marian Wright Edelman, "Protect Children from Unjust Policies." *Washington Post* (Nov 3, 1995).

17. Very restrictive waiver policies were part of the 1988 bill. In response to Clinton's proposals to change welfare, President George H. W. Bush did "come forward with welfare proposals in July 1992 that would have given states increased flexibility" to fashion their welfare programs, but these waivers materialized during the Clinton administration. R. Kent Weaver, *Ending Welfare as We Know It* (Brookings Institution, 2000), 129. See also Donna Shalala, "Welfare Reform: We Must All Assume Responsibility," *Chronicle of Higher Education* (October 4, 1996).

18. Robin Rogers-Dillon, *Welfare Experiments: Politics and Policy Evaluation* (Stanford University Press, 2004).

19. Judith Havermann, "Chief of HHS Objects to Governors' Proposal," *Washington Post* (February 29, 1996).

20. Reed, *All Too Human*, 358–359.

21. Marian Wright Edelman quoted in Children's Defense Fund Press Release (August 22, 1996). For additional critical pronouncements, see Committee on Ways

and Means, "The Dire Predictions Were Wrong: Welfare Reform Is Successful" (Press Release, August 26, 2002), waysandmeans.house.gov/Legacy/fullcomm/107cong/ welfarereskit/predictions.pdf#search='edelman%20JudeoChristian%20welfare'.

22. Robert Sheer, "Terrorism in the Guise of Reform," *LA Times* (July 30, 1996), B7.

23. Shalala, "Welfare Reform."

24. Shalala, "Welfare Reform."

25. Barbara Vobejda, "US to Reward States Moving Welfare Recipients into Jobs," *Washington Post* (February 17, 1998).

26. Peter Edelman, "The Worst Thing Bill Clinton Has Done," *Atlantic Monthly* (March 1997).

27. Primus edited the committee's "Green Book," a resource document published annually that contains comprehensive data on federal entitlement programs, and was also staff director of the House Subcommittee on Human Resources.

28. Arianna Huffington, "Where Liberals Fear to Tread," *Arianna Online* (August 26, 1996), http://www.ariannaonline.com/columns/files/082696.html.

29. For a survey of the literature that supports her position, see Robert Cherry, "Immigration and Race: What We Think We Know," in *The Impact of Immigration on African Americans*, ed. Steve Shulman (Transaction Books, 2004), 137–162.

30. See Peter Edelman, *Searching for America's Heart* (Georgetown University Press, 2003).

31. Edelman, *Searching for America's Heart*, 121.

32. This is a central thesis in Frances Fox Piven and Richard Cloward, *Regulating the Poor: The Functions of Public Welfare (Vintage, 1993)*, and was cited by one of the reviewers of this manuscript.

33. Vernon Briggs, *Immigration and American Unionism* (Cornell University Press, 2001).

34. Sharon Hays, *Flat Broke with Children* (Oxford University Press, 2003), 216–217.

35. For the role that race played in the public discourse, see Martin Gilens, *Why Americans Hate Welfare: Race, Media, and the Politics of Antipoverty Policy* (University of Chicago Press, 1999).

36. Her only reference to Ellwood's views on welfare reform is presented briefly in a footnote:

> The argument regarding welfare reform made in the "Contract [with America]" was largely derived from (conservative) Charles Murray and (liberal) David Ellwood. . . . But Ellwood's proposals were far more generous than the legislation that was finally passed, and he was always more concerned with the possibilities for lowering poverty rates than with the task of reinforcing family values. (Hays, *Flat Broke with Children*, 243 n. 28)

For his views at the time of passage, see David Ellwood, "Welfare Reform as I Knew It," *American Prospect* 7 (May 1996).

37. Randy Albelda ("Fallacies in Welfare-to-Work Policies," in Albelda and Withorn, *Lost Ground*, 82) focuses on the growth of child-only welfare cases, errone-

ously suggesting that these children are not living with a parent or grandparent. In 2001, 62 percent of the children in child-only cases lived with a parent, and another 22 percent lived with a grandparent, while less than 3 percent lived in a household headed by an unrelated adult. Gwendolyn Mink ("Violating Women," in Albelda and Withorn, *Lost Ground*, 96) mistakenly asserts that the growth in foster care adoptions reflects children who would otherwise have been returned to their biological parents. In contrast, Jess McDonald, Sidote Salyer, and Mark Testa ("Nation's Child Welfare System Doubles Number of Adoptions from Foster Care" [Fostering Results, University of Illinois, 2004], http://www.pewtrusts.com/pdf/fostering_results_100903.pdf) are involved with Foster Results, a University of Illinois program focused on reducing the number of foster care children by simultaneously encouraging adoption of "those children who have been 'stuck' in the foster care system" and reducing the number entering by "working to intervene early with at-risk families." While there are a number of concerns with the performance of the foster-care system, they perceive the rise in adoption rates as one of the success stories.

CHAPTER 3

1. Courtland Milloy, "Out from Under the Thumb of White Bias," *Washington Post* (January 26, 2005): B1.

2. Martin Gilens, *Why Americans Hate Welfare* (University of Chicago Press, 1999).

3. Kristin Luker, *Dubious Conceptions: The Politics of Teenage Pregnancy* (Harvard University Press, 1995).

4. Stephan Steinberg, *The Ethnic Myth: Race, Ethnicity, and Class in America* (Antheum, 1981).

5. Louis Wirth, "The Ghetto," *American Journal of Sociology* 33 (July 1927): 61.

6. Louis Wirth, "Urbanism as a Way of Life," in *Community Life and Social Policy*, ed. Elizabeth Wirth Marvick and Albert Reiss (University of Chicago Press, 1956), 128, 130. Reprinted from *American Journal of Sociology* 44 (July 38).

7. John R. Commons, *Races and Immigrants in America* (Macmillan, 1924), 3–4.

8. Gunnar Myrdal, *The American Dilemma* (Macmillan, 1944), 208, 595, 643, 645.

9. Myrdal, *American Dilemma*, 956, 763, 977–978.

10. Walter Jackson, *Gunnar Myrdal and America's Conscience* (University of North Carolina Press, 1990). See also Robert Cherry, "The Culture of Poverty Thesis and African Americans: The Views of Gunnar Myrdal and Other Institutionalists," *Journal of Economic Issues* 29 (December 1995): 1–14.

11. Rebecca Blank, "Selecting among Anti-poverty Policies," *Review of Social Economy* 56 (December 2003): 456.

12. Kerner Commission, *Report of the National Advisory Commission on Civil Disorders* (Bantam Books, 1968), 278.

13. This explanation for weak black student performance is a staple of the *New York Times*. See Bob Hebert, "Breaking Away," *New York Times* (July 10, 2003); and Brent Staples, "How the Racial Literacy Gap Opened," *New York Times* (July 23, 1999). For the controversy stirred when Bill Cosby in 2004 supported this cultural thesis,

see Deepti Hajela, "Cosby Remarks on Blacks Draw Fire, Support," Associated Press Wire Service (May 30, 2004); and Cynthia Tucker, "Bill Cosby's Plain-Spokenness Comes Not a Moment Too Soon," *Yahoo Op-Ed Online* (September 25, 2004). See also Signithia Fordham and John Ogbu, "Black Students' School Success: Coping with the 'Burden of Acting White.'" *Urban Review* (1986): 176–206. For a critique of this cultural explanation for black underperformance, see Philip Cook and Jens Ludwig, "The Burden of 'Acting White': Do Black Adolescents Disparage Academic Achievement?" in *The Black-White Test Score Gap*, ed. Christopher Jencks and Meredith Phillips (Brookings Institution, 1998), 375–400.

14. These views are labeled neo-Malthusian because they harked back to the early stages of industrialization in England when Thomas Malthus claimed that communal norms were responsible for the dysfunctional behavior of the English working class. He railed against parish charity because he believed it allowed the poor to sustain their destructive behavior, including having large families that they could not support.

15. William Julius Wilson, *The Truly Disadvantaged* (University of Chicago Press, 1987).

16. Lawrence Mead, "The New Welfare Debate," *Commentary* 85 (1988): 48.

17. The white women Shipler interviewed had much stronger attachments to work and rarely went on welfare.

18. David Shipler, The Working Poor: Invisible in America (Knopf, 2004), 46.

19. Shipler, The Working Poor, 122.

20. Shipler, The Working Poor, 129.

21. Shipler, The Working Poor, 135.

22. For studies that demonstrate a positive link between self-esteem and employment, see Peter Creed, Tracey Bloxsome, and Karla Johnston, "Self-esteem and Self-efficacy Outcomes for Unemployed Individuals Attending Occupational Skills Training Programs," *Community, Work and Family* 4, no. 3 (2001); and Thomas Li-Ping Tang and Vancie Smith-Brandon, "From Welfare to Work," *Public Personnel Management* 30 (summer 2001).

23. Jason DeParle, *American Dream: Three Women, Ten Kids, and a Nation's Drive to End Welfare (Viking, 2004)*, 21, based on Hortense Powdermaker, *After Freedom: A Cultural Study in the Deep South* (University of Wisconsin Press, 1939). For a criticism of Powdermaker's methodology, see Jane Adams and D. Gorton, "Southern Trauma: Revisiting Caste and Class in the Mississippi Delta," *American Anthropologist* 106 (2004): 334–345.

24. DeParle, *American Dream*, 30, 35.

25. DeParle, *American Dream*, 36.

26. DeParle, *American Dream*, 70.

27. DeParle, *American Dream*, 65.

28. DeParle, *American Dream*, 172.

29. DeParle, *American Dream*, 209.

30. DeParle, *American Dream*, 211.

31. Michael Piore, *Birds of Passage* (Cambridge University Press, 1979).

32. Christopher Jencks, "Crimes and Genes," *New York Review of Books* 12 (February 1987): 33–41. Numerous studies in the 1980s found that the wage rates at

which black youths will accept employment are the same as, if not lower than, the rates at which white youths will accept employment. For a summary of these studies, see Robert Cherry, *Discrimination: Its Economic Impact on Blacks, Women, and Jews* (Heath, 1989), 101.

33. Elijah Anderson, "Some Observations on Black Youth Unemployment," in *Youth Employment and Public Policy*, ed. Bernard Anderson and Isabel Sawhill (Prentice Hall, 1980), 37–46.

34. Robert Cherry, "Race and Gender in Radical Macroeconomic Models: The Case of the Social Structure of Accumulation Model," *Science and Society* 55, no. 1 (Spring 1991): 60–78.

35. John Bound and Richard Freeman, "What Went Wrong? The Erosion of the Relative Earnings of Young Black Men during the 1980s," *Quarterly Journal of Economics* 107, no. 2 (1992): 201–232. Bound and Freeman note that the decline among young white men was only 10 percentage points.

36. Kim Clark and Lawrence Summers, "The Dynamics of Youth Unemployment," in *The Youth Labor Market Problem*, ed. Richard Freeman and David Wise (University of Chicago Press, 1982), 199–230.

37. Becky Pettit and Bruce Weston, "Mass Imprisonment and the Life Course," *American Sociological Review* 69 (April 2004): 151–169.

38. William Julius Wilson, *When Work Disappears* (Vintage, 1996).

39. Joleen Kirshenman and Kathryn Nickerman, " 'We'd Love to Hire Them But...': The Meaning of Race for Employers," in *The Urban Underclass*, ed. Christopher Jencks and Paul Petson (Brookings Institution, 1991), 203–234.

40. Wilson, *When Work Disappears*, 139.

41. Wilson, *When Work Disappears*, xxxiv.

42. Devah Pager, "The Mark of a Criminal Record," *American Journal of Sociology* 110 (March 2004): 937–975.

43. By 2002, the number of homicides in New York City had declined to fewer than 600. Shaila Dewan, "NY Murder Rate Falls Again," *New York Times* (December 24, 2004): B1. For arrest–cocaine link, see Franklin Zimring and Gordon Hawkins, *The Search for Rational Drug Control* (Columbia University Press, 1992), 139.

44. Lawrence Sherman, "Crime and Juvenile Delinquency," in *Family and Child Well-being after Welfare Reform*, ed. Douglas Besharov (Transaction Publishers, 2004), 221–230.

45. Liza Featherstone, *Selling Women Short: The Landmark Battle for Workers' Rights at Wal-Mart* (Basic Books, 2004).

46. For evidence that that there is also a link between employment successes of welfare leavers and a strong work ethic, see Tang and Smith-Brandon, "From Welfare to Work."

47. DeParle, *American Dream*, 177.

48. Shipler, The Disposable Worker, 261.

49. Shipler, The Disposable Worker, 261.

50. DeParle, *American Dream*, 191.

51. Katherine Newman, *No Shame in My Game: The Working Poor in the Inner City* (Russell Sage Foundation, 1999), xv.

52. Newman, *No Shame in My Game*, 25.

53. Mickey Kaus, "The Truth and Consequences of Welfare Reform," *Slate* (November 15, 2004).

54. Kaus, "Truth and Consequences."

55. For juvenile rates, see Peter Reuter, "Drug Use," in *Family and Child Well-being after Welfare Reform*, ed. Douglas Besharov (Transaction Publishers, 2004), 231–246. For arrestee rates, see Zimring and Hawkins, *Rational Drug Control*, and National Institute of Justice, *2000 Arrestee Drug Use Monitoring: Annual Report* (Department of Justice, April 2003).

CHAPTER 4

1. U.S. Census Bureau, *Statistical Abstract of the United States* (Government Printing Office, 1999), tables 93 and 94.

2. Charles Murray, *Losing Ground: American Social Policy, 1950–1980* (Basic Books, 1984).

3. Robert Moffitt, "Incentive Effects of the U.S. Welfare System: A Review," *Journal of Economic Literature* 30, no. 1 (1992): 1–61. See also Sara McLanahan et al., eds., *Losing Ground: A Critique* (Institute for Research on Poverty, University of Wisconsin–Madison, 1985).

4. Ellen Freeman and Karl Rickels, *Early Childbearing* (Sage Publications, 1993), 93.

5. Rebecca Maynard, Reactions to *"Family Formation Issues and Welfare Reform"* by Charles Murray in *The New World of Welfare*, ed. Rebecca Blank and Ron Haskins (Brookings Institution, 2001), 162–163.

6. Another example where state-specific effects are important is crime prevention. Let us suppose that we wanted to test whether more severe penalties are a crime deterrent. However, what if states enact severe penalties in response to high crime rates? Even if they were effective in lowering the crime rates, we would still find that states with high levels of crime tended to have the most severe penalties. As a result, we would find that the level of crime is highest in states that have the most severe penalties even though penalties were an effective crime deterrent.

7. Saul Hoffman and E. Michael Foster, "AFDC Benefits and Non-marital Births to Young Women," *Journal of Human Resources* 35 (2000): 376–391. Hoffman and Foster believe, however, that other socioeconomic factors are far more important, especially when the focus is on teen births. See also Mark Rosenzweig, "Welfare, Marital Prospects, and Nonmarital Childbearing," *Journal of Political Economy* 107, suppl. 6 (1999): S3–S29.

8. Kristin Luker, *Dubious Conceptions: The Politics of Teenage Pregnancy* (Harvard University Press, 1995), 182, 189.

9. Joyce Abma, Anne Driscoll, and Kristin Moore, "Young Women's Degree of Control over First Intercourse: An Exploratory Analysis," *Family Planning Perspectives* 30, no. 1 (1998): 12–18. On a 10-point degree of wantedness scale, 14 percent gave a score of only 1 or 2. Another 20 percent gave a score of 3 or 4, so more than half (57 percent) of these girls did not engage in sexual intercourse primarily because of their own wishes.

10. For women who had their first sexual encounter when they were 16 years old, 10 percent characterized it as involuntary and another 34 percent gave it a rating on the 10-point wantedness scale of 4 or lower. Abma et al., "Young Women's Degree of Control."

11. Kristin Moore, C. Nord, and James Peterson, "Nonvoluntary Sexual Activity among Adolescent Children," *Family Planning Perspectives* 21, no. 3 (1989): 110–114.

12. Abma et al., "Young Women's Degree of Control." Dana Glei ("Measuring Contraceptive Use Patterns among Teenage and Adult Women," *Family Planning Perspectives* 31, no. 2 [1999]: 73–80) found that among sexually active 15- to 19-year-olds, the probability of becoming pregnant in the next 12 months was 50 percent for women who did not used contraception at first intercourse but only 13 percent for those who did.

13. Jacqueline Stock, Michelle Bell, Debra Boyer, and Frederick Connell, "Adolescent Pregnancy and Sexual Risk-Taking among Sexually Abused Girls," *Family Planning Perspectives* 29, no. 5 (1997): 200–203.

14. Jacqueline Darroch, David Landry, and Selene Oslak, "Age Differences between Sexual Partners," *Family Planning Perspectives* 31, no. 4 (1999): 160–167. Glei ("Measuring Contraceptive Use") found that among women 15–17 years old, those who had partners who were at least three years older than them used contraception at only one-third the rate of partners who were closer in age.

15. Darroch et al., "Age Differences between Sexual Partners."

16. Charles Barone, Jeannette Ickovics, Sharon Katz, Charlene Voyce, and Roger Weissberg, "High Risk Sexual Activity among Young Urban Students," *Family Planning Perspectives* 28, no. 2 (1996): 69–74.

17. Abma et al., "Young Women's Degree of Control." These findings contrast with the earlier survey by Moore et al. ("Nonvoluntary Sexual Activity"), which reported the involuntary rate for young black women was one-half the white rate.

18. Robert Griswold, *Fatherhood in America: A History* (Basic Books, 1993), 263; quoted in Maureen Waller, *My Baby's Father* (Cornell University Press, 2002), 163 n.

19. Quoted in Charles Krauthammer, "Teen Pregnancy Is a Cause of Poverty," in *Teen Pregnancy: Opposing Viewpoints*, ed. Stephen Thompson (Greenhaven Press, 1997), 59.

20. William Marsiglio, "Adolescent Males' Orientation toward Paternity and Contraception," *Family Planning Perspectives* 25, no. 1 (1993): 22–31. One can never really disentangle race and class. In particular, white men and black men with low levels of education and weak employment records are not in the same position in the labor market. Black men are much more likely to be continued victims of racial stereotyping by employers, so they have a bleaker outlook than do comparable young white men.

21. Frank Furstenberg, Philip Morgan, Kristin Moore, and James Peterson, "Race Differences in the Timing of First Intercourse," *American Sociological Review* 52, no. 4 (1987): 512, 517.

22. For Gancherov quote, see Michael Males, "Pregnancy Improves Some Teens' Lives," in *Teen Pregnancy: Opposing Viewpoints*, ed. Stephen Thompson (Greenhaven Press, 1997), 47–51.

23. Jody Raphael and Richard Tolman, *Trapped by Poverty, Trapped by Abuse* (Taylor Institute, 1997).

24. "Domestic Violence and Birth Control Sabotage: A Report from the Teen Parent Project" (Center for Impact Research, 2000), http://www.impactresearch.org/documents/birthcontrolexecutive.pdf.

25. Linda Gordon's praise of Ruth Brandwein, ed., *Battered Women, Children, and Welfare Reform* (Sage, 1998), found on its publisher's website: http://www.sagepub.com/book.aspx?pid=4135.

26. Quoted in Robert Cherry, "Rational Choice and the Price of Marriage," *Feminist Economics* 4 (summer 1998): 22.

27. Raphael and Tolman, *Trapped by Poverty*. For evidence that arresting domestic abusers leads to more violent actions if the abuser was unemployed, see Daniel Goleman, "Do Arrests Increase the Rates of Repeated Domestic Violence?" *New York Times* (November 25, 1991): C8. However, arresting employed abusers reduced the subsequent incidence of assault.

28. Gina Wingwood and Ralph DiClemente, "The Effects of an Abusive Primary Partner on the Condom Use and Sexual Negotiation Practices of African American Women," *American Journal of Public Health* 87, no. 6 (1997): 1016–1018.

29. As cited in R. Barri Flowers, *Domestic Crimes, Family Violence and Child Abuse* (McFarland, 2000), table 3.1.

30. As cited in Flowers, *Domestic Crimes*, table 3.2.

31. Raphael and Tolman, *(Trapped by Poverty)*, 14. In a Massachusetts study by Mary Ann Allard, Mary Colten, Randy Albelda, and Carol Cosenza (*In Harm's Way* [McCormack Institute, 1997]), the 15.5 and 1.6 percent of abused and nonabused welfare mothers, respectively, reported that their present or former partner would not like them to have a job or enroll in a job training program.

32. Allard et al. (*In Harm's Way*) found 40 and 27 percent of abused and non-abused recipients, respectively, suffered symptoms of mental depression. In the New Jersey study included in Raphael and Tolman (*Trapped by Poverty*), 31 percent of all recipients but 54 percent of those currently in an abusive relationship indicated that they were currently depressed.

33. Raphael, *Saving Bernice: Battered Women, Welfare, and Poverty* (Northeastern University Press, 2000), 108.

34. Raphael, *Saving Bernice*, 8.

35. Raphael, *Saving Bernice*, 28.

36. Shipler, *The Working Poor: Invisible in America* (Knopf, 2004), 125.

37. Joan Meier, "Domestic Violence, Character, and Social Change in the Welfare Reform Debate," *Law and Policy* 19 (April 1997): 223, 228.

38. Meier, "Domestic Violence," 229.

39. Joe Klein, "Sexual Abuse Is a Factor in Teenage Pregnancy," in *Teen Pregnancy: Opposing Viewpoints*, ed. Stephen Thompson (Greenhaven Press), 73–76.

40. Luker, *Dubious Conceptions*, 146.

41. Luker, *Dubious Conceptions*, 182.

42. Ruth Brandwein and Diana Filiano, "Toward Real Welfare Reform," *AFFILA* 15, no. 2 (2000): 224–243.

43. Jody Raphael and Sheila Haennicke, *Keeping Battered Women Safe through the Welfare-to-Work Journey* (Taylor Institute, 1999).

44. Frank Furstenberg, "The Social Consequences of Teenage Parenthood," in *Teenage Sexuality, Pregnancy and Childbearing*, ed. Frank Furstenberg, Richard Lincoln, and Jane Menken (University of Pennsylvania Press, 1981), 184–210.

45. Jane Menken, "The Health and Social Consequences of Teenage Childbearing," in *Teenage Sexuality, Pregnancy and Childbearing*, ed. Frank Furstenberg, Richard Lincoln, and Jane Menken (University of Pennsylvania Press, 1981), 167–183.

46. Cheryl D. Hayes, ed., *Risking the Future: Adolescent Sexuality, Pregnancy, and Childbearing* (Panel on Adolescent Pregnancy and Childbearing, National Research Council, 1987). http://www.nap.edu/catalog/948.html

47. Frank Furstenberg, J. Brooks-Gunn, and Philip Morgan, *Adolescent Mothers in Later Life* (Cambridge University Press, 1987).

48. Luker, *Dubious Conceptions*, 120.

49. Luker, *Dubious Conceptions*, 122.

50. Arlene Geronimus and Sanders Korenman, "The Socioeconomic Consequences of Teen Childrearing Reconsidered," *Quarterly Journal of Economics* 107, no. 4 (1992): 1187–1214. See also Saul Hoffman, Michael Foster, and Frank Furstenberg, "Reevaluating the Cost of Teenage Childbearing," *Demography* 30, no. 1 (1993): 1–14; Saul Hoffman, "Teenage Childbearing Is Not So Bad After All . . . Or Is It?" *Family Planning Perspectives* 30, no. 5 (1998): 236–239; Joseph Holt, Susan McElroy, and Seth Sanders, "The Impacts of Teenage Childbearing on the Mothers and the Consequences of Those Impacts for Government," in *Kids Having Kids*, ed. Rebecca Maynard (Urban Institute, 2006), 55–94; and Elaine McCrate, "Labor Market Segmentation and Relative Black/White Teenage Birth Rates," *Review of Black Political Economy* 19, no. 2 (1990): 37–53.

51. Geronimus and Korenman, "Socioeconomic Consequences."

52. According to William Darity and Samuel Myers:

> Groups like Planned Parenthood Federation explicitly advocate reduction in the number of children born out of wedlock via family planning measures, including abortion. Such measures, Planned Parenthood Federation spokespersons have argued, will be a crucial step in reducing the supply of welfare-eligible persons. . . . [We] have referred to this outlook as the doctrine of *preemptive extermination of the unborn*, who are anticipated to become part of the permanent poverty population. (*The Underclass* [Garland, 1994], 50)

53. For evidence of the link between welfare reform and teen birth rates, see Robert Kaestner and June O'Neill, "Has Welfare Reform Changed Teenage Behaviors?" NBER Working Paper 8932 (National Bureau of Economic Research, May 2002).

54. Bridget Grant and Deborah Dawson, "Alcohol and Drug Use, Abuse and Dependency among Welfare Recipients," *American Journal of Public Health* 86, no. 10 (October 1996): 1450.

55. D. Gomby and P. Shiono, "Estimating the Number of Substance-Exposed Infants," *Future of Children* 22 (spring 1991).

56. DeParle, *American Dream: Three Women, Ten Kids, and a Nation's Drive to End Welfare* (Viking, 2004), 73.

57. Robert Pear, "Gains Reported for Children of Welfare-to-Work Families," *New York Times* (January 25), 2001.

58. DeParle, *American Dream*, 311.

59. Callie Marie Rennison, "Intimate Partner Violence, 1993–2001," Crime Data Brief NCJ 197838 (Bureau of Justice Statistics, U.S. Department of Justice, February 2003), http://www.ojp.usdoj.gov/bjs/pub/pdf/ipv01.pdf.

CHAPTER 5

1. Mary Jo Bane and David Ellwood, *Welfare Realities* (Harvard University Press, 1994), table 2.3.

2. Kathryn Edin and Laura Lein, *Making Ends Meet: How Single Mothers Survive Welfare and Low-Wage Work* (Russell Sage Foundation, 1997). Laura Connolly and Christine Marston ("Welfare Reform, Earnings, and Income" [Joint Center for Poverty Research, December 2002]) found that among high school graduates, both individual income and family income increased, while for those without a high school degree, individual income rose but family income fell.

3. Christopher Jencks, in Edin and Lein, *Making Ends Meet*, xii.

4. Robert Moffitt and David Stevens, "Changing Caseloads: Macro Influences and Micro Composition," Conference Paper (Federal Reserve Bank of New York, November 17, 2000), 20.

5. Maria Cancian, Robert Haverman, Daniel Meyer, and Barbara Wolfe ("Before and After TANF: The Economic Well-Being of Women Leaving Welfare," Special Report no. 77 [Institute for Research on Poverty, University of Wisconsin-Madison, May 2000]) analyzed the welfare population in Milwaukee during the last quarter of 1995. Among current recipients, they found that 65 percent had been on welfare continuously for more than two years. Over the previous two years, 77 percent had been on welfare for at least 19 months, 41 percent had annual wage income of less than $250, and only 21 percent had annual wage income of more than $3,750.

6. David Ellwood, "Anti-poverty Policy for Families in the Next Century," *Journal of Economic Perspectives* 14 (January 2000): 187–198.

7. Gregory Acs, Norma Coe, Keith Watson, and Robert Lerman, "Does Work Pay?" (Urban Institute, July 1998).

8. See Robert Cherry, "Black Men Still Jobless," *Dollars and Sense* (November–December 1998): 43.

9. In the mid-Atlantic region, the 1992 employment rates of black and white women were 47 and 51 percent, respectively. For data on state employment figures, see Heather Boushey and Robert Cherry, "Exclusionary Practices and Glass Ceiling Effects," in *Prosperity for All? The Economic Boom and African* Americans ed. Robert Cherry and William Rodgers (Russell Sage Foundation, 2001), 160–187.

10. Jencks, in Edin and Lein, *Making Ends Meet*, xx.

11. Irene Browne and Ivy Kennelly, "Stereotypes and Realities: Images of Black Women in the Labor Market," in *Latinas and African American Women at Work*, ed. Irene Brown (Russell Sage Foundation, 1999), 302–326.

12. Sandra Danziger et al., "Barriers to the Employment of Welfare Recipients," in *Prosperity for All? The Economic Boom and African Americans* ed. Robert Cherry and William Rodgers (Russell Sage Foundation, 2001), 245–278.

13. Harry Holzer, Michael Stoll, and Douglas Wissoker, "Job Performance and Retention Among Welfare Recipients" (Urban Institute, June 2001), 2.

14. Danziger et al., "Barriers to the Employment."

15. Interestingly, 30 percent of black male employees and 40 percent of white male employees indicated that over the previous year they had been late, had to change hours, or had been absent because of child care responsibilities. Indeed, the white male rate was slightly higher than the black female rate.

16. Browne and Kennelly, "Stereotypes and Realities"; See also Holzer, Stoll, and Wissoker, *Job Performance and Retention*.

17. Robert Pear, "Welfare Workers Rate High in Job Retention at Companies," *New York Times* (May 27, 1998): B1; Danziger et al., "Barriers to the Employment."

18. Richard Lerman and Caroline Ratcliffe, "Did Metropolitan Areas Absorb Welfare Recipients without Displacing Other Workers?" (Urban Institute, 2000).

19. The 3.5 percentage point employment gap in the mid-Atlantic region was completely eliminated as the black rate increased from 47 to 54 percent, and the South Atlantic region went from equality to a favorable 2 percentage point gap as the black rate increased from 55 to 61 percent, while the white rate only increased to 59 percent.

20. For white never-married women, the rate increased from 52 to 67 percent. Arloc Sherman, Shawn Fremstad, and Sharon Parrott, "Employment Rates for Single Mothers Fell Substantially during Recent Period of Labor Market Weakness" (Center on Budget and Policy Priorities, June 22, 2004).

21. Jason DeParle, *American Dream: Three Women, Ten Kids, and a Nation's Drive to End Welfare (Viking, 2004)*, 210.

22. Rachel Swarns, "City Agrees to Drop Delay in Food Stamp Applications," *New York Times* (April 30, 1999): B3.

23. Rachel Swarns, "Mayor Backs City Policy on Welfare," *New York Times* (November 11, 1998): B6.

24. Rachel Swarns, "U.S. Audit Is Said to Criticize Giuliani's Strict Welfare Plan," *New York Times* (January 20, 1999): A1.

25. Rachel Swarns, "City Agrees to Drop Delay In Food Stamp Applications." *New York Times* (April 30, 1999): B3.

26. Avis Jones-DeWeever, Janice Peterson, and Xue Song (*Before and After Welfare Reform* [Institute for Women's Policy Research, 2003]) estimated that the share of low-income families receiving food stamps declined from 48.1 percent in early 1996 to 36.6 percent in late 1999. The average value of foods stamps per low-income family only fell by about 10 percent so that this decline was disproportionately among those families receiving below average payments.

27. At least some of this decline reflected the lingering effects of the cutoff of immigrant families from the food stamp program. Between 1990 and 1996, 10.9 percent of families receiving food stamps had at least one member who was a noncitizen. In 1998, this share fell to 4.3 percent and had risen back to only 6.4 percent by 2000. U.S. Department of Agriculture, "Characteristics of the Food Stamp Program, 2001,"

Report FSP-03-CHAR (Food and Nutritional Service, January 2003), http://www.fns
.usda.gov.

28. Robert Greenstein and Jocelyn Guyer, "Supporting Work through Medicaid and
Food Stamps," in *The New World of Welfare*, ed. Rebecca Blank and Ron Haskins
(Brookings Institution, 2001), 351.

29. Greenstein and Guyer, "Supporting Work," 352.

30. Sheila Zedlewski, *Recent Trends in Food Stamp Participation: Have New Policies Made a Difference?* (Urban Institute, May 2004).

31. Food and Nutrition Services, *Real Results for Real People: A Record of
Achievement* (U.S. Department of Agriculture, 2005).

32. Zedlewski, *Recent Trends in Food Stamp Participation*; and U.S. Department
of Agriculture, "Monthly Data—National Level, Food Stamp Program" (2005), http://
www.fns.usda.gov/pd/fsmonthly.htm.

33. Gloria Nagle and Bruce Goodro, "After Time Limits" (Massachusetts Department of Transitional Assistance, November 2000).

34. Sheldon Danziger, Colleen Heflin, Mary Corcoran, Elizabeth Oltmans, and Hui-
Chen Wang, "Does It Pay to Move from Welfare to Work?" *Journal of Policy Analysis
and Management* 21 (October 2002): 671–692.

35. Maria Cancian and Daniel Meyer, "Work after Welfare: Women's Work Effort, Occupation, and Economic Well-being," *Social Work Research* 24 (March 2000):
69–86. Though published in 2000, their data measured the employment of welfare
recipients who left in 1987 for five years.

36. Sheldon Danziger, "Welfare Reform: A Fix for All Seasons?" *Milken Institute
Review* 4 (fall 2002): 24–33.

37. Jones-DeWeever et al. (*Before and After Welfare Reform*) compare pre- and
postwelfare reform incomes without including EITC credits. In the report's conclusions,
however, one of the most important recommendations made is to expand the EITC,
which they believe "has been a particularly effective strategy in helping to make work
pay for struggling families" (45). When judging the financial impact of welfare reform, the EITC is ignored in three of the books most critical of welfare reform: Barbara
Ehrenreich, *Nickel and Dimed* (Metropolitan, 2000); Sharon Hayes, *Flat Broke with
Children* (Oxford University Press, 2003); and Randy Albelda and Ann Withorn, eds.,
Lost Ground (South End, 2002).

38. Mark Levitan and Robin Gluck, *Mothers' Work: Single Mothers' Employment
Earnings, and Poverty in the Age of Welfare Reform* (Community Service Society of
New York, 2002).

39. Twenty-seven states have cash reductions of less than $1 for every $2 of wage
income. For summary of states, see Jeffrey Grogger and Lynn Karoly, *Welfare Reform:
Effects of a Decade of Change* (Harvard University Press, 2005), table 2.8.

40. Cancian et al., "Before and after TANF." Wisconsin did not have substantial
disregards in 1995, so this cannot explain the high earnings of mothers while they still
were receiving cash payments. According to Cancian et al., only 21 percent of welfare recipients had annual earnings of at least $3,750, while the average earnings of the
subpopulation of these recipients who left welfare equaled $4,000. In correspondence
with this author, Cancian suggested that the high average for leavers could reflect data

problems caused by the use of income data collected quarterly along with welfare receipt data collected from monthly tabulations.

41. For all black children, between 1995 and 2000, the share living in official poverty fell by 26 percent, while the share living in extreme poverty fell by 33 percent. Using a broader measure of income, the decline in extreme poverty was 18 percent. Children's Defense Fund, "Analysis Background: Number of Black Children in Extreme Poverty Hits Record High" (April 2003); and Melissa G. Pardue, "Sharp Reduction in Black Child Poverty Due to Welfare Reform," Backgrounder no. 1661 (Heritage Foundation, June 12, 2003).

42. Scott Winship and Christopher Jencks, "Understanding Welfare Reform: The Critics of Welfare Reform Were Wrong," *Harvard Magazine* (November–December 2004). Of interest, in 2000 Jencks was still pessimistic about reform and, like other critics, emphasized the adverse consequences to the poorest single mothers and the limited economic benefits to many others. Christopher Jencks and Joseph Swingle, "Without a Net," *American Prospect* 11 (January 3, 2000): 37–41.

43. Sandi Nelson, "Trends in Parents' Economic Hardship" (Urban Institute, March 18, 2004).

44. Jennifer Van Hook, "Welfare Reform and the Long-Term Stability in Food Security among Children of Immigrants," Joint Center for Poverty Research Working Paper 352 (University of Chicago, January 2004).

45. Winship and Jencks, "Understanding Welfare Reform."

46. Lisa Pohlmann, *Welfare Reform: Lessons from Maine* (Maine Center for Economic Policy, March 2002).

47. Julie Altman and Gertrude Goldberg, "The Quality of Life of Former Public Assistance Recipients in Dutchess County, New York" (Adelphi School of Social Work, April 2003). In Massachusetts, those who left welfare before reaching time limits were twice as likely to consider themselves both financially and emotionally better off than to consider themselves worse off on each of these measures. By contrast, those who left welfare because they had reached their time limits were equally split as to whether their financial or emotional well-being had improved or was worsened after leaving welfare.

48. Winship and Jencks, "Understanding Welfare Reform."

49. June O'Neill and M. Anne Hill ("Gaining Ground, Moving Up," Report No. 35 [Manhattan Institute Civic, March 2003]) estimate that 44 percent of the employment gains were the result of welfare legislation while less than 10 percent was the result of a stronger economy. Clinton's Council of Economic Advisors ("Economic Expansion, Welfare Reform, and the Decline in Caseloads: An Update" [Executive Office of the President, 1999]) estimated that 35 percent of the change in caseloads was due to welfare reform while only 9 percent was due to a stronger economy. Similar results appear in Geoffrey Wallace and Rebecca Blank, "What Goes Up Must Come Down? Explaining Recent Changes in Public Assistance Caseloads," in *Economic Conditions and Welfare Reform*, ed. Sheldon Danziger (W.E. Upjohn Institute, 1999). For a full set of estimates, see Rebecca Blank, "Evaluating Welfare Reform in the United States," *Journal of Economic Literature* 90 (December 2002): table 6. For dissenting views that find that economic growth, not welfare reform, was most responsible, see Stephen Bell,

"Why Are Welfare Caseloads Falling?" Discussion Paper (Urban Institute, March 2001); and Jonathan Pingle, "What If Welfare Had No Work Requirements?" Working Paper (Federal Research Board, 2003).

50. Gary Burtless, "The Labor Force Status of Mothers Who Are Most Likely to Receive Welfare: Changes Following Reform," Brookings Web Editorial (Brookings Institution, March 30, 2004).

51. Kathryn Porter and Allen Dupree, "Poverty Trends for Families Headed by Working Single Mothers," Priorities Report 01-144 (Center on Budget and Policy, August 2001). Note that this result is after the doubling of the EITC in 1993 and before the rebound of food stamp participation rates.

52. For references that use the Porter–Dupree paper to support this claim, see Karen Christopher, "Welfare as We (Don't) Know It," *Feminist Economics* 10 (July 2004): 143–172; and Charles Price, "Reforming Welfare Reform Post-secondary Education Policy," *Journal of Sociology and Social Welfare* (September 2005). For a critique of Christopher, see Robert Cherry, "Assessing Welfare Reform Data," *Feminist Economics* 13 (April 2007): 379–389.

53. Danziger et al., "Does It Pay to Move from Welfare to Work?"

54. In Baltimore, Moffitt and Stevens ("Changing Caseloads") found the share of welfare recipients that had at least a high school degree remained constant between 1995 and 1999. In Wisconsin, Cancian et al. ("Before and After TANF,) found that the share fell from 56 to 46 percent between 1995 and 1997. Cynthia Miller ("Leavers, Stayers, and Cyclers" [Manpower Demonstration Research Corporation, November 2002]) found that, across 12 programs studied by the Manpower Demonstration Research Corporation, only 45 percent of stayers but 53 percent of leavers had at least a high school degree. For a study that finds little change, see Sheila Zedlewski and Donald Alderson, "Do Families on Welfare in the Post-TANF Era Differ from Their Pre-TANF Counterparts?" *Assessing the New Federalism*, Discussion Paper 01–03 (Urban Institute, 2001).

55. Danziger et al., "Does It Pay to Move from Welfare to Work?"

56. Erin Burchfield and Sarah Yatsko, *From Welfare Check to Pay Check* (Economic Opportunity Institute, October 2002).

57. Referenced by Ron Haskins, "The Effect of Welfare Reform on Family Income and Poverty," in *The New World of Welfare*, ed. Rebecca Blank and Ron Haskins (Brookings Institution, 2001).

58. Deanna Lyter, Melissa Sills, Gi-Taik Oh, and Avis Jones-DeWeever, *The Children Left Behind: Deeper Poverty, Fewer Supports* (Institute for Women's Policy Research, 2004), extrapolation from table 10.

59. Among welfare leavers, 61.3 percent had been poor while on welfare but 42.7 percent remained poor after leaving. By contrast, 7.7 percent were extremely poor while on welfare but 10.5 percent were extremely poor after leaving. Cynthia Miller, "Leavers, Stayers, and Cyclers." Similarly, in Massachusetts, though the majority of leavers raised their incomes, Nagle and Goodro ("After Time Limits") found that the amount of severe food insecurity increased, as well. Among those who left welfare, 22 percent experienced severe food insecurity after they left, but only 14 percent remember experiencing it when they were still on welfare.

60. Haskins, "Effects of Welfare Reform."

61. Referenced in Haskins, "Effects of Welfare Reform."

62. Bruce Meyer and James Sullivan, "The Well-Being of Single-Mother Families after Welfare Reform," Policy Brief no. 33 (Brookings Institution, 2005).

63. A 9.8 estimate for 1999 is found in Pamela Loprest, "Disconnected Welfare Leavers Face Serious Risks" (Urban Institute, August 21, 2003). A 12 percent estimate for 1997–1999 is found in Pamela Loprest, "Making the Transition from Welfare to Work," in *The Next Act*, ed. Alan Weil and Kenneth Feingold (Urban Institute, 2002).

64. Meyer and Sullivan, *The Well-being of Single-Mother Families*; Kasia Murray and Wendell Primus, "Recent Data Trends Show Welfare Reform to Be a Mixed Success" (Joint Economic Committee, 2005). For a contrarian view, see Richard Bavier, "Welfare Reform Data from Survey of Income and Program Participation," *Monthly Labor Review* (July 200): 13–24.

65. DeParle, *American Dream*, 287.

66. Grogger and Karoly, *Welfare Reform*, table 4.2.

67. Loprest, "Making the Transition from Welfare to Work." For further evidence sanctions, see Chi-Fung Wu, Maria Cancian, and Daniel Meyer, "Sanction Policies and Outcomes in Wisconsin," *Focus* 23 (Winter 2004): 38–40; and Bong Joo Kee, Kristen Slack and Dan Lewis, "Sanctions Policies and Outcomes in Illinois," *Focus* 23 (Winter 2004): 41–43.

68. U.S. Department of Health and Human Services estimated that 10 percent of child-only cases were due to the sanctioning of their mothers. "Characteristics and Financial Circumstances of TANF Recipients, July-September 1999" (Administration for Children and Families, Office of Planning, Research and Evaluation, 1999).

69. DeParle, *American Dream*, 211.

70. Ehrenreich, *Nickel and Dimed*, 3.

71. Ehrenreich, *Nickel and Dimed*, 194.

72. For evidence, see Robert Cherry, "African Americans and the Social Benefits of Tight Labor Markets," *WorkingUSA* 5 (fall 2001): 106–118.

73. Anu Rangarajan and Robert Wood, "Current and Former WFNJ Clients" (Mathematica, 2000), http://www.mathematica-mpr.com/; Nagle and Goodro, "After Time Limits."

74. For women followed in a Manpower Demonstration Research Corporation study, the average income increase between 1998 and 1999 was 23 percent; for those who relied solely on wage income, the increase was 38 percent. Ellen Scort et al., "Welfare Recipients Struggle to Balance Work and Family," *Poverty Research News* 6 (July–August 2002): 12–15.

75. Erin Burchfield and Sarah Yatsko, *From Welfare Check to Pay Check* (Economic Opportunity Institute, October 2002).

76. Katherine Newman and Chauncy Lennon, "Working Poor, Working Hard: The Trajectories of the Bottom of the American Labor Market," in *Social Inequalities in Comparative Perspective*, ed. Fiona Devine and Mary Waters (Blackwell, 2004), 116–140.

77. Newman and Lennon, "Working Poor, Working Hard," 128. They also followed 93 workers who had been rejected for employment in 1993. In 1997, 47 percent

were unemployed, with most having worked only intermittently during the previous four years.

78. Loprest, "Making the Transition from Welfare to Work." Also see Isabel Sawhill, "From Welfare to Work," *Brookings Review* (summer 2001): 4–7.

79. For a summary of these state EITC programs, see National Women's Law Center, "Lower Your Taxes or Increase Your Refund," http://www.nwlc.org/details .cfm?id=2860&section=tax.

80. Community Service Society of New York, *The Unheard Third: Bringing the Voices of Low-Income New Yorkers to the Policy Debate* (Community Service Society, October 2004).

81. Pohlmann, *Welfare Reform*, table 7. Between one in six and one in four Maine working welfare leavers did experience these hardships, although at lower rates than did welfare recipients on each of these measures.

82. Average of two alternative measures in Heather Boushey, Chauna Brocht, Bethney Gundersen, and Jared Bernstein, *Hardships in America: The Real Story of Working Families* (Economic Policy Institute, 2001), table 7. When family income rose above $30,000, less than one percent of these families had at least two critical hardships. Thus, only after families have left the near-poor income range do critical hardships became rare.

CHAPTER 6

1. Richard Freeman and William Rodgers, "The Fragility of the 1990s Economic Gains" (paper presented to Allied Social Science Association, January 8, 2005). Moreover, Freeman and Rodgers found that almost 30 percent of the job growth since the end of the recession has been created by the temporary help sector. By contrast, during the first three years of the recovery from the 1990–1991 recession, only 10 percent of the new jobs were in temporary help services.

2. Heather Boushey, "Last Hired, First Fired: Job Losses Plague former TANF Recipients," Brief 171 (Economic Policy Institute, December 12, 2001). Between February and November 2001, employment in personal supply services fell from 3.73 to 3.28 million; in the hotel and lodging sector, from 1.95 to 1.85 million. From August to October 2001, employment in restaurants and bars fell from 8.28 to 8.19 million, and in general merchandise stores, from 2.80 to 2.76 million.

3. It is true that among those workers who have been unemployed for at least six months, the female share was higher during the 2001–2004 economic slowdown than during the 1990–1993 slowdown. This increase is not because the 2001–2004 slowdown was harsher to women than the previous slowdown. It was the result of women becoming a more active part of the labor force. A decade earlier, a much larger share left the active labor force when they suffered unemployment, some cycling back onto welfare. Today, fewer unemployed women are willing or able to shift to welfare, so they remain actively engaged in job searching, causing them to remain on the unemployment rolls longer.

4. Robert Lerman, "How Did the 2001 Recession Affect Single Mothers?" *Single Parents' Earnings Monitor* (Urban Institute), January 2005.

5. Heather Boushey and David Rosnick, "For Welfare Reform to Work, Jobs Must Be Available," Issue Brief (Center for Economic and Policy Brief, April 1, 2004).

6. To judge the impact of the economic slowdown on welfare leavers, we must assume that they keep their share of total employment in each of these nine sectors.

7. Shawn Fremstad, Sharon Parrott, and Arloc Sherman, "Unemployment Insurance Does Not Explain Why TANF Caseloads Are Falling as Poverty and Need Are Rising" (Center on Budget and Policy Priorities, October 12, 2004).

8. The increase in the extreme poverty rate is also sensitive to the income measure used. In particular, the increase during the economic slowdown was much more substantial if a broader income measure is used rather than a pure cash income measure. For example, a Children's Defense Fund paper ("Analysis Background: Number of Black Children in Extreme Poverty Hits Record High" [April 2003]) found that the extreme poverty rate for black children rose to the highest recorded levels during the 2001 recession if this broader income measure was used, whereas it was still more than one-third below peak levels if the pure cash income measure is used.

9. Quoted in Leslie Kaufman, "Are Those Leaving Welfare Better Off Now? Yes and No," *New York Times* (October 20, 2003): B1.

10. Lerman, "How Did the 2001 Recession Affect Single Mothers?"

11. Anu Rangarajan and Carol Razafindrakoto, "Unemployment Insurance as a Potential Safety Net for TANF Leavers: Evidence from Five States" (Mathematica Policy Research Inc., September 2004).

12. Vicky Lovell and Maurice Emsellem, "Florida's Unemployment Insurance System" (Institute for Women's Policy Research, 2004).

13. Rangarajan and Razafindrakoto, "Unemployment Insurance as a Potential Safety Net."

14. Lovell and Emsellem, "Florida's Unemployment Insurance System," 10–11.

15. "Why Unemployment Insurance Matters to Working Women and Families An Important Tool in the Work-Family Balance" (National Education and Law Projects, 2005); and "Unemployment Benefits for Domestic Violence Survivors: What Are Its Costs?" (National Education and Law Projects, 2005).

16. Unfortunately, the Florida House refused to allow the bill to come to a vote, so two years later the legislation was still pending.

17. White House press briefing (June 8, 2005), http://www.whitehouse.gov/news/releases/2005/06/20050608-4.html.

18. White House press briefing (June 8, 2005).

19. This position was strongly influenced by Martin Feldstein ("The Economics of the New Unemployment," *Public Interest* 33 [1973]: 1–21), who would become head of the Council of Economic Advisors under President Ronald Reagan.

20. See Laura D'Andrea Tyson, "Five Myths about Inflation," *New York Times* (November 13, 1994): A24; and editorial, "A Valuable Voice for the Fed," *New York Times* (January 29, 1996): A23.

21. George Akerlof, William Dickens, and George Perry, "Low Inflation or No Inflation: Should the Federal Reserve Pursue Complete Price Stability?" Policy Brief no. 4 (Brookings Institution, August 1996).

22. Joseph Stiglitz, "Reflections on the Natural Rate Hypothesis," *Journal of Economic Perspectives* (winter 1997): 3–10. For a more general background of this viewpoint, see Robert Eisner, "A New Vision of NAIRU," in *Improving the Global Economy*, ed. Paul Davidson and Jan Kregel (Edward Algar, 1997), 196–230.

23. See Jared Bernstein, *All Together Now: Common Sense for a Fair Economy* (Economic Policy Institute, 2006); and Robert Cherry and Jared Bernstein, "When Is a Soft Landing Too Hard?" *Viewpoints* (January 21, 2001), http://www.epi.org/content .cfm/webfeatures_viewpoints_soft_landing.

24. Take a bond that pays interest of $5,000 annually over a 20-year period. How do investors judge the fair price it should pay for this bond? In 2004, the competitive rate of return on 20-year bonds was 5 percent. As a result, investors paying $100,000 for the bond would be receiving the necessary 5 percent rate of return. Thus, the fair market price for this bond in 2004 would have been $100,000. Now suppose that in 2006 the competitive return rose to 6.25 percent. In this environment, a 20-year bond promising $5,000 annual interest payments would no longer sell for $100,000 since investors would not accept a 5 percent rate of return. Only at a sale price of $80,000 would investors receive the necessary 6.25 percent rate of return (5,000/80,000).

25. Edward Wolff, "Recent Trends in Wealth Ownership," in *Assets for the Poor*, ed. Thomas Shapiro and Edward Wolff (Russell Sage Foundation, 2001), tables 2.1 and 2.6.

26. James Tobin, "On Improving the Economic Status of the Negro," in *The Negro American*, ed. Talcott Parsons and Kenneth Clark (Houghton Mifflin, 1963), 462–463.

27. Quoted in Louis Uchitelle, "Hiring Pace Picks Up Last Month," *New York Times* (July 9, 2005): C1.

28. Quoted it David Leonhardt, "Suggesting No Let Up, Fed Raises Rate Again," *New York Times* (August 10, 2005): C1.

29. Bureau of Labor Statistics, Table D19. http://www.bls.gov/web/cpseed19.pdf.

CHAPTER 7

1. David Moberg, "Martha Jernegons's New Shoes," *American Prospect* (June 19, 2000).

2. Heather Boushey, "Staying Employed after Welfare," EPI Briefing Paper no. 128 (Economic Policy Institute, June 2002).

3. Toby Parcel and Elizabeth Menaghan, "Effects of Low-Wage Employment on Family Well-Being," *Future of Children* 7 (spring 1997): 116–121.

4. Martha Zaslow and Carol Emig, "When Low Income Mothers Go to Work: Implication for Children," *Future of Children* 7 (spring 1997): 112.

5. Zaslow and Emig, "When Low Income Mothers Go to Work," 113.

6. Rachel Schumacher, Danielle Ewen, and Katherine Hart, "All Together Now: State Experiences in Using Community-Based Child Care to Provide Pre-kindergarten," CLASP Policy Brief No. 5 (Center for Law and Social Policy, February 2005), http:// www.clasp.org/publications/cc_brief5.pdf.

7. Timothy Smith, Anne Kleiner, Basmat Parsad, Elizabeth Farris, and Bernard Greene, "Prekindergarten in U.S. Public Schools: 2000–2001: Statistical Analysis

Report," NCES 2003-019 (National Center for Education Statistics, U.S. Department of Education, March 2003), http://nces.ed.gov/pubs2003/2003019.pdf.

8. Katherine Magnuson and Jane Waldfogel, "Early Childhood Care and Education," *Future of Children* 15 (spring 2005): 174–175.

9. Administration for Children and Families, "Head Start Impact Study: First Year Findings" (U.S. Department of Health and Human Services, June 2005), http://www.acf.hhs.gov/programs/opre/hs/impact_study/reports/first_yr_finds/firstyr_finds_title.

10. Cited in Magnuson and Waldfogel, "Early Childhood and Education," 175. For the cited studies, see William Gormley and Ted Gayer, "Promoting School Readiness in Oklahoma," mimeo, Georgetown University, 2003; and Arthur Reynolds et al., "Long-term Effects of an Early Childhood Intervention on Educational Achievement and Juvenile Arrests," *Journal of the American Medical Association* 285 (2001): 2339–2346.

11. Magnuson and Waldfogel, "Early Childhood and Education," 176.

12. For a broad discussion of improving child care center quality, see Katie Hamm, Barbara Gault, and Avis Jones DeWeever, "In Our Own Backyards: Local and State Strategies to Improve the Quality of Family Child Care" (Institute for Women's Policy Research, 2005).

13. Michelle Chan, "Debate over Renewing Welfare Reform Reveals Cracks in the System," *New Standard* (April 30, 2005); Margy Waller, "The Federal Welfare Debate: Is Congress Deserting Working Families?" (paper presented at the Illinois Welfare Policy Symposium, Brookings Institution, March 4, 2005).

14. Waller, "The Federal Welfare Debate."

15. Karen Schulman and Helen Blank, "Child Care Assistance Policies, 2001–2004; Families Struggling to Move Forward, States Going Backward." (National Women's Law Center Issue Brief, September 2004) http://www.nwlc.org/pdf/childcaresubsidyfinalreport.pdf

16. Waller, "The Federal Welfare Debate," 5.

17. Hannah Matthews and Danielle Ewen, "Child Care Assistance in 2005: State Cuts Continue." (Center for Law and Social Policy, November 1, 2006) 3. For somewhat different figures, see Gina Adams and Monica Rohacek, "Child Care and Welfare Reform," in *Welfare Reform: The Next Act*, ed. Alan Weil and Kenneth Finegold (Urban Institute, 2004), 121–141.

18. See Suzanne Heilbrun and Barbara Bergman, *America's Child Care Problem: The Way Out* (Palgrave Macmillan, 2002).

19. Data from U.S. Department of Health and Human Resources, "Child Care and Development Fund Statistics" (Agency for Family and Children). For 2004, see: http://www.acf.hhs.gov/programs/ccb/data/ccdf_data/04acf800/table1.htm. For 2001, see: http://www.acf.hhs.gov/programs/ccb/data/ccdf_data/01acf800/chldser1.htm.

20. Magnuson and Waldfogel, "Early Childhood and Education," table 1.

21. David Ellwood and Jeffrey Liebman, "Middle Class Parent Penalty: Child Benefits in the U.S. Tax Code," NBER Working Paper 8031 (National Bureau of Economic Research, December 2000).

22. Ellwood and Liebman, "Middle Class Parent Penalty," table 2.

23. Elaine Maag, "State Tax Credits for Child Care" (Urban Institute, July 2005). http://www.urban.org/UploadedPDF/1000796_Tax_Fact_7-11-05.pdf.

24. These areas are the District of Columbia, Maryland, Minnesota, New Jersey, New York, and Vermont. Wisconsin, Kansas, and Massachusetts offer refundable credits of 14–15 percent of the federal EITC, and Illinois, Indiana, New Mexico, Oklahoma, and Rhode Island offer refundable credits of 5–7 percent of the federal EITC. Iowa, Maine, and Oregon offer small nonrefundable credits. Tax Credit Resources, "State EIC Programs: An Overview" (date accessed 2007), http://www.taxcreditresources.org/pages.cfm?contentID=39&pageID=12&Subpages=yes.

25. Robert Greenstein and Isaac Shapiro, "New Research Findings on the Effects of the Earned Income Tax Credit," Report No. 98-022 (Center on Budget and Policy Priorities, 1998); John Karl Scholz, "The Earned Income Tax Credit: Participation, Compliance, and Antipoverty Effectiveness," *National Tax Journal* 47, no. 1 (1994): 59–81. For studies that measured the positive employment effect, see Jeffrey Liebman and Nadia Eissa, "Labor Supply Response to the Earned Income Tax Credit," *Quarterly Journal of Economics* 112 (May 1996): 605–637; Bruce Meyer and Daniel Rosenbaum, "Welfare, the Earned Income Tax Credit, and the Supply of Single Mothers," manuscript (Northwestern University, 1999).

26. U.S. House Ways and Means Committee, *Green Book* (1998), table 7.3.

27. Liebman and Eissa, "Labor Supply Response."

28. Robert Cherry and Max Sawicky, "Giving Tax Credit Where Credit Is Due: 'Universal Unified Child Credit' That Expands the EITC and Cuts Taxes for Working Families," EPI Briefing Paper no. 91 (Economic Policy Institute, April 2000), http://www.epinet.org/content.cfm/briefingpapers_eitc.

29. See Rahm Emanuel, "The Democrats Can Win," *Wall Street Journal* (October 15, 2003).

30. David Kirp, "Before School," *Nation* (November 21, 2005): 24–30.

31. When I went to tax accountants, they could not immediately calculate the benefits in New York, and a national organization that has written detailed booklets to inform the public of DCAP benefits had a critical error regarding the impact of DCAP on the federal child tax credit.

32. For a comparison with the child-related benefits of United Kingdom, Canada, and Australia, see Kenneth Battle and Michael Mendelson (ed.), *Benefits for Children: A Four Country Study* (Caledon Institute of Social Policy, 2001).

CHAPTER 8

1. For an evaluation of LIFETIME, see Avis Jones-DeWeever and Barbara Gault, *Resilient and Reaching for More: Challenges and Benefits of Higher Education for Welfare Participants and Their Children* (Institute for Women's Policy Research, April 2006), http://www.iwpr.org/pdf/D466.pdf.

2. Joe Kincheloe, *What Do We Tell the Workers? The Socioeconomic Foundations of Work and Vocational Education* (Westview Press, 1999), 130.

3. Kincheloe, *What Do We Tell the Workers*, 123.

4. James Rosenbaum, *Beyond College for All* (Russell Sage, 2001), table 3.3.

5. Rosenbaum, *Beyond College for All*, 83.

6. Kincheloe consistently mentions ex-Klansman David Duke and the authors of *The Bell Curve*, Charles Murray and Richard Hernnstein, as prominent supporters of vocational tracking. Thus, if you favor expanding vocational programs, you must be supporting these racists.

7. W. Norton Grubb and Norman Lazerson, *The Educational Gospel: The Economic Power of Education* (Harvard University Press, 2004), 3.

8. Grubb and Lazerson, *The Educational Gospel*, 94. For proponents of this "cooling out" hypothesis, see S. Brint and J. Karabel, *The Diverted Dream* (Oxford University Press, 1989); K. J. Dugherty, *The Contradictory College* (State University of New York Press, 1994); and A. Nora, *Reexamining the Community College Mission* (American Association of Community Colleges Press, 2000). Mariana Alfonso, Thomas Bailey, and Marc Scott ("The Educational Outcomes of Occupational Sub-baccalaureate Students: Evidence from the 1990s," *Economics of Education Review* 24 [2005]: 197) do find that students enrolled in *vocational* associate degree programs fare have lower success rates than comparable students enrolled in *academic* associate degree programs. They do note, however, that the study had poor controls for student academic skills and suggested that the reason for the disparity in success rates may be "that community colleges have yet to figure out and implement the optimal approach to provide direct occupational preparation within an institutional structure that continues to rest on a foundation oriented towards academic education."

9. Grubb and Lazerson (*The Educational Gospel*, 217) write that academic programs built on the strengths of working class students "would become second-class alternatives like the dumping ground of traditional voc ed or the occupational programs in community colleges criticized for cooling out nontraditional students." Elsewhere, Grubb ("From Isolation to Integration: Postsecondary Vocational Education and Emerging Systems of Workforce Development," *New Directions in Community Colleges* 115 [fall 2001]: 27–37) discusses how to make vocational training more educational by shifting it to the community colleges from job training sites.

10. Rosenbaum, *Beyond College for All* 74.

11. Among part-timers who were required to take a math remediation course, after five years fewer than 9 percent had attained an associate degree and fewer than 4 percent either were enrolled in or had completed a four-year college degree program.

12. Eric Bettinger and Bridget Long, "Remediation at the Community College: Student Participation and Outcomes," *New Directions in College Communities* 129 (spring 2005). After five years, only 16 percent had completed an associate degree and fewer than 7 percent either were enrolled in or had completed a four-year college degree program. See also Thomas Bailey, Davis Jenkins, and Timothy Leinbach, "Is Student Success Labeled Institutional Failure?" CCRC Working Paper no. 1 (Columbia University Community College Research Center, Columbia University, June 2005).

13. G. Norton Grubb et al., *Honored but Invisible* (Routledge, 1999), table 5.1.

14. Robert McCabe, *No One to Waste* (Community College Press, 2000).

15. Southern Regional Educational Board, "Fact Book" (June 28, 2005), table 38.

16. Thomas Bailey et al. ("Educational Outcomes of Postsecondary Occupational Students," CCRC Brief no. 22 [Columbia University Community College Research Center, August 2004]) found that for those who entered community colleges in 1989, only 44 percent were successful after five years, while for those who entered in the early 1990s, 54 percent were successful after six to eight years.

17. Rosenbaum, *Beyond College for All*, 112.

18. Rosenbaum, *Beyond College for All*, table 9.5.

19. Derek Neal and William Johnson, "The Role of Pre-market Factors in Black-White Earnings Differences," *Journal of Political Economy* 104 (October 96): 869–895. For a criticism of this and similar studies, see William Rodgers and William Spriggs, "Communications," *Industrial and Labor Relations Review* 55 (April 2002): 533–542.

20. June O'Neill, "The Role of Human Capital in Earnings Differences between Black and White Men," *Journal of Economic Perspectives* 4 (fall 1990): 25–46.

21. Grubb et al., *Honored but Invisible*, 351.

22. Grubb et al., *Honored but Invisible*, 354–355.

23. Anita Mathur et al., "Credentials Count: How California's Community Colleges Help Parents Move from Welfare to Self-Sufficiency" (Center for Law and Social Policy, May 2002). The authors do not dwell on these failure rates but instead focus on earnings outcomes. The earnings growth of even those who completed zero credits was quite robust during the economic boom. While they infer that this wage growth was due to the college experience, it probably had much more to do with the robust job market.

24. McCabe, *No One to Waste*, 41.

25. Nancy Ritze, "The Evolution of Developmental Education at the City University of New York and Bronx Community College," *New Directions for College Communities* 129 (spring 2005).

26. Ritze, "The Evolution of Developmental Education."

27. Rosenbaum, *Beyond College for All*, 56.

28. Grubb and Lazerson, *The Educational Gospel*, 49.

29. Gayle Hamilton, "Moving People from Welfare to Work: Lessons from the National Evaluation of Welfare-to-Work Strategies" (Manpower Demonstration Research Corporation, July 2002), aspe.hhs.gov/hsp/newws/synthesis02/index.htm.

30. Hamilton, *Moving People from Welfare to Work*, 117.

31. Hamilton, *Moving People from Welfare to Work*, 119.

32. For a critique of the Manpower Development Research Corporation evaluations, see Erika Kates, "Debunking the Myth of the Failure of Education and Training for Welfare Recipients," in *Shut Out*, ed. Valerie Polakow et al. (SUNY Press, 2004).

33. At public two-year colleges, 21 percent of these students have no financial aid and another 47 percent receive grants but have no loans. By contrast, at proprietary schools, only 4 percent of these students have no financial aid and only 14 percent received grants and do not have student loans. National Center for Education Statistics, "National Postsecondary Student Aid" (U.S. Department of Education, 2004), tables 74 and 76.

34. National Center for Education Statistics, "Students at Private, For-Profit Institutions," NCES 2000-175 (U.S. Department of Education, Office of Educational Research and Improvement, November 1999), table 2.

35. Stephanie Riegg Cellini, "The Impact of Taxpayer Dollars on the Market for Sub-baccalaureate Education" (UCLA Department of Education, July 2005).

36. Quoted in Karen Arenson, "Speedy Growth in Career Schools Raises Questions," *New York Times* (July 12, 2005).

37. U.S. House of Representatives, "Enforcement of Federal Anti-Fraud Laws in For-Profit Education," Hearing before the Committee on Education and the Workforce, Serial No. 109-2 (Government Printing Office, March 1, 2005).

38. Quoted in Arenson, "Speedy Growth."

39. Charles Price, "Reforming Post-secondary Education Policy," *Journal of Sociology and Social Welfare* 32 (September 2005); and Charles Price et al., "Continuing a Commitment to the Higher Education Option" (Howard Samuels State Management and Policy Center, April 2003).

40. Mark Greenberg, Julie Strawn, and Lisa Plimpton, "State Opportunities to Provide Access to Postsecondary Education under TANF" (Center for Law and Social Policy, 2000); Center for Law and Social Policy, "Forty States Likely to Cut Access to Postsecondary Training and Education Under House Welfare Bill" (June 19, 2002), table 1, http://www.clasp.org/publications.php?id=9&year=2002.

41. Thomas Brock, Lisa Matus-Grossman, and Gayle Hamilton, "Welfare Reform and Community Colleges: A Policy and Research Context," *New Directions for Community Colleges* 116 (December 2001): 13.

42. Charles Outcalt and James Schimer, "Understanding the Relationships between Proprietary Schools and Community College," *Community College Review* 31 (summer 2003): 56–74.

43. Stated in Outcalt and Schimer "Understanding the Relationship."

44. Ben Brown, "A Smart Path—That Isn't 'College,'" *USA Today* (January 11, 2005): 11A.

45. Karen Pagenette and Cheryl Korzell, "The Advanced Technology Program: A Welfare-to-Work Success Story," *New Directions for Community Colleges* 116 (December 2001): 49–59.

46. John Ream, Brenda Wagner, and Robin Knorr, "Welfare to Work: Solutions or Snake Oil?" *New Directions for Community Colleges* 116 (December 2001): 61–66.

47. Brown, "A Smart Path."

48. Mariana Alfonso, Thomas Bailey, and Marc Scott, "The Educational Outcomes of Occupational Sub-baccalaureate Students: Evidence from the 1990s," *Economics of Education Review* 24 (April 2005): 197 (emphasis added).

49. Louis Uchitelle, "College Still Counts, Though Not as Much," *New York Times* (October 2, 2005).

50. Bureau of Labor Statistics, News Releases, "Usual Weekly Earnings," Table 4. http://www.bls.gov/news.release/wkyeng.to4.htm.

CHAPTER 9

1. Robert Rector and Melissa Pardue, "Understanding the President's Healthy Marriage Initiative," Report no. 1741 (Heritage Foundation, March 26, 2004).

2. Mary Leonard, "Bush Seeks $1.5 Billion to Back Marriages" *Boston Globe* (January 15, 2004).

3. Leonard, "Bush Seeks $1.5 Billion."

4. Spencer Hsu, "Marriage Fund for Poor Proposed," *Washington Post* (July 22, 2005): B5.

5. Wade Horn, "Wedding Bell Blues: Marriage and Welfare Reform," *Brookings Review* 19 (summer 2001): 39–42.

6. Rector and Pardue, "Understanding the President's Healthy Marriage Initiative," 6.

7. Rector and Pardue, "Understanding the President's Healthy Marriage Initiative," 6.

8. Mary Parke and Theodora Ooms, "More than a Dating Service" (Policy Brief, Center for Law and Social Policy, October 17, 2002).

9. Katherine Boo, "The Marriage Cure: Is Wedlock Really a Way Out of Poverty?" *New Yorker* (August 15, 2003): 108.

10. Boo, "The Marriage Cure," 109.

11. Boo, "The Marriage Cure," 109–110.

12. Laura Wherry and Kenneth Finegold, "Marriage Promotion and Living Arrangements of Black, Hispanic and White Children," Report B-61 (Urban Institute, September 2004).

13. See Robert Wood, "Marriage Rates and Marriageable Men: A Test of the Wilson Hypothesis." *Journal of Human Resources* 30 (Winter 1995):163–193.

14. Kathryn Edin and Laura Lein, *Making Ends Meet* (Russell Sage Foundation, 1997).

15. These earlier interviews are recounted in Kathryn Edin, "A Few Good Men: Why Poor Women Don't Marry or Remarry," *American Prospect* 11 no. 4 (January 3, 2000): 26–42.

16. According to the 2000 census of the entire population, there are 97 white women for every 100 white men but 109 black women for every 100 black men.

17. For a more formal marriage model that finds the level of inequality in the typical marriage is a function of the relative supply of men willing and women willing to marry, see Robert Cherry, "Rational Choice and the Price of Marriage," *Feminist Economics* 4 (spring 1998): 27–49.

18. Edin, "A Few Good Men," 28.

19. Edin, "A Few Good Men," 29.

20. Institute for Research on Poverty, "Expectations of Marriage among Unmarried Couples: New Evidence from Fragile Families Study," *Focus* 22 (summer 2002): 13–17.

21. Kathryn Edin, Paula England, and Kathryn Linnenberg, "Love and Distrust among Unmarried Parents" (paper presented at the National Poverty Center Conference on Marriage and Family Formation among Low-Income Couples, Washington, D.C., September 4–5, 2003).

22. Edin et al., "Love and Distrust," 7.

23. Edin et al., "Love and Distrust," 10.

24. Kathryn Edin, Laura Lein, Timothy Nelson, and Susan Clampet-Lundquist, "Talking with Low-Income Fathers," *Poverty Research News* 4 (March-April 2000): 13

25. Edin et al., "Talking with Low-Income Fathers," *Poverty Research News* 4 (March-April 2000): 12.

26. Edin et al., "Talking with Low-Income Fathers," 10–11.

27. Edin et al., "Talking with Low-Income Fathers," 10–11.

28. The contrast between Edin's ("A Few Good Men") earlier interviews with these later interviews ("Talking with Low-Income Fathers") no doubt reflects differences between the voices heard: the mothers in the earlier interviews versus the men in the later interviews. The differences, however, may also reflect different time periods. In the late 1980s, noncustodial fathers were members of the postmigration generation. Men from this generation were victims of the joblessness and crack cocaine culture that pervaded inner-city black communities. With a more favorable economic situation and a less pervasive drug culture, the post-welfare reform fathers that the Edin research team and David Pate (footnote 30) interviewed were likely to be less irresponsible and less violent.

29. Edin et al., "Talking with Low-Income Fathers," 12. Their conclusion does mention in passing, "Often fathers described scenarios of being barred from their lives owing to their economic marginality and personal problems (substance abuse, violence)." The clear intention of the article, however, is to present these fathers in the most sympathetic light possible, so I have excluded this sentence from the concluding paragraph.

30. David Pate, "The Life Circumstances of African American Fathers with Children on W-2," *Focus* 22 (summer 2002): 28.

31. Critical Resistance, "2003 Prison and Jail Fact Sheet," http://www.criticalresistance.org/media/CR%202003%20Prison%20Fact%20Sheet.pdf#search='2003%20prison%20and%20jail%20fact%20sheet'.

32. Rebekah Levine Coley and Lindsay Chase-Lansdale, "Father's Involvement with Their Children over Time," *Poverty Research News* 4 (March-April 2000): 12–15. Also see David Ellwood and Christopher Jencks, "The Uneven Spread of Single Parent Families" in *Social Inequality* ed. Kathryn Neckerman (Russell Sage Foundation, 2004).

33. Wherry and Finegold, "Marriage Promotion."

34. Wherry and Finegold, "Marriage Promotion," 3.

35. Wade Horn and Isabel Sawhill, "Fathers, Marriage, and Welfare Reform," in *The New World of Welfare*, ed. Rebecca Blank and Ron Haskins (Brookings Institution, 2001), 421–441.

36. Edin et al., "Love and Distrust."

37. Institute for Research on Poverty, "Expectations of Marriage," 15.

38. Edin et al., "Love and Distrust," 14. For further elaboration, see Kathryn Edin and Maria Kefalas, *Promises I Can Keep: Why Poor Women Put Motherhood Before Marriage* (University of California Press, 2005).

39. Gregory Acs and Sandi Nelson, "What Do 'I Do's Do? Potential Benefits of Marriage for Couples with Children," Report B-59 (Urban Institute, May 24, 2004).

40. Catherine Kenney and Sara McLanahan, "Are Cohabiting Relationships More Violent than Marriages?" Working Paper 265 (Joint Center for Poverty Research, January 8, 2002).

41. Acs and Nelson, "What Do 'I Do's Do?"

42. Ron Haskins and Isabel Sawhill, "Work and Marriage: The Way to End Poverty and Welfare," *Welfare and Beyond* 28 (September 2003).

43. Chien-Chung Huang, "Impact of Child Support Enforcement on Nonmarital and Marital Births" (Rutgers University, November 2001).

44. Vicki Turetsky, "The Child Enforcement Program" (Center for Law and Social Policy, October 2005).

45. Irwin Garfinkel, Theresa Heintze, and Chien-Chung Huang, "The Effect of Child Support Payments on Mothers' Income," *Poverty Research News* 5 (May-June 2001): 5–8.

46. Turetsky, "The Child Enforcement Program."

47. For the one million estimate, see Turetsky, "The Child Enforcement Program"; for the half million estimate, see Center for Law and Social Policy, "Child Support Substantially Increases Economic Well-Being of Low- and Moderate Income Families: Research Fact Sheet" (2005).

48. Elaine Sorensen, "Child Support Gains Some Ground," *Snapshots III of America's Families*, no. 11 (October 2003), http://www.urban.org/uploadedpdf/310860_snapshots3_no11.pdf.

49. Center for Law and Social Policy, "Child Support Substantially Increases."

50. Garfinkel et al., "The Effect of Child Support Payments"; also see Center for Law and Social Policy, "Child Support Payments Benefit Children in Non-economic as well as Economic Ways: Research Fact Sheet" (2005).

51. Huang, "Impact of Child Support Enforcement."

52. Vicki Turetsky, "Parental Conflict, Domestic Violence and Child Support Policies: What the Research Says" (Center for Law and Social Policy, October 2003).

53. Turetsky, "Parental Conflict."

54. Turetsky, "Parental Conflict."

55. Pate, "Life Circumstances," 30.

56. Shaun Fremstad and Wendel Primus, "Strengthening Families" (Center on Budget and Policy Priorities, January 22, 2002). Unfortunately, as part of the new reauthorization bill, Wisconsin can only pass through the state portion of child care payments until 2008, at which time they could also pass through the federal portion.

57. Maria Cancian and Daniel Meyer, "The Economic Circumstances of Fathers with Children on W-2," *Focus* 22 (summer 2002): 19–24.

58. Elaine Sorensen and Chava Zibman, "Poor Dads Who Don't Pay Child Support: Deadbeat or Disadvantaged?" (Urban Institute, April 1, 2001).

59. Elaine Sorensen, "Helping Poor Nonresident Dads Do More" (Urban Institute, May 2, 2002).

60. Paula Roberts and Elaine Sorensen, "Strategies for Preventing the Accumulation of Child Support Arrears and Managing Existing Arrears" (Center for Law and Social Policy, October 6, 2005).

61. Sorensen and Zibman, "Poor Dads Who Don't Pay Child Support."

62. Abbey Frank, "Where the Funds Are: Potential Use of Child Support Funds for Transitional Jobs Programs" (Center for Law and Social Policy, September 2004).

63. Horn and Sawhill, "Fathers, Marriage, and Welfare Reform," 424–425.

CHAPTER 10

1. Greenberg dislikes participation rate requirements because they can be met either by enrolling more recipients or by cutting the caseload, regardless of whether the leaver attained employment. This provided a real incentive to reduce caseloads since the TANF funds could be used for other more desirable activities. In addition, participation is a lousy measure of performance, but the federal government has been unwilling to judge whether certain work-related activities are effective.

2. Elisa Minoff, "Participation in TANF Work Activities in 2004" (Center for Law and Social Policy, March 23, 2006).

3. Quoted in Sharon Parrott, "Conference Agreement Imposes Expensive New TANF Requirements" (Center on Budget and Policy Priorities, December 18, 2005).

4. Parrott, "Conference Agreement."

5. The penalty is reduced by the degree the state's rate is more than half of its required rate, in this case half of 45 percent. As a result, the 30 participation rate is one-third greater than 22.5 percent. In addition, the penalty is reduced by the percentage the increase in those participating in work activities has grown by more than 15 percent. The state's participation rate rose by 20 percent—from 25 to 30 percent—which is one-third above the 15 percent.

6. Lisa Schott, "Up-Front Programs for TANF Applicants," Center on Budget and Policy Priorities (January 16, 2007) 1.

7. Schott, "Up-Front Programs."

8. Abbey Frank, "Increasing Opportunities: Creating and Expanding Transitional Jobs Programs for TANF Recipients under the Deficit Reduction Act." (Center for Law and Social Policy, January 18, 2007).

9. Danielle Ewen and Hannah Matthews, "Toward a Decade of Indifference: Administration Budget Ignores Child Care Needs of Working Families" (Center for Law and Social Policy, February 10, 2006).

10. Ewen and Matthews, "Toward a Decade of Indifference."

11. Hannah Matthews and Danielle Ewen, "Child Care Assistance in 2005: State Cuts Continue" (Center for Law and Social Policy, November 1, 2006).

12. Sharon Parrott and Isaac Shapiro, "Unshared Sacrifice" (Center on Budget and Policy Priorities, November 2, 2005).

13. For a comprehensive survey of research on the impact of immigration on black workers, see Robert Cherry, "Immigration and Race: What We Think We Know," in *The Impact of Immigration on African Americans*, ed. Steve Shulman (Transaction Books, 2004), 137–162. See also Barry Chiswick, "The Worker Next Door," *New York Times* (June 3, 2006).

14. Timothy Egan, "The 110th Congress: For $7.93 an Hour It's Worth a Trip Across State Lines" *New York Times* (January 11, 2007).

15. Heather Boushey and John Schmitt, "Impact of Proposed Minimum-Wage Increase on Low-Income Families" (Center for Economic and Policy Research, December 2005).

16. Jason Furman and Sharon Parrott, "A $7.25 Minimum Wage would be a Useful Step in Helping Working Families Escape Poverty" (Center on Budget and Policy Priorities, January 5, 2007).

17. See Jonathan B. Forman, *Making America Work* (Urban Institute, 2006).

18. Mary Gatta, *Not Just Getting By: The New Era of Flexible Workforce Development* (Lexington Books, 2005), 5.

19. Gatta, *Not Just Getting By*, 7.

20. Ellen Duke, Karin Martinson, and Julie Strawn, "Wising Up: How Government Can Partner with Business to Increase Skills and Advance Low-Wage Workers" (Center for Law and Social Policy, April 6, 2006).

21. Andrea Eger, "Pre-school Access Lauded," *Tulsa World* (November 22 2004), http://www.captc.org/pubpol/childcare/World_NIEER_Nov22.pdf#search='childcare%20enrollment%20Texas%20Georgia%20Oklahoma.

22. Rachel Schumacher, Danielle Ewen, Katherine Hart, and Joan Lombardi, "All Together Now: State Experiences in Using Community-Based Child Care to Provide Pre-kindergarten" (Center for Law and Social Policy, May 2005).

23. Noelle Straub, "Tester Touts Middle-Class Tax Cut" *Billings Gazette* (February 16, 2007). http://www.billingsgazette.net/articles/2007/02/16/news/state/40-tester.txt.

24. For a summary of the conference, see Theodora Ooms et al., "Building Bridges: A Preliminary Guide" (Center for Law and Public Policy, December 7, 2006).

25. Sharon Parrott and Arloc Sherman, "TANF at 10" (Center on Budget and Policy Priorities, August 17, 2006), figure 1.

Index